ALSO BY JONATHAN MAHLER

Ladies and Gentlemen, the Bronx Is Burning

The Challenge

The
CHALLENGE

HAMDAN *v.* RUMSFELD
AND THE FIGHT OVER
PRESIDENTIAL POWER

Jonathan Mahler

Farrar, Straus and Giroux
New York

Farrar, Straus and Giroux
18 West 18th Street, New York 10011

Copyright © 2008 by Jonathan Mahler
All rights reserved
Distributed in Canada by Douglas & McIntyre Ltd.
Printed in the United States of America
First edition, 2008

Portions of this work originally appeared, in somewhat different form,
in the June 13, 2004, January 8, 2006, and July 9, 2006, issues of
The New York Times Magazine.

Library of Congress Cataloging-in-Publication Data
Mahler, Jonathan, 1969–
    The challenge : Hamdan v. Rumsfeld and the fight over presidential power /
Jonathan Mahler — 1st ed.
        p.   cm.
    "Portions of this work appeared, in somewhat different form, in the June 13,
2004, January 8, 2006, and July 9, 2006 issues of The New York Times Magazine."
    Includes index.
    ISBN-13: 978-0-374-22320-5 (hardcover : alk. paper)
    ISBN-10: 0-374-22320-3 (hardcover : alk. paper)
    1. Hamdan, Salim Ahmed, 1970– —Trials, litigation, etc.   2. Rumsfeld, Donald,
1932– —Trials, litigation, etc.   3. Military courts—United States.   4. Jurisdiction—
United States.   5. War on Terrorism, 2001—Law and legislation—United States.
6. International and municipal law—United States.   7. Combatants and
noncombatants (International law).   8. Chauffeurs—Legal status, laws, etc.
I. Title.

KF225.H36M34   2008
343.73'0143—dc22

                                                                    2008003063

Designed by Robert C. Olsson

www.fsgbooks.com

1   3   5   7   9   10   8   6   4   2

For Danielle

He that would make his own liberty secure must guard even his enemy from oppression, for if he violates this duty he establishes a precedent that will reach to himself.

—Thomas Paine, July 7, 1795

CONTENTS

The Challenge

Prologue

JUST OUTSIDE the Old City of Sana, a maze of densely packed, intricately adorned stone houses and centuries-old shops that rise like drip castles from narrow cobblestone streets, sits the modern Martyrs' Mosque. If the Old City evokes Yemen's cosmopolitan days at the center of the world's spice trade in 1000 B.C., the scene outside the Martyrs' Mosque, an imposing ash-colored monolith built to honor the country's holy warriors, speaks to its more recent history as the poorest of the Arabian Peninsula states. The big open square that fronts the mosque is a gathering place for the dispossessed. Homeless people lie on flattened cardboard boxes with gasoline cans repurposed as water jugs beside them. Yemeni music issues from loudspeakers fastened to the handlebars of three-wheeled cycles pedaled by cassette vendors. *Dababs*—minivans stuffed with passengers that career around Sana's crowded streets—jockey for fares. The smells of grilling meat and corn on the cob commingle with perfumed oil, urine, and exhaust.

There are no women here, only young men and boys. And while roughly 40 percent of Yemeni men are unemployed, everyone seems to be in a big hurry, hustling around, often holding hands, always in standard Yemeni dress: sandals, white robes, and Western-style blazers with the labels showing just above the left cuff. Long curved daggers known as jambiyas, reminders of the country's enduring tribal culture, hang from belts. Cheeks bulge with khat, a narcotic plant that brightens the mood and sends the mind in every direction, a mental state reflected in the combination of aimlessness and restlessness on display here.

In 1996, Salim Hamdan, a twenty-six-year-old Yemeni with a thick mustache and kinky black hair, was one of these men.

He was born hundreds of miles from Sana in the Wadi Hadramawt, a primitive tribal region in the mountainous desert of southeastern Yemen that has been inhabited since 1000 B.C. Physically, the Hadramawt is breathtaking: its small villages are improbably perched atop soaring cliffs overlooking a valley carved up by intersecting watercourses—or wadis—that centuries ago represented a marvel of irrigation, exploiting fitful, seasonal rains to create thousands of acres of arable land. The Hadramawt's most valued crop was an indigenous tree, *Boswellia sacra*, the source of frankincense, which was in high demand in pharaonic Egypt and ancient Rome. But the rise of Christianity—the early leaders of the Christian church considered incense burning a pagan ritual—and the decline of the overland camel trade put an end to the region's long era of prosperity. Today the landscape of the Hadramawt is mostly barren; the scarce supply of water is used to irrigate the khat crops.

Hamdan's father was a farmer and shopkeeper, and the family lived modestly in a small mud-brick home on a mountainside terrace. Both of Hamdan's parents died from illnesses that were poorly treated—his mother when he was seven, his father when he was eleven. With no other family nearby, Hamdan went to live with relatives in Mukalla, a bleak port city of about one hundred thousand people on Yemen's southern coast. By that point he had already quit school, not unusual in the Hadramawt, where the imperatives of helping one's family earn money far outweigh the comparatively abstract virtues of an education.

Within a few years Hamdan was on his own, living on the streets of Mukalla and working odd jobs. Then, in 1990, when he was twenty, he joined a mass migration north. Yemen, which had long been divided into two separate nations, the Islamic North Yemen and the Marxist South Yemen, had just become officially unified as the Republic of Yemen, and there was a widespread sense that Sana, the nation's new capital, would soon be booming. As it turned out, the job prospects were not very promising, particularly for someone with Hamdan's limited qualifications. Like thousands of others, he found his way to the Martyrs' Mosque, where he worked part-time as a *dabab* driver, dividing his paltry income between the mattress he rented in a crowded boardinghouse in Sana and his daily supply of khat, which he chewed by the fistful.

Then one day the low-hanging horizon of Hamdan's life lifted. He was recruited for jihad.

Jihad has an almost mythic appeal in Yemen, its roots running all the way back to the seventh century, when the Prophet Muhammad is said to have declared, "Allah, give me fighters from behind me," his back turned conspicuously to Yemen.

In its more modern incarnation, jihad can be traced to 1967, when a civil war broke out between the Islamic North and the Marxist South Yemen. It didn't take long for North Yemen's rulers to exploit the conflict's religious undertones. By the time the Soviets invaded Afghanistan in 1979, many young Yemenis already accepted that it was their duty as Muslims to confront unbelievers. Over the next several years, scores of young Yemeni men answered their clerics' calls for jihad. Afghanistan's mujahedeen received support from many Arab countries, as well as from the United States, but the Yemenis were among the fiercest of the so-called Afghan-Arab fighters. Unlike the jihadis from the wealthier states in the Persian Gulf, they were accustomed to hard living, and the rugged, mountainous terrain of Afghanistan was similar to that of their homeland.

After the Soviets withdrew from Afghanistan in 1989, many of these Yemeni jihadis returned home heroes. Their exalted stature was further cemented in 1994, when the still-simmering tensions between the country's Islamists and Marxists erupted anew into a full-fledged civil war and they played a critical role in defeating the Communists.

Though Hamdan was not especially religious, he enthusiastically embraced the idea of jihad, with its promise of paid and meaningful work. His recruiter, one of the leaders of the group, was a self-assured young man named Nasser al-Bahri. Although two years his junior, al-Bahri, who was born in Yemen but grew up in an upper-middle-class family in Jidda, Saudi Arabia, was far more worldly and sophisticated than Hamdan and was without question the most educated person he had ever met. Al-Bahri had studied business in college, but he was also deeply steeped in the Koran, having become a devout Muslim as a teenager in rebellion against his bourgeois upbringing. He spoke comfortably and forcefully about the plight of Muslims all over the world, and he had traveled extensively to places as far as Bosnia and Somalia to defend his oppressed Islamic brethren.

In 1996, Hamdan, al-Bahri, and a group of about thirty-five other Muslims, mostly Yemenis with a smattering of Saudis, convened in Jalalabad, Afghanistan, with the intention of going to Tajikistan to fight alongside the country's small Islamic insurgency against its Russian-backed government. They started out in jeeps and then, when the roads were impassable, on foot. For six months they traversed Afghanistan's mountainous, often snow-covered terrain. But to cross the Tajik border, they needed the permission of Ahmed Shah Massoud, the legendary anti-Soviet guerrilla commander who controlled the northeast quadrant of Afghanistan and was himself Tajik. Massoud refused to grant it. He had just forged a precarious alliance with his former enemy, Russia, and was relying on the Russians to defeat their common enemy in Afghanistan, a rising militia of Islamic radicals known as the Taliban.

At loose ends and casting about for a cause, one of the jihadis suggested that they go see a man named Osama bin Laden, at the time a well-known sheikh who led a militant group of itinerant Muslim holy warriors called al Qaeda. As luck would have it, bin Laden had recently been expelled from Sudan at the urging of the American government and relocated to Afghanistan, where he had earned his reputation fighting the Soviets during the 1980s. Word was that he was now enlisting soldiers for a new crusade to drive the United States from the Arabian Peninsula.

Soon al-Bahri, Hamdan, and the rest of the jihadis were making their way back through Afghanistan toward Jalalabad, near the base of the Hindu Kush Mountains, where bin Laden had set up camp in the caves of Tora Bora.

The group arrived in late 1996, days before Ramadan, the holiest time of year. They were demoralized, exhausted, and far from home, and in bin Laden they found a leader who saw strength and virtue in their suffering. He too had endured hardships: the Sudanese had stripped him of his fortune; his homeland of Saudi Arabia had stripped him of his citizenship; and his close friend and military chief, Abu Ubaydah, had just been killed in a ferry accident. He understood what the jihadis had been through and the purpose they were seeking. "On the existential plane, bin Laden was marginalized, out of play, but inside the chrysalis of myth that he spun about himself he was becoming a representative of all persecuted and humiliated Muslims," wrote Lawrence Wright in *The Looming Tower*, a history of al Qaeda.

The Yemeni jihadis held a special appeal to bin Laden. His father had been born in the Hadramawt, and as a radical sheikh in Saudi Arabia in the late 1980s he had taken it upon himself to end his ancestral homeland's flirtation with communism and purge it of nonbelievers by inciting and bankrolling attacks on its socialist leaders. What's more, only a smattering of Egyptians and Algerians had followed bin Laden to Afghanistan. To sell his new crusade to young Muslims, he was going to need support from the Arabian Peninsula, on whose behalf the campaign was being waged. "Bin Laden had just declared war on America, but no one cared because the young people from the Arabian Peninsula were not there," al-Bahri later recalled. "He urgently needed men from the Arabian Peninsula."

For three days bin Laden preached to his prospective recruits about the religious imperative of reversing America's presence in the Persian Gulf. He quoted the Prophet Muhammad's injunction, uttered on his deathbed: "Let there be no two religions in the Arabian Peninsula." Bin Laden spoke too about the need to change the nature of the fight against Islam's enemies. New kinds of training camps would be required. Conventional skills such as map reading and weapons training were no longer enough. They would also need to focus on fighting in cities and preparing for martyrdom operations, which meant learning how to blend in with civilian populations and attack civilian targets. Jihadis would be trained in bomb making, hijacking, assassination, even suicide bombing.

And bin Laden always kept broader war strategies in mind. "He said we must carry out painful attacks on the United States until it becomes like an agitated bull," al-Bahri recalled, "and when the bull comes to our region, he won't be familiar with the land, but we will."

SEVENTEEN OF THE ORIGINAL thirty-five jihadis decided to stay with bin Laden in Afghanistan; Hamdan, along with al-Bahri, was among them. For the next several years he worked for bin Laden mostly as a driver and bodyguard, first in Jalalabad, then, when bin Laden relocated for security reasons, at Tarnak Farms, a walled al Qaeda compound thirty minutes outside Kandahar. Hamdan had a Taliban-issued permit to carry a Russian-made pistol. His al Qaeda alias was Saqr al-Jedawi—"the hawk." As for al-Bahri—or Abu Jandal, as he was known inside the organization—he rose quickly through al Qaeda's ranks, becoming one of bin Laden's personal bodyguards after he subdued a Sudanese man who had assumed a hostile tone with the sheikh.

Tucked into a vast expanse of treeless desert and sagebrush, Tarnak Farms was a bleak and isolating place. But while those inside the compound existed in a world outside of time, bin Laden was busy raising his international profile. In 1998 he and a handful of other radical Islamic leaders—the International Islamic Front for Jihad Against Jews and Crusaders, they called themselves—issued a fatwa: "The ruling to kill the Americans and their allies—civilian and military—is an individual duty for every Muslim who can do it in any country in which it is possible to do it." Shortly after, in August 1998, al Qaeda carried out its first major strike, the simultaneous bombing of the American embassies in Tanzania and Kenya.

In 1999, at bin Laden's urging and with his financial help, al-Bahri and Hamdan became brothers-in-law, a development that took al-Bahri completely by surprise. He had been in a mountain town in Yemen, delivering a five-thousand-dollar dowry for bin Laden's fourth wife, when Hamdan tracked him down and told him that the sheikh had sent him with money and instructions for them to marry a pair of Yemeni sisters.

Prologue

After the wedding, Hamdan and al-Bahri returned to Afghanistan with their brides. Hamdan's wife, Um Fatima, was reluctant to go and shocked at the primitive conditions in which she was expected to live and raise a family. The house they were to live in was made of mud, its floors were dirt, and there was no running water. Um Fatima soon had a daughter to look after; the two would spend most of their days alone inside while Hamdan drove bin Laden around Afghanistan to rally the troops. When her husband *was* around, he usually wouldn't return until early evening, often with his clothes stained with grease from fixing the various cars and trucks on the compound. Um Fatima periodically complained about their life in Afghanistan. Hamdan told her to be patient, that one day they would move back to Yemen.

Al-Bahri moved around a lot as well. In the wake of the 1998 embassy attacks, bin Laden put him in charge of al Qaeda's guesthouses in Kabul and Kandahar. With his natural charisma, religious knowledge, and military expertise, he seemed an obvious choice to inspire and train the new generation of jihadis who were now pouring into Afghanistan. He and Hamdan did what they could to look after each other's families. When al-Bahri's first son was born, it was Hamdan who carried him to bin Laden so the sheikh could feed him bits of a masticated date from his own mouth and then bless him, according to the Islamic custom.

In the summer of 2000, Hamdan and al-Bahri returned to Sana with their wives for a family wedding. Within weeks of their arrival, a boat filled with explosives rammed into an American naval destroyer, the USS *Cole*, on a refueling stop in the Yemeni port of Aden. Al Qaeda was quickly identified as the culprit, and Yemeni intelligence started rounding up suspected extremists. Trying to flee to Afghanistan, al-Bahri got as far as the airport before being arrested.

The police came to Hamdan's in-laws' house looking for him too, but he and Um Fatima had already taken her family on a religious pilgrimage to Mecca. From Saudi Arabia, Hamdan and his wife returned to Afghanistan and bin Laden.

Months later, in the days leading up to September 11, Hamdan was part of a small motorcade of al Qaeda leaders, including bin Laden and his top lieutenant, Ayman al-Zawahiri, who drove into the mountains above Khost in order to watch the planes crash into the World Trade Center and the Pentagon on satellite TV. Unable to get a signal, they followed the news of 9/11 on the radio. After each strike, bin Laden held up another finger for his joyful, incredulous followers, promising yet another one.

For the next several weeks, the motorcade moved from one guest-house to the next as bin Laden and Zawahiri celebrated the success of the operation and readied their remaining fighters for America's imminent invasion. On October 7, with the ruins of the Twin Towers still burning, Al Jazeera broadcast bin Laden's prerecorded message to the world. "There is America, hit by God in one of its softest spots," he said. "Its greatest buildings were destroyed. Thank God for that. There is America, full of fear from its north to its south, from its west to its east. Thank God for that. These events have divided the whole world into two sides—the side of the believers and the side of the infidels . . . Every Muslim has to rush to make his religion victorious. The winds of faith have come."

In late November, with U.S.-backed Northern Alliance forces sweeping across Afghanistan, bin Laden ordered his men to evacuate their families from Tarnak Farms. On November 24, 2001, Hamdan returned to Kandahar, the last Taliban stronghold, for his young daughter and his wife, who was eight months pregnant at the time. With American B-52s circling the skies overhead, they made their way east in a silver Japanese hatchback through the Maruf mountains, alongside the throng of refugees heading toward Pakistan in the bitter cold, their backs laden with belongings. As they closed in on the border, Hamdan let his wife and daughter out of the car and then turned around.

Over the course of the next several weeks, Um Fatima traveled deeper into Pakistan in the back of a pickup truck with a group of Afghan refugees. Entering her ninth month of pregnancy, she became so hysterical that some sympathetic strangers in Karachi bought her and her daughter a plane ticket home. Upon arriving in Sana she was interrogated for five hours about her husband's whereabouts. Um Fatima said she assumed he was dead.

Two and a half months later, she received a letter from Hamdan on

International Committee of the Red Cross stationery. "My sweetheart, peace and blessings be upon you," it began. "I did not die. Allah prescribed a new life for me. Now I am a detainee with the Americans."

Within hours of leaving his family at the border, Hamdan had been captured by Northern Alliance soldiers who found two surface-to-air missiles in the trunk of his car. They hogtied him with electrical wire, placed a hood over his head, and soon turned him over to the American forces for a five-thousand-dollar bounty. During his early interrogations Hamdan gave the same story that other detainees were giving: that he was in Afghanistan working for a Muslim charity. After about a month had passed, though, another detainee identified him as bin Laden's driver, Saqr al-Jedawi. Hamdan acknowledged that he had worked for bin Laden and attended al Qaeda training camps.

For the next six months Hamdan was held at Bagram Air Base and at a U.S. prison camp in Kandahar. In early May 2002 he was transferred to the newly built American detention facility, Camp Delta, on Guantánamo Bay, Cuba. For a year and a half, Hamdan lived in one of Delta's main cellblocks, forty-eight six-by-eight-foot cells divided by wire mesh walls. In December 2003, he was moved out of Guantánamo's general population and into pretrial solitary confinement. Of the thousands of detainees in U.S. custody, President Bush had chosen him to be the first Arab defendant in America's first war crimes trials in more than fifty years.

ONE

The JAG

LT. CMDR. CHARLES SWIFT came bounding down the hallway of his JAG detachment at Mayport Naval Station in Jacksonville, Florida, early on the morning of September 11, 2001, a backpack slung over his shoulder and a large Starbucks coffee doused with half-and-half in his hand. He wore blue shorts, a faded white polo shirt, and boat shoes. At forty-one he had the padding and confident posture of the formerly athletic, along with a weathered complexion and an overgrown crew cut of sandy hair. As he made his way toward his office, his gait was unmistakable; he didn't so much walk as bounce on the balls of his feet, his toes pointed out.

Swift's mind was whirring. He had a big trial about to get under way, the court-martial of a chief petty officer who'd been accused of stealing thirty-five thousand dollars from the cash register at a gas station where he'd been moonlighting. The defendant had confessed to the crime, but Swift was trying to stave off a bad conduct discharge and save the man's pension by arguing that he suffered from a clinical compulsive disorder; his client had used all of the money he'd stolen to buy women's underwear on eBay. Swift had lined up a psychiatrist who was going to testify that it was an illness that could be treated through therapy. During his opening statement, which Swift was still formulating in his head, he was going to talk about the goals of punishment—to encourage rehabilitation, not to satisfy a desire for retribution—and the importance of helping people.

Inside his office, Swift fished a Jay-Z CD out of one of the piles on the desk, tore open a fresh pack of Nicorette—he'd recently quit Copenhagen—and removed a crisp white uniform from a hanger on the back of his door. Swift had learned long ago that the only way to keep his uniform clean was to keep it in plastic until the last possible moment. Since then, changing into his dress whites had become part of his pretrial ritual, along with listening to rap music, which, as he liked to say, put him in the mood to take down the man.

Swift made his way down the hall of the single-story concrete building, toward the military courtroom. On his way he noticed a cluster of people gathered around a television set, watching smoke pour out of a skyscraper. One of them said that there had been an accident; an airplane had flown into the World Trade Center.

Swift, whose wife was training to become a commercial pilot, knew that planes didn't veer so far off their flight paths accidentally. He also remembered the car bomb that had gone off in a garage under the Twin Towers in 1993. "That's a terrorist attack," he announced to the cluster of people before heading down the hall to the courtroom.

Once there, Swift urged the judge to postpone the proceedings but was refused, and jury selection began as scheduled. It wasn't until both towers and the Pentagon had been hit that all nonessential personnel were ordered off the base and he went home.

Swift's wife's flight school, which was three hours away in Vero Beach, was closed indefinitely, and she soon joined him in Jacksonville. They watched the news coverage of the attacks in horror: the jumpers falling through the sky, the towers collapsing in on themselves, the ash-caked swarms emerging dazed from lower Manhattan.

When Swift set out for work the following morning in his silver Honda convertible, he saw a line of cars four miles long waiting to be searched by military police at the entrance gates to Mayport and turned back around. His commanding officer, Capt. Bill Sweeney, called him at home a few hours later to find out why he wasn't at work. "The last thing you need right now is a defense lawyer," Swift told him.

CHARLIE SWIFT—no one except his wife and parents called him Charles—was, by both reputation and self-profession, one of the most zealous defense attorneys in the JAG Corps. The notion of law school had first occurred to him in 1990, when he was a twenty-nine-year-old surface warfare officer, the navigator of a Navy frigate called the *Rathburne*. One of Swift's collateral duties was chief legal officer, so when a few of the *Rathburne*'s sailors were arrested one night in a port town in Malaysia for smoking pot, it fell to him to negotiate their release. Swift made a time-honored defense lawyer's argument on their behalf: because the sailors had only one joint among them, only one of them could be guilty of possession. By sunrise he had managed to spring two of the men and got the third moved out of the prison's basement.

At the time, Swift's commitment to the Navy was nearing its end, and he was coming to the conclusion that he should probably leave the military. He was a natural seaman, a gifted ship handler and engineer who invariably excelled at tasks that interested him. But he had an exceptionally low tolerance for tasks that didn't and an almost involuntary disregard for military decorum. As a result, his performance had been erratic, as underscored by his wildly inconsistent fitness reports, the Navy's version of annual performance reviews.

At the end of Swift's first year of duty, his commanding officer rated him the top junior officer on his ship, the *Niagara Falls*. Not long after, the *Niagara*, which carried supplies to the Navy's South Pacific fleet, came under new command. Because this was the tropics and the ship was always loaded with groceries, roaches were a problem. The most efficient way to fumigate was to keep most of the crates of food on one side and spray the other, giving the *Niagara* a permanent list. On his second day on post, Swift's new commanding officer ordered him to fix it. Swift told him that that wasn't necessary; the ship had plenty of reserve stability. "I don't give a damn," the CO shot back. "I want that list off my ship." Swift left his CO's stateroom and returned a few hours later with a stack of charts and graphs, intending to demonstrate why the list wasn't affecting the *Niagara*'s performance. When the junior officers were next ranked, he had dropped to dead last.

Swift's law school options had been limited. He had performed well on the Law School Admission Test, but to call his college career undistingished would be generous; it had been an almost crushing disaster.

When Swift arrived at the United States Naval Academy in 1980, he more or less fitted the profile of the average incoming midshipman. He had grown up in Franklin, a small town in western North Carolina, where he was an Eagle Scout and varsity athlete with obvious intellectual aptitude. As it turned out, though, Swift, the adopted son of a forest scientist and schoolteacher, was utterly ill-suited to the academy. The physical challenges were not an issue: Swift, a standout wrestler who had worked summers at a ruby mine in Franklin, was fit and strong and had a high threshold for pain. But nearly everything else was.

Swift's problems started not long after he and the rest of his class assembled inside the gates of the academy, a formation of granite buildings and manicured playing fields on the banks of the Severn River in Annapolis, Maryland, and took an oath to defend the Constitution. The best way to get through plebe year was to lie low, but this was impossible for Swift: he walked funny, his uniform was never squared away, and his cover—or cap—was usually askew. It wasn't just that he didn't look the part, though. He also struggled to march in step and stumbled through his chow calls, a morning ritual in which plebes are forced to stand at full attention and recite an endless stream of information—the day's menu in the mess hall, the names of the officers of the watch, how many days until Navy beats Army—with upperclassmen's jaws in their faces. Plebes were expected to limit their answers to questions from upperclassmen, preferably to "No, sir!," "Aye, aye, sir!" or "No excuse, sir!" But Swift, an impulsive and compulsive talker, had trouble keeping his word count down. It wasn't long before people were calling him N.T., for Charles "Not Too" Swift.

It was sometimes hard to tell whether Swift was simply tone-deaf to the academy's peculiar subculture or deliberately defying it. "Charlie was in great shape physically, and he knew his ships and aircrafts, but he was a little spacey," recalled Gina DiNicolo, one of his closest friends at the academy and his date to the first dance of his plebe year, despite the taboo against dating fellow midshipmen. "He wasn't weak, but he was different, and the attitude was: He's different, he must suffer."

And he did. Hazing had long since been banned from the Naval Academy, replaced by a kinder, gentler form of persecution known as plebe indoctrination. The second semester of Swift's plebe year, however, coincided with the publication of James Webb's *A Sense of Honor*, a bestselling novel set at Annapolis during the Vietnam War that inspired upperclassmen to revive such long-dormant practices as forcing plebes to sleep naked on their metal bedframes.

When a roommate of Swift's came in for some particularly harsh abuse, an investigation was launched. Swift elected to tell the truth rather than protect the upperclassmen who had been accused of the misconduct. Soon Bancroft Hall, the massive dormitory that housed all forty-eight hundred of the academy's midshipmen, became a gauntlet of upperclassmen looking to mess with *him*. His chow calls were extended so that he'd receive demerits for being late for morning formation, his uniform and room inspections continued until an infraction was discovered, and he was overloaded with mandatory "professional reports" on arcane naval subjects.

Somehow he made it to the Herndon Monument Climb, the June ritual in which outgoing plebes knock a "Dixie cup"—the white canvas hat worn by first-year midshipmen—off a lard-slathered twenty-one-foot-tall obelisk. Swift's difficulties outlasted the ordeal of plebe year, though. Often they were self-inflicted and alcohol-related. He spent the better part of his junior year on campus restriction and disciplinary probation after racking up a string of offenses: an admiral's wife busted him skinny-dipping with a group of strippers; he was arrested after getting into a fistfight at a bar in Georgetown; he was hospitalized with alcohol poisoning.

Swift was scraping bottom academically too. The academy system rewarded nothing so much as efficiency; though it would not be diagnosed until many years later, Swift suffered from acute attention deficit disorder. He had a tendency to drift off during lectures and was easily distracted from his homework. He had succeeded in high school by virtue of his raw intelligence, but at the academy, where midshipmen were allotted just three hours a day to study, his difficulty in maintaining concentration proved a severe liability. In four years Swift flunked three classes—chemistry, thermodynamics, and celestial navigation—and was sent before two academic review boards, where he was grilled by a panel of officers who were responsible for determining whether he should be separated or retained. The second time, his junior year, he almost certainly would have been expelled had it not been for the intervention of his uncle, a distinguished Annapolis graduate and two-star admiral. "I'm going to see you one more time," Bud Edney, the commander of the midshipmen, told Swift at the time, "when I hand you your diploma or when I separate you."

Swift may never have made it had it not been for Deborah Breaden, a petite brunette whom he met one Saturday night at a dance at Dahlgren Hall, an old armory that doubled as a campus bar and disco on weekends. A week later Swift took Debbie, a senior in high school who lived with her grandmother in Annapolis, to the Ring Dance, the formal ceremony where juniors are presented with their class rings. "I fell head over heels with the guy immediately," Debbie later recalled. "He just seemed to exude this incredible energy. The best way to describe him—even though it's a word usually used for women—is 'vivacious.'"

Swift's performance at the academy instantly improved. He now had an incentive to keep his weekend privileges, and for the first time he was focused on his future.

Few midshipmen actually enjoy being at the academy: the saying goes that it is the only institution of higher learning where you can get a $250,000 education shoved up your ass one nickel at a time. Yet by the time they are done, even those who hate the academy the most— perhaps especially those who hate the academy the most—tend to recognize that it has changed them.

The Naval Academy's goal isn't simply to educate midshipmen. It is to develop them "morally, mentally, and physically" to defend their nation. Between the culture, the coursework, and the ubiquitous reminders of heroism—the ribbons that decorate the uniforms of instructors, the monuments that dot the campus—it is a lesson that usually sticks. "The Academy reinforced your love of country," wrote Robert Timberg, an Annapolis alumnus, in his book *The Nightingale's Song*. "It was not blind affection, and certainly not an overweening patriotism. You knew the United States had its faults, serious ones . . . But you also felt an optimism that the country could come to grips with its problems if given a chance. That was your job, to give it a chance. You were to be its protector, and that seemed like a worthwhile way for a man to spend his life."

In addition to bestowing midshipmen with this new sense of duty and optimism, Annapolis left many with profound, if ambivalent, feelings about it. Swift was no exception. As a plebe he had hung a sign in his room that read YOU ARE BEING PAID $545 A MONTH TO GET OUT OF BED and signed his letters home "A citizen of Stalingrad." Yet nine months after graduating—960th out of a class of 1,006—he donned his dress whites and married Debbie beneath crossed swords in the Naval Academy's chapel.

LAW SCHOOL WAS A STRUGGLE for Swift too. He had a knack for spotting issues and grasping concepts, but he was frustrated by the formality of legal writing and became tangled up in his own thoughts. He fell behind in classes that failed to hold his interest. His grades suffered, awakening in him feelings of inferiority and self-doubt that he chased away by drinking rather than studying, which only accelerated his downward spiral. Debbie grew concerned about his sinking self-esteem, not to mention the increasing amount of time he was spending in bars. She was teaching grade school at the time and had encountered several children with ADD. It occurred to her that Swift had all the same symptoms, both good and bad: restlessness, distractibility, forgetfulness, and a tendency toward addictive behavior on one side of the ledger; intuitive intelligence and creativity on the other. She suggested that he get tested, and he came up positive.

The diagnosis came almost as a relief to Swift. Gradually, with the encouragement of Debbie and a couple of his professors, he began to turn things around. He stopped drinking and discovered that by writing out his briefs as if they were mathematical equations rather than essays, he could avoid tying himself up in knots.

In 1993, Swift graduated from Seattle University Law School with honors. He wasn't planning to return to the military, but a job that he'd been counting on in a small division of the Justice Department that specialized in maritime law fell through. After two miserable months as an associate at a medium-size law firm in Tacoma, he sent in an application to the JAG Corps.

Created by George Washington in 1775, the JAG Corps likes to call itself the oldest law firm in the nation, but for the better part of its first two centuries it was largely devoid of lawyers. Soldiers accused of misconduct were effectively at the mercy of their commanders. This was by design. The court-martial system existed to advance the principal goal of military justice, which was to enforce discipline, not to dispense justice. The public raised few objections. The military was a small, distinct society. What it did to keep the country safe was its business.

World War II ushered in sweeping changes, though. Sixteen million Americans from every class and professional background answered the call to serve. Many were exposed to the military's conception of justice—during the war, there was an average of sixty court-martial trials a day—and few liked what they saw. What's more, America emerged from the war as the premier superpower, the world's defender of freedom. To meet the nation's new responsibilities, the armed forces would need to expand, and these new peacetime recruits could not be expected to sign away all of their rights in order to join the military.

And so James Forrestal, America's first secretary of defense, appointed a committee chaired by a Harvard law professor and former Army major, Edmund Morgan, to rewrite the rules of the country's 175-year-old system of military justice. The resulting document, the Uniform Code of Military Justice, was signed into law in May 1950. Among other things, it created a court of military appeals and provided service members with many of the protections of the Bill of Rights. Eighteen years later, against the backdrop of the ongoing civil rights struggle and a war in Vietnam whose protesters included members of the armed forces, came a fresh push for additional reforms. In 1968, Congress passed a new statute stipulating that counsel in court-martial trials could no longer be line officers without any formal legal training. They would have to be attorneys, serving under the command of their service's top lawyer, the judge advocate general; hence the now-familiar acronym JAG.

Swift returned to the Navy as a lieutenant. For his first case, he was detailed to serve as assistant counsel to a veteran JAG named Brent Pope, who was defending a sailor whose two teenage stepdaughters had accused him of sexually molesting them, a crime that carried a possible sentence of twenty-five years. Swift and Pope arrived at the sailor's Coast Guard base in Kodiak, Alaska, with every intention of persuading him to plead guilty. In a matter of minutes, though, Pope had gotten into a fight with the prosecuting JAG. "Fuck this," he told Swift. "Let's not make a deal. Let's try this thing."

The trial started a couple of weeks later. Swift felt sick to his stomach and confessed to Pope that he was nervous. He found Pope's response strangely calming. "You're not even going to remember that guy's name in three years," Pope said, gesturing at their client. "But he's going to remember yours for the rest of his life."

While digging for dirt on the stepdaughters, Swift discovered that the older one had once accused some boys of raping her but had later admitted that the sex was consensual. It was a defense lawyer's dream—a preexisting pattern of false sexual allegations—but the judge wouldn't allow them to introduce the false police report into evidence. Pope told Swift not to worry and called as a witness the cop who had taken the report. Pope's first question was whether he had an opinion about the girl's credibility. The prosecutor objected, citing lack of foundation. Pope asked the judge for permission to lay the foundation and then proceeded to ask the cop how he knew the girl. Out tumbled the story of the recanted rape charge. The prosecution demanded a mistrial. The judge refused, though she did call the defense counsel into her chambers for a lecture. After dressing Pope down for his slippery tactics, she turned toward Swift. "And you," she said, "are learning all of his bad habits." To Swift, now in Pope's thrall, this was high praise.

The daily proceedings were front-page news in the *Kodiak Daily Mirror*. Swift hadn't expected to do much more than keep track of the evidence and take notes, but Pope suggested that he cross-examine the older girl's child psychiatrist, a key witness for the prosecution. When Swift pressed her about her patient's credibility, the psychiatrist said the girl was getting better; she now told the truth at least 50 percent of the time. Impressed with Swift's performance, Pope asked him to give the closing argument too. Swift flipped a coin in front of the jury box. "That's what the prosecutor's idea of justice is," he said. Their client was acquitted on all but one minor charge, and Swift knew that he'd discovered his calling.

Guilty pleas are common in the JAG Corps. As far as the military justice system has come, commanders are still responsible for deciding whom to prosecute and on what charges, meaning that mounting a vigorous defense is tantamount to challenging a superior officer. Swift contested almost every case that crossed his desk, from the ship supervisor of a ballistic missile submarine who had tested positive for cocaine to a petty officer who had confessed to stealing the offering from a church, burning down the building, and then gambling away the money in Las Vegas. Swift threw himself completely into each one, spending hours with his clients to earn their trust. Every case, whether it involved murder or lewd behavior in a public park, was an epic battle with life-or-death stakes. "It's you and me versus the infinite resources of the United States government" is the way he put it to his clients.

Trial work is generally considered an entry-level job in the Navy JAG Corps. The mission of the U.S. Navy is to maintain maritime superiority and defeat any threat to the nation's free use of the high seas. Accordingly, the high-status JAG jobs entail advising line commanders on the legality of live military actions, not prosecuting or defending wayward service members. But Swift had no desire to be anywhere but the courtroom. He treated every trial like a wrestling match, starving himself beforehand and then binge-eating afterward.

By the time Swift arrived at Mayport in the summer of 2000, he had racked up a long list of improbable acquittals and had been promoted to lieutenant commander. He was also a familiar figure among the Navy's top brass. Swift's last tour before Florida was an unexpectedly high-profile one: he had been the senior JAG at Roosevelt Roads Naval Station in Puerto Rico. It had started out as a sleepy assignment—he and Debbie bought a twenty-one-foot sailboat and were able to cruise the Caribbean on weekends with their scuba gear, and Debbie got into underwater photography—but in April 1999 a Marine fighter jet conducting a training exercise over Vieques, a satellite island that served as a weapons-testing ground for the U.S. military, missed its target with a pair of five-hundred-pound bombs, killing a local civilian. Demonstrators organized mass sit-ins on the target range, and Vieques became an international cause célèbre. The White House had to grapple with the decision of whether to cave in and halt the bombing exercises, which it had every legal right to conduct, or risk alienating the Puerto Rican population, a particular concern to President Clinton, whose wife was running for the U.S. Senate in New York.

Swift participated in weekly strategy meetings with admirals from the Pentagon and senior officials from the Justice Department and tried to explain to the steady stream of celebrity protesters, from the Reverend Jesse Jackson to the pop star Ricky Martin, why they were wrong. The pleasure he took in being part of such a high-profile story was offset, if only partly, by the frustration of finding himself in an unwinnable fight against politics.

TWO

The Trials

SHORTLY AFTER NOON on Friday, September 14, 2001, a day of mourning and remembrance across the United States, President Bush stood beneath the soaring arched roof of Washington's National Cathedral and called America to prayer, even as he summoned it to battle. "In every generation the world has produced enemies of human freedom," the president said, as a driving rain pummeled the cathedral's massive stained glass windows. "They have attacked America because we are freedom's home and defender. And the commitment of our fathers is now the calling of our time."

Later that afternoon, Bush boarded Air Force One and flew to New York to visit the smoldering ruins of Ground Zero. Amid chants of "U-S-A! U-S-A! U-S-A!" from mud-streaked rescue workers who were still pulling bodies from the debris, the president delivered an impromptu address with a bullhorn. "I can't hear you!" one of the workers shouted. "I can hear *you*," Bush now famously shouted back. "The rest of the world hears you. And the people who knocked these buildings down will hear all of us soon." Late that night, Bush retreated to Camp David with his war cabinet for the weekend to plan the country's response to the most devastating attack on American soil in the nation's history, one that claimed the lives of nearly three thousand men, women, and children.

Buried in that day's *Washington Post*, amid the avalanche of post-9/11 coverage, was a report on one possible post-9/11 initiative: the president was considering trying certain suspected terrorists as war criminals before military tribunals rather than in America's civilian courts.

The idea had come from the former attorney general William Barr, who had explored the possibility of convening military tribunals for the Libyan terrorists accused of blowing up a New York–bound Pan Am airliner over Lockerbie, Scotland, during his tenure at the Justice Department in the late 1980s. "People were referring to the 9/11 attacks as criminal acts, talking about the World Trade Center as a crime site," Barr later recalled. "I didn't think we should get too locked into that model. This was more of a military conflict."

The proposal instantly found traction among the president's senior legal advisers, including Alberto Gonzales, and, most significant, the vice president's chief counsel, David Addington. Though he held a position that did not ordinarily entail shaping policy and was unknown to most Americans, the lanky, bearded Addington had quickly emerged as a powerful player in the post-9/11 White House. In addition to his close relationship with Vice President Dick Cheney, Addington had a forceful personality and a wealth of national security experience, particularly when compared with his untested counterpart, Gonzales.

Five days after *The Washington Post* story ran, Addington, Gonzales, and Timothy Flanigan, President Bush's deputy counsel, summoned Pierre-Richard Prosper, the thirty-seven-year-old head of the State Department's war crimes office, to a meeting at the White House. Prosper too had been mulling the possibility of trying terrorists before military tribunals. It was already clear that U.S. forces would be moving into Afghanistan. From a security perspective alone, he couldn't imagine bringing hundreds of captured terrorists, perhaps even bin Laden himself, onto U.S. soil and exposing them to civilian judges and jurics.

At the end of the meeting, Prosper was charged with convening an interagency task force to study the idea more closely. For the next several weeks his team of lawyers from the State, Justice, and Defense departments, as well as the White House and National Security Council, met regularly in a conference room on the seventh floor of the State Department. There they discussed the pros and cons of military tribunals relative to the administration's other prosecutorial options for terrorists, including federal trials or an international criminal tribunal, which the United Nations was advocating. The issues were endless, the opinions in the room diverse: Where would the tribunals be held? What would the charges be? Who would define the rules of evidence?

The White House quickly grew impatient with Prosper's consensus-seeking and time-consuming brain trust. The American bombing campaign in Afghanistan was already under way, and special operations forces were preparing for a ground assault. Terrorists could be in U.S. custody in a matter of weeks. And so, even as Prosper and his group debated the merits and efficacy of the tribunals, the president's senior legal advisers forged ahead with the idea on their own.

By this point, a small group of lawyers—Gonzales; Flanigan; the Pentagon's general counsel, William J. Haynes; and John Yoo, a deputy assistant attorney in the Office of Legal Counsel, the division of the Justice Department that provides legal advice to the executive branch—had already coalesced around Addington to help plot the administration's legal strategy in the emerging global war on terror. The War Council, as the group called itself, had eagerly embraced military tribunals as a linchpin of its plans. The reasons for this were largely strategic, informed by both the short- and long-term goals of the Bush White House.

On an immediate and symbolic level, convening the nation's first war crimes trials since World War II would put the fight against Islamic extremism in the same class as the fight against Nazism and thus telegraph to the world a moral comparison that would be hard to ignore.

Practically, the War Council believed the traditional tools of law enforcement—search warrants, criminal indictments, federal trials—were no longer enough when it came to dealing with a stateless enemy that deliberately blended into the civilian population and was committed to the destruction of America. This was a real war, not a metaphorical one, and these were wartime courts. In broad terms, certain rights that would be considered fundamental in a civilian court wouldn't apply. If defendants were suspected terrorists, they couldn't very well be permitted to see all of the evidence against them, as some of it would no doubt be classified for national security reasons. Because the War Council determined that military tribunals would not have to be governed by statute, the trial system could be built to conform to the particular circumstances of the war on terror. The tribunals could be closed to the public to minimize propaganda efforts by the defendants. What's more, the evidentiary standards could be flexible. So, for example, judges could be empowered to admit an al Qaeda document discovered in a cave in Afghanistan even if the prosecution was unable to show its chain of custody.

Finally, but by no means least significant, because the trials would be overseen by the executive branch, they were consistent with the administration's broader goal of reasserting and expanding the president's powers in the aftermath of September 11. For both the vice president and his chief counsel, this was a preoccupation that long predated the terrorist attacks. It could in fact be traced back to the constitutional culture wars of the mid-1980s. At the time, Cheney was a Wyoming congressman and the ranking Republican on the House Intelligence Committee, and Addington, who had recently emerged from Duke University Law School into the dawn of the Reagan era, was one of the committee's young Republican staffers. Both men were ardent champions of the Reagan Doctrine, the president's ambitious and aggressive strategy to confront Soviet power worldwide, stepping up the arms race and taking the fight to the countryside of the third world, to places like El Salvador, where a Soviet-backed insurgency threatened to topple the ruling regime. More fundamentally, both Cheney and Addington believed that matters of national security should be left almost entirely in the hands of the president.

The mid-1980s were years of open hostility between the Republican administration and a Democratic House of Representatives that looked warily at Reagan's annual military budget increases and smelled another Vietnam in El Salvador. Things came to a head in late 1986, when news broke that the administration had been covertly funding the contras, the Nicaraguan forces that were opposing Marxist revolutionaries in neighboring El Salvador. Congress promptly launched an investigation led by the House Intelligence Committee. The resulting 427-page report, released almost a year later, was withering, accusing the president of violating American law and flouting the will of Congress—in sum, abusing his executive authority.

There was another way to look at the Iran-contra affair, though: that it was Congress that had overstepped its authority by interfering in the conduct of U.S. foreign policy. This view found its most forceful articulation in a separate, dissenting report commissioned and overseen by Cheney, with research and legal support from Addington. Their dissent argued that the Constitution gave the president all the power he needed to sell arms to the contras whether Congress approved or not. Not that President Reagan was entirely safe from blame. The report criticized him not for openly defying Congress's will, but for doing so clandestinely, which amounted to a "less-than-robust defense of his office's constitutional powers." It was a mistake that the president had repeated, the report continued, by cooperating with congressional investigators rather than simply invoking his executive privilege.

Even in the early weeks after 9/11, the echoes of the Reagan Doctrine were impossible to miss in the Bush administration's evolving approach to fighting terrorism, in the president's religiously charged vocabulary of good and evil, but also in his administration's broader strategy to encourage the spread of democracy in the Islamic world. Cheney and Addington had been on the margins of the White House during the Reagan years, doing what they could in their limited capacities to empower the president to combat communism. Now they were in position to do a good deal more to help President Bush defeat radical Islam.

WITH PROSPER AND HIS GROUP hunkered down in the State Department, the president's senior legal advisers got to work laying the foundation for military tribunals on their own. Their first call was to the thirty-four-year-old John Yoo.

A former clerk for Justice Clarence Thomas and Berkeley law professor whose academic work focused on foreign affairs and presidential war powers, Yoo had already been called on to draft an overarching opinion defining the scope of the president's authority to answer the 9/11 attacks. The lengthy memo, which Yoo delivered to the White House counsel's office on September 25, 2001, was to serve as the legal scaffolding for the global war on terror. Its conclusion was that President Bush possessed the authority to respond to 9/11 in any way he deemed necessary and appropriate, and that not even laws passed by Congress could limit this authority. ("The power of the President is at its zenith under the Constitution when the President is directing military operations of the armed forces, because the power of the Commander in Chief is assigned solely to the President," Yoo had written.)

As he set out to assess the legality of trying terrorists before military tribunals—or military commissions, as the administration had taken to calling them—Yoo enlisted the help of his friend and colleague Patrick Philbin, with whom he had clerked on the D.C. circuit court of appeals for Judge Laurence H. Silberman. The thrust of their determination was that military commissions were without question a legitimate course of action. Their November 6 memo remains classified, but Tim Golden, a reporter for *The New York Times*, quoted it as saying that the 9/11 attacks were "plainly sufficient" for applying the laws of war and that the president has "inherent authority" to authorize the commissions.

The White House assigned the Pentagon's general counsel and a protégé of Addington's, William J. Haynes, the task of figuring out how the commissions would work. The Uniform Code of Military Justice gives the Army authority over military commissions, so Haynes reached out to the Army's judge advocate general, Gen. Thomas Romig. Haynes stressed to Romig that the project was top secret. For now he could bring only a few officers into the loop. Romig chose the Army's head of criminal law, Col. Lawrence Morris, to lead the small team.

Morris was an expert in military justice, but he knew almost nothing about military commissions. He soon discovered that they had been around for more than 150 years, since the Mexican-American War of 1847.

Morris spent a few weeks poring over historical documents at the

National Archives warehouse in suburban Maryland and then racing back to his office in Rosslyn, Virginia, to brief Haynes on his progress. "I kept expanding on an outline of talking points I would use with Mr. Haynes," Morris later remembered. "What was this mechanism? What was it used for before? How can we make it work now?"

By the end of October, Morris had closed in on one especially relevant precedent. In most cases military commissions had been used either in American-occupied territories or in states under martial law, in short, when no other alternative was available. In the summer of 1942, however, a group of German saboteurs had landed by submarine in the United States with plans to blow up bridges, airplane plants, and railroad hubs around the country. The day after their arrival one of the men, George Dasch, had a change of heart and called the Federal Bureau of Investigation's New York office to notify it of the group's intentions. The FBI dismissed him as a crackpot, so he hopped on a train to Washington, checked into the Mayflower Hotel, and told his story to the FBI in person. Dasch was again met with skepticism. Only after he pulled eighty thousand dollars in cash from his briefcase did the FBI start to take him seriously.

Like modern-day terrorists, the saboteurs wore no uniforms and targeted civilians. While they were subject to criminal prosecution in the U.S. courts, which were open and functioning, President Roosevelt had instead elected to try them before a military commission of seven Army generals, and the Supreme Court, in a case called *Ex parte Quirin*, had given him the unanimous go-ahead to do so.

When Morris and Haynes discussed the case, Haynes seemed especially interested in the language of President Roosevelt's order authorizing the commission to try the saboteurs. Morris soon learned why. On Saturday, November 10, 2001, he was called to the Pentagon to comment on a confidential draft copy of a similar order authorizing the use of commissions to try non-American prisoners in the war against terrorism. It was written by Addington but had been closely modeled after Roosevelt's of 1942.

The three-page order was ready for President Bush's signature on the morning of November 13, 2001. Bush was about to leave for his ranch in Crawford, Texas, but Northern Alliance forces were already rolling into Kabul. There was no time to lose. Bradford Berenson, an associate White House counsel, raced into the Oval Office with the final draft, and the president signed it minutes before climbing into Marine One, which was idling on the White House lawn.

It was a "military order," meaning that its authority was derived from the commander-in-chief clause of the Constitution, which gives the president control over the nation's military. The order was applicable to all noncitizens who the president had "reason to believe" were affiliated with al Qaeda or had engaged in or aided and abetted acts of terrorism against the United States. The details on the trials themselves were sparse. The order did not say where the commissions would take place, what the charges would be, or who would serve as the attorneys. It did enumerate a few of the rules, though: the president himself would choose whom to try; hearsay evidence would be admissible; a majority of votes would be adequate for a guilty verdict; the jurisdiction of the war crimes courts would be exclusive, meaning that there would be no appeals to the U.S. courts; and sentences would include life in prison and death.

THE CREATION of the commissions had been an extraordinarily secretive process. Secretary of State Colin Powell and National Security Adviser Condoleezza Rice were among the many senior officials who didn't know about the administration's plans to go forward with the idea until after the president had signed the order.

Prosper too had been given no advance notice. His interagency task force had completed an analysis of the president's various options for trying suspected terrorists in late October that never even started its journey up the chain of command to the White House. "I had no idea the order was being signed until I saw it on CNN," Prosper recalled.

Nevertheless, with the military order in place, Prosper was assigned a new task. Later that month, while visiting his parents in upstate New York over Thanksgiving, he got a call on his secure cell phone from Marc Grossman, the undersecretary of state for political affairs. Grossman patched in Gen. Peter Pace, the chairman of the Joint Chiefs of Staff, who told Prosper that U.S. forces had picked up a few hundred prisoners in a recent battle at Mazar-e Sharif in northern Afghanistan. The theater commander, Tommy Franks, wanted them out of his area of operations, and there were too many to stow on an aircraft carrier in the Arabian Sea. "What should he do with them, Pierre?" Grossman asked.

Back in Washington, Prosper reassembled his task force and presented it with a new question: Where should the United States detain captured combatants, pending their possible trial by military commission? Wherever the facility was located, it would have to be large and secure, as it was an obvious target for another terrorist operation. It was still possible that the conflict would spill out of Afghanistan, so the most convenient option—moving detainees to a secure facility in a neighboring country, such as Pakistan—was out of the question. The group looked into using a U.S. military base in Frankfurt, but there was a risk that the German government might try to exert a degree of authority over the facility. It also considered and ruled out some of the smaller islands in the Pacific, including the Marshall Islands: some lacked the necessary infrastructure; others simply demanded too much money.

Someone suggested Guantánamo Bay, a U.S. naval station in the southeastern corner of Cuba. As a military base on a dusty piece of windswept property surrounded on three sides by water, it was certainly secure. It didn't have much in the way of infrastructure, but it could easily be outfitted with some sort of temporary prison. And it was a three-hour flight from Florida, making it relatively remote yet convenient enough for intelligence officials and interpreters.

The Defense Department liked the idea, but there was one outstanding issue. More than just a prison camp, Guantánamo Bay was going to be, in the words of one of its future commanders, "the interrogation battle lab for the war on terror." Al Qaeda was a secretive organization whose members had been trained to resist interrogation. In order to break them down, interrogators were going to need a tightly controlled environment, safe from outside interference from third parties—most notably civilian judges and defense lawyers. "Any insertion of counsel into the subject-interrogator relationship . . . can undo months of work and may permanently shut down the adversarial process," one Defense Department intelligence official later explained.

Even though the administration didn't intend to disclose the names of the detainees, it recognized that it would be only a matter of time before their identities started leaking out and human rights and civil liberties lawyers set about trying to challenge their detentions. The administration wanted to be sure that these lawyers didn't find a foothold in America's civilian courts. So the critical question was: Did the jurisdiction of the federal courts extend to Guantánamo Bay, which the United States leased from Cuba?

In late December, Yoo and Philbin were called on to provide an answer. Their search quickly led them to a 1950 Supreme Court case known as *Johnson v. Eisentrager*. Lothar Eisentrager was a German intelligence officer based in Shanghai who ran the Nazi espionage operations for the Far East during World War II. When Germany surrendered in the spring of 1945, Eisentrager and a number of other China-based German soldiers signed on to help the Japanese military. They were arrested the following year by the American Military Mission in China, accused of violating the terms of their country's unconditional surrender and prosecuted as war criminals before a U.S. military commission sitting in Shanghai. The majority of them were convicted, sentenced, and repatriated to Germany, where they were incarcerated in an Allied prison.

From there they filed suit against the United States in federal district court in Washington, D.C., challenging the lawfulness of their trial and imprisonment. The case eventually made its way to the Supreme Court, which ruled that the federal courts had no jurisdiction over the suit because the Germans had been captured, tried, and punished outside the sovereign United States.

The same could be said of any claim brought by the Guantánamo detainees—that is, as long as Guantánamo was not part of the sovereign United States. Yoo and Philbin determined that it was not. America's long-term lease for the property, they wrote, "expressly provides that 'the United States recognizes the continuance of the ultimate sovereignty of the Republic of Cuba'" over the base. "The great weight of legal authority," they concluded, suggested that Guantánamo Bay was beyond the "territorial jurisdiction" of the federal courts.

Yoo and Philbin's opinion cleared the way for the first planeload of prisoners to touch down on Guantánamo on January 11, 2002. They were initially housed at Camp X-Ray in open-air cells divided by barbed wire–topped chain-link fencing. Within a matter of months there were more than three hundred detainees on Guantánamo. Camp X-Ray was at maximum capacity, and ground had been broken on a more permanent facility, Camp Delta. Its opening in May ushered in the arrival of hundreds more prisoners in the war on terror, including a Yemeni man named Salim Hamdan.

DAYS AFTER PRESIDENT BUSH signed the November 13 military order, Colonel Morris and his growing staff of JAGs were relocated to an empty office in the basement of the Pentagon to continue their work on the commissions. Morris divided the JAGs into teams based on their areas of expertise, and they set about creating what was essentially a new judicial system from scratch. It was a daunting task. The terrorists who were going to find themselves in the dock might have committed unspeakable atrocities, but what specific crimes were they guilty of? And what rights were they entitled to? In short, how could the JAG teams prevent any terrorists from going free without sacrificing the legitimacy of the trials?

Inside the Pentagon, a rift quickly opened over the commissions between the military lawyers and the political appointees. General Romig, as well as the top lawyers of the Air Force and Navy, Maj. Gen. Thomas Fiscus and Rear Adm. Donald Guter, had been taken aback by the president's military order. They thought that the commissions should take into account the dramatic changes in military and international law that had occurred since the time of the Nazi saboteurs—most prominently, the advent of the Geneva Conventions and the Uniform Code of Military Justice. "We wanted the trials to draw on our current state of jurisprudence, not something that happened fifty years ago," Guter later recalled. "We didn't want it to look like we were moving back in time in terms of due process because for sure that criticism would come down on the military, not the administration." In his meetings with Haynes as well as Yoo and Philbin, Morris too made clear his concerns that the trials might be perceived as unfair. He thought the commissions should more closely resemble conventional court-martial trials for American servicemen than the trial convened by FDR for the Nazi saboteurs.

The political appointees grew frustrated with the military lawyers' skepticism and increasingly cut them out of the conversations over the shape of the commissions. Once the procedures had been finalized, Morris's team was supposed to serve as the Defense Department's "executive agent" for the trials—in effect, to run and oversee them. But Defense Secretary Donald Rumsfeld had second thoughts about this plan. In early 2002 the Pentagon started dismantling Morris's team. The Defense Department's general counsel's office was going to be in charge of the commissions instead.

Morris was reassigned, and his notes were turned over to Col. William Lietzau, a war crimes expert who had been pulled out of his command of a Marine boot camp battalion in San Diego and summoned to the Pentagon's general counsel's office in January 2002 to help drive the commission process forward. Lietzau shared some of his fellow military lawyers' concerns about the president's order. "The language felt anachronistic," Lietzau would remember. "We should have been talking about grave breaches of Geneva, and it looked like they just cut and pasted from the *Quirin* order." Nevertheless, over the course of the next several months he worked closely with Haynes and one of the Pentagon's deputy general counsels, Paul "Whit" Cobb, to develop the legal machinery for the commissions.

Slowly, over the course of dozens of drafts, a trial system started to take shape. On March 21, 2002, the Defense Department unveiled Military Commission Order No. 1, a sixteen-page list of trial procedures for the commissions. At the press conference accompanying their release, Secretary Rumsfeld emphasized morality over might and underscored America's commitment to conducting full and fair trials. "We are a nation of laws," he said, peering over the top of his rimless spectacles. "We have just been attacked by lawless terrorists. The manner in which we conduct trials under military commissions will speak volumes about our character as a nation, just as the manner in which we were attacked speaks volumes about the character of our adversaries."

THREE

VUCA

LIEUTENANT COMMANDER SWIFT rose instinctively when Capt. Dan McCarthy, a superior officer and the chief JAG prosecutor at Mayport, appeared in his doorway one afternoon in the spring of 2002. McCarthy, a strapping former college basketball star, put Swift at ease and took a seat. Like Swift, McCarthy was an Annapolis graduate who had gone back to law school and then joined the JAG Corps. They often went up against each other during trials but were cordial, even friendly, outside the courtroom. On Sundays, Swift sometimes watched Jacksonville Jaguars games at McCarthy's house, and they occasionally jogged together around the base.

"Ever heard of *Ex parte Quirin?*" McCarthy asked.

"No, sir," Swift replied.

"Well, you might want to look at it," McCarthy said, dropping the sixty-year-old Supreme Court opinion and a lengthy background report of the case on Swift's desk. "It's going to be the basis for the military commissions."

Swift had heard, vaguely, about the commissions, though he'd missed the news of President Bush's military order authorizing their use. A congenitally poor sleeper who was often stretched out on his couch until almost dawn watching the History Channel or DVDs of *The West Wing,* he stayed up late that night reading *Quirin.*

As Colonel Morris had discovered only six months earlier while doing research for the administration at the National Archives, Swift soon learned that Richard Quirin was one of eight Nazi saboteurs arrested in the United States and designated to stand trial before a military commission convened in 1942 by President Roosevelt. But while Morris had been focused on justifying the use of military commissions to prosecute suspected terrorists, Swift gravitated instantly to the story of the defense lawyer assigned to defend the saboteurs, an Army colonel in the legal affairs department of the War Department named Kenneth Royall.

Soon after the saboteurs had been arrested by the FBI and subsequently transferred to the custody of the military, an envelope had arrived from the White House for Royall. Inside was a letter signed by the president ordering him to defend the saboteurs before a military commission, as well as a presidential proclamation denying the men access to the civil courts. Royall instantly recognized his dilemma. His duty was to vigorously defend the accused, which meant trying to get the case moved to the civil courts, where they would have more rights. Yet his own commander in chief had explicitly precluded that possibility. Royall decided to write a letter to Roosevelt asking him to reconsider the proclamation. The president responded, via his secretary, that he would not. As for how Royall should proceed, FDR told him to use his judgment. Royall wrote the president again, this time politely informing him that his duty to his clients compelled him to seek a determination on the legality of the commission.

The Supreme Court heard the case, *Ex parte Quirin,* in a special summer session. The verdict was quick and unanimous, with the justices finding that FDR's commission was legal. The defendants were subsequently found guilty in their military commission. Six were executed.

By the time he finished reading, Swift was in a lather. It looked to him like a quintessential political trial. America's sabotage statute carried a maximum sentence of thirty years. If the president removed the saboteurs from the civil system, though, he could hang them and, in so doing, make an example of them. (There was also the fact that a public trial—open to the media—would most likely have destroyed the popular perception that the saboteurs had been apprehended in a heroic FBI sting.)

To judge by its rules, Swift thought, the commission could easily have been mistaken for something out of Stalin's Soviet Union; among other things, the defendants had been put to death without any sort of appeal. As for the Supreme Court's unanimous decision validating the lawfulness of the commission, it seemed a clear product of what was known in the military as undue command influence; for the justices to have ruled otherwise would have meant contradicting a direct order from the nation's commander in chief.

Swift's first stop the next morning was McCarthy's office. "Do we really want to be doing this, sir?" he asked.

For the next thirty minutes they discussed the wisdom of trying terrorists as war criminals. "I'm sure the Defense Department will do the right thing," McCarthy told Swift as he left.

Swift didn't give much more thought to military commissions until early 2003, when his detailer, the officer tasked with doling out his assignments, told him that the Navy was considering nominating him to serve as one of the defense attorneys. Swift reminded him that he was scheduled to start a yearlong graduate program in trial advocacy at Temple University in Philadelphia in April. His detailer assured him that it would be a short tour, no more than six weeks, because the first group of defendants all were going to plead guilty.

Swift was ambivalent. He was tempted by the romantic appeal of the assignment, which put him in mind of John Adams defending the British redcoats after the Boston Massacre. But how historic could a guilty plea be? Debbie thought it was a bad idea. "If you want to do it, fine," she told Swift, "but you're going to make a lot of enemies in the Navy. This will kill your career."

A couple of months later Swift had just returned from a court-martial trial in Georgia when his secretary informed him that he'd received a call from a colonel at the Pentagon. "Oh, yeah?" said Swift. "What was *he* wrongfully accused of?" Swift's secretary told him it wasn't that kind of call. The colonel was Will Gunn, the Air Force JAG who had recently been named chief defense counsel for the military commissions.

Swift called Gunn back, and they spoke for an hour or so. Swift came on strong. "He certainly struck me as unusual," Gunn later remembered. "It's not every day that a lieutenant commander volunteers that he's a member of the ACLU."

Gunn knew that the Defense Department wanted defense lawyers who would be "loyal to the military commissions process," not "Johnnie Cochran types," as Haynes, the Pentagon's general counsel, had put it to him. Still, Gunn liked Swift's enthusiasm. His fitness reports as a military lawyer were unimpeachable; one of Swift's commanding officers in Mayport had described him as the most impressive litigator she had ever seen. Perhaps most of all, the services had not exactly flooded Gunn with candidates. The word inside the JAG Corps was that the commissions were going to be a career buster. From the Navy, only Swift and one other lawyer agreed to have their names put forward.

When he arrived at his office the next morning, a Friday, Swift had an e-mail from Gunn asking him to report for duty on Monday. At his farewell party his staff presented him with a raincoat—there were rumors that the terrorists being held on Guantánamo Bay had taken to showering prison guards with urine and feces—and a humidor filled with short, slender cigarillos, a winking reference to Swift's habit of smoking cigars in a gazebo outside Mayport's military courtroom while waiting out juries.

COLONEL GUNN had not sought out the job of chief defense counsel and had accepted the position only after months of on-and-off conversations with the Defense Department and no shortage of personal searching. A graduate of the Air Force Academy and Harvard Law School, he had been steadily climbing the military hierarchy for more than twenty years and was on track to make general, perhaps even become the Air Force's first African-American judge advocate general. From the moment he'd been approached about the assignment, he knew the risks to his career were high, the rewards at best uncertain. A born-again Christian, Gunn had prayed daily about whether to withdraw his name from consideration. He had decided not to, though, and so, on a sunny Monday morning in March 2003, he found himself in a conference room on the ground floor of the Pentagon, addressing his new team of defense lawyers for the first time.

Gunn hoisted his brittle six-foot-seven-inch frame out of his chair and wrote four letters on a big white blackboard: *VUCA*. It was an acronym that he'd learned a few years earlier in a graduate course at the Industrial College of the Armed Forces: Volatile. Uncertain. Complex. Ambiguous. It seemed to apply perfectly to the situation in which he and his four new defense attorneys, two Navy JAGs and two Air Force JAGs, now found themselves.

Gunn told his lawyers what the Defense Department had been telling him: the trials would most likely be starting on Guantánamo Bay in a matter of weeks. The four JAGs spent the morning brainstorming about how to gear up. They all agreed that the public's expectations would be low; military lawyers were not exactly considered the cream of the legal profession under the best of circumstances, let alone when their clients were suspected terrorists. There was an endless number of practical matters to discuss: Would they have time to interview witnesses? Did they have a travel budget? Would the government monitor conversations with their clients? The broader issues were more daunting: How were they going to go about countering the widespread perception that their eventual clients were already guilty, given that both the president and Secretary Rumsfeld were referring to the detainees on Guantánamo as "the worst of the worst"?

At around noon the four JAGs broke for a sandwich in the Pentagon's food court. When they returned, Gunn announced that he'd been ordered to send them all home and that he'd be in touch soon with more information.

Swift and the other Navy JAG, Lt. Cmdr. Philip Sundel, figured there could only be one explanation for their abrupt dismissal: the administration had decided against doing the commissions after all. After a week of silence, though, Gunn called the Navy JAGs and told them to come back. When they did, they learned that the staff of four had been reduced to just the two of them; the two JAGs from the Air Force had been vetoed by the Department of Defense.* For Swift and Sundel, it was the first glimpse of the highly politicized process they were about to wade into, not to mention the all-powerful role the administration would play in it. Not only was the Defense Department writing the rules and running the prosecutions, it was vetting the defense attorneys.

There were no press releases or news conferences announcing Swift's and Sundel's appointments. In fact the two JAGs were explicitly barred from speaking to the media. For the next couple of months they were left more or less alone in their new jobs. With no clients, no regular contact with their superiors, and no clear instructions from above, they watched the invasion of Iraq unfold on CNN and started educating themselves. Stacks of printed documents were soon rising from their desks. They studied the Geneva Conventions and the laws of war and immersed themselves in the two-hundred-plus-year history of U.S. military commissions, as well as international war crimes tribunals—Nuremberg, Tokyo, and elsewhere. They sought out experts on Arab and Islamic culture to help them prepare to meet their eventual clients and looked for international and humanitarian law conferences to attend. Gaining admission to these conferences, however, proved harder than they had anticipated. When Swift tried to sign up for a seminar being run by the International Committee of the Red Cross on the legal status of the Guantánamo detainees, he was told that the conference was for humanitarian law professionals only.

"I have been assigned to the military commissions as a defense counselor," Swift replied. "Since you're probably going to be talking about what a lousy job I'm going to do, I'd like to be there." He and Sundel both went.

Despite their diametrically different personalities and working styles, a bond quickly developed between the two JAGs. Small, wiry, and laconic, Sundel had grown up in the Bronx and graduated from Bates College in Maine. He'd wanted to be a fighter pilot but wound

---

* Haynes overruled their appointment when he learned that one had been accused of drunk driving and that both had recently been passed over for promotion. Already anticipating the inevitable criticism that the administration had stacked the deck against the defendants, he wanted all the defense lawyers to possess unassailable service records. For his part, Gunn figured that because their military careers had stalled out they would be less likely to be burdened by concerns about professional advancement.

up at Miami University Law School after failing a vision test at the Navy's flight school in Pensacola. Sundel had some grounding in war crimes and international law from a year spent working for the United Nations as an investigator for the international criminal tribunals in Rwanda. Having done two tours of duty as an appellate lawyer, he was also accustomed to spending his days researching, thinking, and taking notes.

Swift had a harder time adjusting to the rhythm of his new job. He had taken a laws of war seminar at the Naval Justice School years earlier but otherwise hadn't had any exposure to the Geneva Conventions. He also felt left out of the larger story of Iraq, which had pushed Afghanistan and Guantánamo Bay to the margins. "There's a big war going on, and I'm reading about in *The Washington Post*," Swift later recalled. "I really felt useless." Full of zeal and impatience, he was constantly peering over the partition that separated his cubicle from Sundel's to blurt out his latest ideas and racing down the hall to run his notions by Gunn.

Sundel's responses were often monosyllabic, but he usually welcomed the interruptions. For Gunn, who was busy building a staff and figuring out how to navigate the hierarchy of the Pentagon, Swift's intrusions were more trying. "There were times when I wondered whether I'd made the right choice with respect to Charlie," Gunn would remember. "He'd come into my office and pontificate for an hour about some idea. It was hard to get a word in edgewise; you're just sort of waiting for him to take a breath. I was trying to build a team, so I wanted to listen, but at the same time I needed to get work done."

Swift gradually settled into a routine. Having assumed that he wasn't going to be in Washington for long, he had decided against getting his own apartment and had moved from his uncle's house to his grandmother's basement in Falls Church, Virginia. On Friday afternoons he would drive to Delaware to spend the weekend with Debbie, who had an internship at a flight simulator in Wilmington and was sharing a condominium with two other pilots until Swift finished his tour on the commissions. On Monday morning he would wake up before dawn and drive back to the Pentagon. Weeknights he'd jog across the Potomac or paddle a canoe around the small lake beside his grandmother's house.

Come May, Swift and Sundel still had no clients. By this point the prison camp on Guantánamo Bay had been open for sixteen months, and civil libertarians and human rights activists were no longer the only ones criticizing the administration's detention policies. Having given President Bush plenty of slack in the aftermath of 9/11, the media were now pressing the administration to begin sorting out the six-hundred-plus prisoners being held on Guantánamo. Even Secretary of State Powell warned Rumsfeld that the indefinite detentions threatened to undermine U.S. efforts to build a broad coalition against terrorism.

At the end of the month, in an effort to signal that the commission process was moving forward, the Defense Department introduced Gunn to the media. At the press conference, Gunn told reporters that he had not asked for the assignment and acknowledged that the real "glamour job" was prosecuting terrorists, not defending them. Nevertheless, Gunn made it clear that his team didn't intend to roll over.

"Colonel," one reporter asked, "as a uniformed member of the U.S. military and knowing what these folks have been accused of, in this building, in New York City, and around the world, how can you and the folks on your team really generate the passion to feel that these people deserve to be defended, let alone to actually go in to work every day for as long as it takes to defend them in that zealous way that you talk about?"

"We do that, first of all, because we believe in this country, and we believe in what this country espouses as its key values," Gunn answered. "And among those key values is the concept that every individual accused of a crime is presumed to be innocent."

It was a stirring response, but as far as Swift and Sundel were concerned, Gunn was playing right into the government's hands. By suggesting that a zealous defense would even be *possible*, he was legitimizing the president's military commissions.

THE DEFENSE DEPARTMENT continued to define the workings of the commissions over the course of the spring. Public pressure from such unlikely quarters as the conservative columnist William Safire had prompted Secretary Rumsfeld to consult with an array of legal experts about the trials. The procedures had improved since the president's original military order. According to the new rules, defendants would be presumed innocent until proved guilty, they would have the right to hire civilian lawyers to defend them, the trials would be at least partly open to the media, a unanimous verdict would be required for the imposition of a death sentence, and there would be some sort of appeals process.

Swift still didn't like what he saw. Among other shortcomings, defendants would not necessarily be able to see the evidence against them, hearsay would be permitted, and the appeals process consisted of a four-member review panel handpicked by the defense secretary. More fundamentally, the Defense Department—in effect, the prosecution—was not only defining the crimes worthy of trial by commission but doing so only after hundreds of suspects were already in custody and had been repeatedly interrogated. That was ex post facto law; crimes could be retrofitted to suit the prisoner.

Swift mentioned some of his concerns about the emerging system to the chief prosecutor, an Army colonel named Frederick Borch. "If you've got a problem with the hearsay rules, you can argue at the commission that hearsay evidence is unreliable," Borch told him one afternoon. "That's what they did at the Tokyo tribunals."

"But, sir, the defense lost every single challenge at the Tokyo tribunals," Swift replied. "Are we supposed to just run a losing play?"

Swift and Sundel lobbied Gunn to be more outspoken about the commissions, to call them what they believed they were—kangaroo courts—but Gunn thought there was a difference between enabling a vigorous defense and criticizing the system. And anyway, he wasn't allowed to speak to the media without a Pentagon spokesman present.

In the face of Swift and Sundel's continuous complaints about the process, a number of Pentagon officials began to wonder if they'd been premature in bringing defense counsel on board. While it was important to signal that suspected terrorists would be given proper legal representation, there was an obvious danger in having idle defense lawyers hanging around, looking for ways to undermine the system before the trials had even gotten under way.

The Pentagon tried to keep Swift and Sundel busy by ordering them to draft memos analyzing the various trial procedures. The JAGs refused. As they saw it, their job as defense lawyers was to exploit the holes in the system, not to help the government patch them up, which they saw as akin to being asked to build a better mousetrap for their eventual clients. The Defense Department told Swift and Sundel that until they had clients, they were staff attorneys, not defense lawyers. The distinction became a bone of contention when Swift attended a legal conference at Harvard and made a point of identifying himself as "defense counsel for the military commissions" rather than a staff attorney for the Defense Department. Word got back to the Pentagon, as Swift had no doubt that it would, and Borch fired off an angry memo to Gunn. "Quite honestly," it read, "Lt. Cmdr. Swift's description of his job title is not only wrong, but it seems calculated to be provocative if not offensive."

On Thursday, July 3, 2003, it finally looked as if the JAGs were going to get clients. They sat in the back row of the Pentagon briefing room for the announcement that the president had designated the first six detainees to be tried before military commissions. The Defense Department spokesman declined to identify the prospective defendants, but news soon broke in England that two of them, Feroz Abbasi and Moazzam Begg, were British citizens. Over the weekend the British papers were crowded with photos of Abbasi and Begg and their children, interviews with their families, and angry denunciations of the "show trials" and "death chambers" that awaited them.

Back at work on Monday, Swift and Sundel watched the British Parliament grill Prime Minister Tony Blair about the commissions on C-SPAN. It was the last thing Blair needed. His popularity was already tumbling as the war in Iraq, which he had supported over the objections of the majority of the British populace, devolved into a quagmire. Bush had no desire to alienate Blair, a trusted ally in the war on terror. The commissions were put on hold as the shuttle diplomacy got under way.*

Swift and Sundel spent the next couple of weeks debating the future of the commissions. Sundel had always been skeptical that the trials were ever going to become a reality. He figured it made much more sense for the United States to simply hold the detainees until the end of hostilities, as it was entitled to do under international law. After the British debacle, he was more doubtful than ever. Swift disagreed. "These are political trials," he insisted. "Sooner or later the president is going to have to be able to announce to the American public that the architects of 9/11 are dead, and 'died without a trial in U.S. custody on Guantánamo Bay' doesn't sound very good, so what other choice does he have?"

---

* Abbasi and Begg were never tried and were eventually released from Guantánamo in January 2005.

FOUR

The Professor

ONE AFTERNOON in late May 2003, Colonel Gunn received an e-mail from a law professor at Georgetown named Neal Katyal. "I hope this e-mail reaches you," it began, "as I've tried to find your contact info from a variety of different sources . . . I'm writing, in the event that you do lead the defense team at the military tribunals, to offer my help."

"I am forwarding your e-mail to Lieutenant Commanders Swift and Sundel," Gunn replied. "They're going to be handling the first cases so they'll be the ones calling the shots on case strategies."

After reading the forwarded e-mail, Sundel tossed a copy of an April 2002 article from *The Yale Law Journal* onto Swift's desk. Swift glanced at the cover page. It was titled "Waging War, Deciding Guilt: Trying the Military Tribunals." He recognized one of the authors, Laurence H. Tribe, the highly regarded Harvard law professor who had argued dozens of high-profile cases before the Supreme Court and written the definitive textbook on American constitutional law. But the name of the other author, Neal Kumar Katyal, meant nothing to him. "He's wrong," said Sundel, who had first come across the article weeks earlier. "But it's worth reading anyway."

Swift started reading. The thrust of the argument was that by unilaterally authorizing the commissions, drawing up their rules and procedures, and foreclosing any sort of appeal to an independent judicial body, the president had violated bedrock principles of the constitutional system. "Central among those principles," Katyal and Tribe wrote, "is that great power must be held in check and that the body that defines what conduct to outlaw, the body that prosecutes violators, and the body that adjudicates guilt and dispenses punishment should be three separate entities."

According to Katyal and Tribe, the military commissions weren't just ill-advised; they were illegal. The president's commander-in-chief powers, enshrined in Article II of the Constitution, gave him the authority to capture and detain enemy combatants, but *dispensing* justice was up to Congress because only Congress could make laws. The authors argued that without specific congressional authorization—or, at the very least, a formal declaration of war from Congress, which would give the president additional emergency powers—the president lacked the constitutional authority to convene these military commissions.

Sundel didn't buy it. He regarded the September 18, 2001, congressional resolution authorizing the president to use "all necessary and appropriate force" against those responsible for the attacks of 9/11 as the functional equivalent of a declaration of war. As he saw it, Congress's so-called AUMF—Authorization for Use of Military Force—gave the president all the power he needed to create the commissions.

After reading the article, Swift was inclined to agree with Sundel. He had no shortage of complaints about the trials, but one thing he didn't doubt was his commander in chief's authority to convene them. The nation was at war, and military commissions were part of the president's wartime arsenal.

Nevertheless, the JAGs figured they needed all the help they could get. Sundel called to set up a meeting. Katyal was on his way to the hospital with his wife, who was about to give birth to their second child, Calder, when he got the message. He called Sundel back a few days later, and they agreed to get together at his office at Georgetown.

UNLIKE HIS COAUTHOR Laurence Tribe, Neal Katyal had yet to write a book or argue a case before the Supreme Court. Still, at thirty-three, he was something of a rising star in the world of constitutional law. His résumé was glittering. The son of first-generation

Indian immigrants who had settled in a largely Jewish suburb of Chicago, Katyal attended Dartmouth College and Yale Law School and followed a pair of prestigious clerkships, including one on the Supreme Court, with a stint at the Clinton Justice Department. In the fall of 2000 he served as co-counsel for Al Gore in the 2000 Florida recount case.

Katyal's path to the law had presented itself early. When he was a freshman in high school in suburban Chicago, an uncle suggested that he join the debate team to help him overcome his extreme shyness. Katyal took to it immediately and went on to become the captain of the Dartmouth debate team and a third-place finisher three years running in the national collegiate forensics championships.

Law school was the logical next step. Katyal attended Yale, a cluster of ivy-cloaked neo-Gothic buildings in downtown New Haven. In contrast with Harvard, whose cutthroat atmosphere was immortalized in the film *The Paper Chase* and in Scott Turow's *One L*, Yale Law actively cultivated an unhurried, contemplative culture. Dean Guido Calabresi welcomed Katyal's class, the Class of 1995, by informing its members that they were now officially "off the treadmill." Simply possessing a Yale J.D. was enough to open any professional door, so forget about grades—all of Yale's classes were pass/fail anyway—and find and explore your passions.

It did not take Katyal long to discover his. Constitutional law tends to inspire dramatically different reactions among law students. Many find it infuriating; aspiring lawyers tend to crave logic, and con law, in which hour after bewildering hour is spent trying to reconcile seemingly contradictory Supreme Court opinions interpreting what the framers meant by this article or that clause, can be maddeningly illogical. Katyal, however, found it irresistible and completely submerged himself in it, while doing virtually no work for the rest of his classes.

Katyal had always taken a single-minded approach to his interests. So while he didn't have many, those that he did have were tirelessly pursued to the point of mastery. He had been an avid music fan since high school, tracking down obscure bootleg tapes of college rock bands like the Violent Femmes, lurking in underground record stores, and sleeping outside for U2 tickets during a postgraduation trip to

Europe. Skiing had become a parallel obsession. Feeling guilty that he couldn't teach his son how to play football or baseball, Katyal's father decided they should take up skiing. He taught first himself and then Katyal at a small mountain about an hour from their house. Though Katyal was not especially athletic, he took to it and was soon branching out to tackle mountains in the West, taking mogul lessons, and generally doing everything he could to conquer the sport. Later he entered the fetishist's world of wine appreciation, reading Robert Parker's one-thousand-plus-page book *Bordeaux* cover to cover, making a list of all the wines that received Parker's highest rating, and then taking wine-tasting classes until he could tell the difference between a first- and second-growth Bordeaux without looking at the bottles.

Katyal approached constitutional law, with its seemingly inexhaustible trail of obscure precedents and subtle doctrines, with the same methodical zeal. During the very first week of classes he stayed up all night studying *Roe v. Wade*. The next day, his constitutional law professor, Akhil Amar, asked the class why the suit had been brought against Henry Wade, the district attorney of Dallas County, rather than the state of Texas. Katyal raised his hand and answered that it was because of the Eleventh Amendment, which, Katyal explained, gave the states immunity from suits. Amar asked Katyal to read the amendment out loud. The language seemed murky. Amar pressed Katyal on his interpretation of the amendment. "Well, there's this case called *Hans v. Louisiana*," Katyal replied, citing an 1890 decision in which the Supreme Court had definitively ruled that the amendment prohibits citizens from suing states.

"So why can Jane Roe sue Wade if she can't sue Texas?" Amar asked next. "That's because of *Ex parte Young*," Katyal answered, referring to a 1908 Supreme Court opinion that gave citizens the right to sue state officials for injunctive relief. Amar had been asking this series of questions for years; no student before Katyal had ever managed to answer them all.

Within weeks of arriving at Yale, Katyal was working on his first piece of original constitutional scholarship, an argument that the authors of the Thirteenth Amendment intended to abolish not just slavery but forced prostitution. It was accepted for publication by *The Yale*

Law Journal in January, and secured for Katyal his class's first invitation to join the editorial staff of Yale's most prestigious law journal.

There are generally two ways to approach the study of the Constitution. One can treat it as a "living," or evolving, text, designed to accommodate historical change. As Justice William Brennan, one of the leading exponents of this approach, once put it, "The genius of the Constitution rests not in any static meaning it might have had in a world that is dead and gone, but in the adaptability of its great principles to cope with current problems." Or one can limit one's reading of the document to the actual words on the page and the "original intent" of their authors. Katyal gravitated toward the latter. He was struck by the framers' expansive sense of liberty and equality and captivated by the process of trying to understand their vision for the nation they had summoned into being with these four pages of parchment. Its forty-four hundred words, plus amendments, and the history that underlay them contained the answers to all of the great social and political questions that the United States had faced since its founding.

Katyal had two judicial heroes. The first was Thurgood Marshall, who as the head of the National Association for the Advancement of Colored People had been the architect of *Brown v. Board of Education*. Reading about *Brown*, Katyal was awed by Marshall's patient, incremental approach. "A lot of people seek revolution in the courts, and in general they fail," Katyal would later observe. "The genius of Marshall's strategy was to take the long view, to realize that he wasn't going to overturn segregation in one fell swoop. Instead of making dramatic claims or being histrionic, he made subtle use of his advocate's pen and his oral skills to gradually build momentum."

Marshall was appointed to the Supreme Court after *Brown v. Board of Education*. As a jurist, though, he was too activist for Katyal's taste. On the Court he preferred his other hero, Justice John Marshall Harlan II, who tempered his iconoclasism with a profound respect for the political process. As Katyal saw it, the framers had conjured a nation in which power was to be derived from the people. To honor this vision, judges needed to encourage the democratic dialogue, not to sap the will of the populace to act by legislating from the bench. This perspective was reinforced during Katyal's Supreme Court clerkship with Justice Stephen Breyer, who spoke frequently about the need for the courts to trust the political branches.

Following his Supreme Court clerkship, Katyal, then twenty-seven, deferred a professorship at Georgetown Law to take a job at the Justice Department. During law school he had interned for Vice President Gore and had gotten to know Gore's general counsel, Kumiki Gibson, who recommended him for the position. As she put it to Deputy Attorney General Eric Holder, he could wait his whole life and never get a better referral than Katyal.

Unfortunately, Katyal's first few months on the job were squandered. The very day he arrived in January 1998 happened to be the same day that the independent counsel Kenneth Starr decided to put a tap on Linda Tripp's phone to record her conversations with Monica Lewinsky. The request went straight to Holder's office, and Holder essentially disappeared into the nascent Lewinsky scandal, leaving Katyal with nothing to do. Most of his new colleagues—career government lawyers with decades of service under their belts—wrote him off as an overpedigreed political appointee and offered little help keeping him busy. After four months Katyal told Holder that he was bored and planned to quit.

The next morning Holder gave Katyal his first meaningful assignment: the United States might soon be given an opportunity to take custody of several leaders of the Khmer Rouge, the genocidal regime that had ruled Communist Cambodia in the late 1970s, but no one at the Justice Department had been able to find a legal means by which to detain and prosecute them. By noon Katyal had come up with a solution. A few hours later he was summoned to the White House Situation Room to brief a group of generals and officials from the State Department, Pentagon, and intelligence agencies on his plan.

For the next sixteen months Katyal worked virtually nonstop on this and other issues, arriving in his office by seven every day and rarely leaving before midnight. His years as a debater had made him an unusually efficient researcher, and he was quickly able to master a diverse array of complicated subjects and turn around detailed legal opinions at a pace Holder had never before seen. Katyal was politically precocious as well, and he became Holder's go-to guy on many of the department's most sensitive matters.

For a lifelong Democrat, Katyal was a strong believer in executive authority and unusually hawkish on matters of national security. One of his early assignments at the Justice Department was to head the team charged with formulating the department's policy toward the independent counsel statute, which was about to lapse. The statute, which empowered court-appointed lawyers to investigate claims of executive branch misconduct, was a cornerstone of the post-Watergate campaign to curb the White House's power, and most Democrats viewed it as a critical check against the abuse of executive authority. Katyal, however, believed that it created a dangerous institution unaccountable to the American people that could very easily prevent the president from performing his duties. After a sustained campaign, he managed to sway some stalwart advocates of the statute inside the administration and in the end convinced the Justice Department not to support its renewal.

Katyal found himself in another ideological battle after al Qaeda bombed two U.S. embassies in East Africa in the summer of 1998. The attacks created a divide inside the administration between those advocating a military approach to the terrorist threat and those who continued to believe that the best way to handle bin Laden was to bring him to justice in an American courtroom. Katyal aligned himself with the hawks, arguing that it was time to abandon the law enforcement approach to fighting terrorism and that existing laws posed no barriers to doing so. His position put him at odds with Attorney General Janet Reno and most of his colleagues in the Justice Department, who believed that lethal force should be used on bin Laden and his lieutenants only if necessary during their capture or in the face of an imminent threat on the United States. They were concerned about the risk of collateral damage—five years earlier a Clinton-approved air strike on the headquarters of Iraq's intelligence services had inadvertently killed a prominent Iraqi female artist—and about running afoul of Executive Order 12333, which banned assassinations.

Katyal contended that the executive order didn't apply to military targets and that even if it did, Clinton could simply rescind or modify it. More broadly, Katyal argued that from James Madison onward, American and international law had embraced a robust form of self-defense, one that recognized the need for preemption, or, in the technical terminology of international law, "anticipatory self-defense." This battle ended in defeat for Katyal. President Clinton ultimately took a much more restrained position vis-à-vis bin Laden.*

In the spring of 1999, Katyal met the woman he wanted to marry, Joanna Rosen, a doctor from New York and the sister of a friend, the law professor and writer Jeffrey Rosen. Katyal knew their relationship would never survive his all-consuming government job, so he decided to leave the Justice Department.

His final assignment, in the summer of 1999, came directly from the White House. Thirty-six years earlier President John F. Kennedy had summoned 250 leading American lawyers to the East Room of the White House to mobilize them to become more involved in the civil rights struggle. President Clinton now wanted to make another call to America's lawyers—in the very same White House room—urging them to devote more energy and resources to pro bono work. Katyal was asked to write his speech, which the president delivered on July 20. "One of the best things Dr. King ever said was that 'the arc of the moral universe is long, but it bends toward justice,'" the speech concluded. "Our nation's lawyers have bent that arc toward justice."

AFTER LEAVING the Justice Department, Katyal started his academic career at Georgetown, and for the next year he taught, wrote law review articles, and commuted to San Francisco, where Joanna was practicing medicine. The two were married in the summer of 2000 near Joanna's family's country house in Woodstock, New York, and lived together in his Dupont Circle apartment in Washington, D.C., until September 2001, when he returned to Yale as a visiting pro-

---

*Katyal's 1998 bin Laden memo remains classified, but a member of the 9/11 Commission, Col. Len Hawley, came across it during his research and was struck by its prescience, calling the memo a "very remarkable analysis of the terrorist threat that called for a very assertive role for law enforcement and justice." Few people in government, Hawley said, "had the imagination to think about this threat as being as serious as it turned out to be."

fessor. It was there, after having been up much of the night with their infant son, Rem, that Joanna woke him up with the news that two airplanes had just slammed into the World Trade Center.

For Katyal, the emotional impact of 9/11 was magnified by the recent birth of their first child. He was also plagued by regret over his failure to sell the White House on his aggressive stance toward bin Laden. Most of all, though, he was frustrated to no longer be working in government. Eager to be somehow involved in the post-9/11 effort, Katyal suggested to his constitutional law class that they write letters to the families of the victims, offering their help securing any benefits or social services. It was a far cry from helping shape the nation's response to the terrorist threat, but it was at least something.

President Bush, meanwhile, moved swiftly and boldly to answer the 9/11 attacks, signing a broad Memorandum of Notification authorizing the CIA to use lethal covert action against al Qaeda and other terrorist organizations and ordering the military to begin preparations for an air and ground assault in Afghanistan. On September 24, 2001, the president invoked his authority under the International Emergency Economic Powers Act to freeze the assets of twenty-seven organizations and individuals suspected of helping finance terrorism, including a number of Muslim charities and international businesses with direct ties to the leadership of several Arab countries. There was a major domestic component to the emerging war on terror as well, its centerpiece being the USA PATRIOT Act, which gave the federal government sweeping new law enforcement powers that would have been inconceivable in the pre-9/11 era.

Yale was a liberal school—"Save America, Close Yale Law School," read one conservative bumper sticker in the 1980s—and many students were shocked at what they were witnessing. Secret searches! The infiltration and surveillance of religious and political groups! The indefinite detention of American citizens, without access to counsel! It was a return to the Nixon era, only worse.

Katyal thought the administration's actions were not only legal but appropriate, and he always went to class ready to explain why. The framers of the Constitution had endowed the head of the federal government with broad discretionary power for precisely such moments. As Alexander Hamilton had written in *The Federalist Papers*, a strong presidency "is essential to the protection of the community against foreign attack." The 9/11 attacks plainly justified an aggressive military response. Domestically, a readjustment of the delicate balance between civil liberties and national security was inevitable during wartime. To Katyal, the PATRIOT Act, which came in for especially harsh criticism at Yale, seemed perfectly within constitutional bounds. So-called sunset clauses had been attached to most of the act's more controversial provisions, so there would soon be a chance to revisit their relative costs and benefits. Most of all, Congress had passed the legislation. This was precisely how the democratic process was meant to work.

But the president's November 13 order authorizing military commissions struck Katyal as something altogether different. The moment he first learned about the commissions from the news crawl on CNN, he logged on to the White House website to read the full text of the order and was flabbergasted.

Even while the framers had sought to empower the president, they had taken care to prevent government repression by containing his ability to unilaterally restrict individual liberties. This had been driven home for Katyal during law school, when he spent a year and a half working on a piece of scholarship about the early history of the Constitution. Reading through the framers' papers at a number of different historical archives on the East Coast, Katyal had developed a theory that the president, Congress, and the judiciary were like three separate light switches. In order for the government to deprive an individual of his liberties, as was sometimes necessary for national security, all three needed to be flipped to the "on" position: Congress had to pass a bill, the president had to enforce it (not veto it), and the courts had to deem the action constitutional. By contrast, not only had the president not consulted Congress about the tribunals, but he was explicitly asserting that the courts would have no jurisdiction over them.

Katyal printed out fifteen copies of the president's military order for the students in his constitutional law class, who had been teasing him about his support for Bush's draconian antiterrorism policies and presidential war powers in general. "Ha!" he said, distributing them around the classroom. "I finally found something that I think is blatantly unconstitutional."

CONGRESS TOO had been taken aback by the president's military order. In the wake of September 11, lawmakers had gone out of their way to provide the executive branch with everything it said it needed to confront the new terrorist threat, not simply empowering the president to answer the attacks with military force but allocating forty billion dollars for the war on terror and passing the PATRIOT Act in record time and with almost unanimous support. (Only one senator, Wisconsin's Russ Feingold, cast his vote against it.)

In late October and early November, though, it had emerged that in the midst of this period of almost unprecedented cooperation between the White House and Congress, the executive branch had been amassing additional antiterrorism tools by quietly issuing new directives via the *Federal Register*. Thus, without any public debate, the administration had claimed the authority to monitor conversations between federal prisoners and their lawyers without a court order; to withhold the identities of American citizens whom it was detaining; and to round up some five thousand Muslim students in the United States for questioning. And it had raised the bar for reporters and watchdog organizations to obtain government documents by narrowly reinterpreting the Freedom of Information Act.

In the face of this lengthening list of unilateral actions, Congress's united front of goodwill toward the executive branch began to fracture. "I have felt a growing concern that the trust and cooperation Congress provided is proving to be a one-way street," Senator Patrick J. Leahy, the Democratic chairman of the Judiciary Committee, warned Attorney General John Ashcroft in early November 2001. The November 13 military order pushed Leahy over the edge, prompting him to convene the first congressional hearings on the president's antiterrorism policies since September 11.

When Katyal heard about the hearings, he called someone he

knew at the Senate Judiciary Committee to volunteer his help. He eventually spoke with Bruce Cohen, the chief counsel for the committee's Democrats, and outlined some of his concerns about the commissions. Cohen asked him to come down and testify.

Joanna was initially worried about Katyal's safety: two senators, including Leahy, had just been sent envelopes containing anthrax powder. She ultimately relented, though, and Katyal agreed to testify. But testifying didn't just mean showing up. He would have to prepare a written statement due at the Judiciary Committee on November 23, the day after Thanksgiving, only a week away.

While Katyal was racing to get up to speed on military commissions, a friend suggested that he look at an article in the *Journal of Supreme Court History* about the *Quirin* decision. Katyal was already acquainted with the *Quirin* case, but this article focused on the actions of a particular justice, Felix Frankfurter, who had pushed for the military commission for the Nazi saboteurs only to regret the decision afterward. Frankfurter had been such a strong advocate of the commission, in fact, that he had personally encouraged FDR's secretary of war to convene it and then fumed at the saboteurs' gall for petitioning the Supreme Court to hear their challenge to its legality. While the justices were working on their opinion in *Quirin*, Frankfurter wrote a memo to his colleagues in the form of an imagined dialogue with the Nazi saboteurs, referring to them as "damned scoundrels" before dismissing all their claims out of hand: "You've done enough mischief already without leaving the seeds of a bitter conflict involving the President, the courts and Congress after your bodies will be rotting in lime."

But not long after the Court's unanimous opinion had been issued, Frankfurter asked Frederick Bernays Wiener, a noted expert on military law, for his thoughts on the case. Wiener told him that FDR's order establishing the commission had violated the Articles of War—the precursor to the Uniform Code of Military Justice—and was thus "palpably illegal." Frankfurter was apparently persuaded by Wiener's analysis. Years later, he ruefully acknowledged that the *Quirin* experience was "not a happy precedent." The article made a powerful impression on Katyal, who knew how extraordinary it was for a Supreme

Court justice to express second thoughts about a decision. (As the embroidered pillow in Justice O'Connor's chambers put it, "Maybe in error, never in doubt.")

Katyal and his family spent Thanksgiving at his in-laws' small apartment on the Upper East Side of Manhattan. For three days Katyal emerged from his room only to eat and go for a run in Central Park. He packed everything he could into his written testimony, citing Frankfurter's second thoughts about the *Quirin* precedent, quoting the framers on the dangers of concentrating too much power in one branch of the government, and detailing the various deficiencies of the proposed trials. He sent a near-final draft of the testimony to Harold Koh, a distinguished law professor at Yale, who told him that it was way too long. Katyal thanked him for his input but decided not to cut it. He finished his fortieth and final draft at midnight on November 22. It was twenty-two single-spaced pages, including twenty-four footnotes citing case law dating back to 1863. "Our enemies will call them 'show trials,'" Katyal wrote of the proposed commissions; "our friends will wonder why American justice cannot handle those who are obviously culpable."

In the hallway outside the hearing room of the Dirksen Senate Office Building on the morning of the hearing, Katyal ran into Brad Berenson, the associate White House counsel, whom he knew from the 2000 election dispute. "I was with you guys all of the way in the war on terror—the authorization for the use of military force, the war in Afghanistan, the PATRIOT Act," Katyal said. "But these commissions defy constitutional belief. I hate coming out against the government right now, but we've got to put *some* limits on presidential power."

"I understand," Berenson replied, "but we've had military commissions since the founding, and there's no way that the courts are going to stop them."

THE HEARING ROOM filled quickly. Senate Democrats had been clamoring for Ashcroft, but the administration instead sent as its first witness his formidable aide, Michael Chertoff, the head of the Justice Department's Criminal Division. A wiry, serious-looking man with a wispy beard and an agile mind, he spoke almost all morning, defending the commissions and the administration's domestic counterterrorism policies in measured yet forceful tones. "We are at war," Chertoff said. "Our homeland was suddenly and deliberately attacked from abroad on September 11, resulting in the intentional murder of thousands of unarmed civilians. Osama bin Laden has candidly said he intends to continue his attacks as long as he and his organization are able. In view of such circumstances, military commissions are a traditional way of bringing justice to persons charged with offenses under the laws of armed conflict."

Katyal didn't have much time, and he focused on the big picture: that by unilaterally authorizing the commissions, the president had overstepped his constitutional authority, and it was up to Congress to set things straight. "Throughout history there have been times when this country has had to dispense with civil trials and other protections," Katyal said. "Yet those circumstances have been rare, carefully circumscribed, and never unilaterally defined by a single person. A tremendous danger exists if the power is left in one individual to put aside our constitutional traditions when our nation is at crisis. The safeguard against the potential for this abuse has always been Congress's involvement in a deep constitutional sense."

Katyal was asked just one question, by Senator Feingold, who wanted him to comment on the administration's claim that it needed to move quickly in the war against terror and that the congressional decision-making process was inherently slow. Katyal answered by saying that what might seem expedient now could prove time-consuming later if the courts were to find the military order unconstitutional.

Ashcroft appeared before the committee the following week and assumed a far more combative posture than Chertoff. He opened with a message to the administration's critics—"Your tactics only aid the terrorists, for they erode our national unity and diminish our resolve"—and went on to aggressively defend the use of military commissions: "When we come to those responsible for this, say, who are in Afghanistan, are we supposed to read them the *Miranda* rights, hire a flamboyant defense lawyer, bring them back to the United States to create a new cable network of Osama TV or what have you, provide a worldwide platform from which propaganda can be developed?"

The attorney general's scorched earth testimony destroyed whatever political will Congress might have possessed to regulate the commissions. The war in Afghanistan was going well, and the popularity of the president, a decisive and plainspoken leader prone to neither introspection nor self-doubt, was surging; his approval rating among *Democrats* was running at four to one. National emergencies—from the Civil War to the Great Depression to the cold war—have always produced a hunger for aggressive leadership and a willingness to tolerate whatever sacrifices such leadership entailed. So if President Bush wanted to suspend certain rights for suspected terrorists after September 11, it seemed a small price to pay for the security of the nation. "We're an open society," as the president liked to say, "but we're at war."

Back in New Haven, Katyal e-mailed Laurence Tribe, who had also testified at the hearings, and suggested that they coauthor a law review article on military commissions. Assuming the trials were imminent, they wrote the article in a matter of weeks and rushed it into print in *The Yale Law Journal*. Months passed, though, with no further word on the commissions. Katyal figured the administration had abandoned the idea. A year and a half later he read about Colonel Gunn's appointment and tracked him down at the Pentagon.

FIVE

The Civil Power

ONE AFTERNOON in late May 2003, a day as sticky as flypaper in Washington, Swift and Sundel went to meet Katyal in his office at the Georgetown University Law Center. Katyal looked much younger than they'd imagined. Slender, with sloping shoulders, he had neatly combed black hair and wore rectangular wire-rimmed glasses. His dark skin barely betrayed the shadow of a beard. On his wall hung a personalized photograph of a smiling man in a black robe, Justice Stephen G. Breyer.

Katyal had set out bottles of water for the JAGs on a small round table in his office, and the three of them sat down to discuss the commissions. Katyal was instantly impressed by Sundel. He had a confident yet understated manner, and he obviously knew the Geneva Conventions and the laws of war cold. Katyal liked Swift too. "A deeply human person who wears his emotions on his sleeve" is how he later described him. But Swift was blustery and imprecise, and Katyal worried about how much he would be able to contribute.

For their part, the two JAGs were both impressed by Katyal. He was only thirty-three years old but conveyed the wisdom and authority of a much older person. In law school Katyal's natural reserve, combined with his unremitting drive and ambition and his prodigy's command of the Constitution, had been off-putting to some of his classmates, who considered him arrogant. Since then the affect of his confidence had mellowed and matured; being around him, the JAGs felt instantly reassured and deferential.

The three lawyers continued to meet regularly over the course of the summer. Katyal prepared a packet of Supreme Court opinions and relevant law review articles to help educate the JAGs on the constitutional issues surrounding the commissions. Sundel, meanwhile, taught Katyal about the laws of war and the Uniform Code of Military Justice. They debated what exactly constituted an armed conflict and hashed out the various arguments against the legality of the commissions. Sundel continued to impress Katyal. He was a creative legal thinker, but careful and methodical as well. In one of their early meetings he brought in a paragraph buried in the Uniform Code of Military Justice stating that the UCMJ applied to anyone within any leased territory of the United States—a seemingly explicit refutation of the government's claim that the Guantánamo detainees were not entitled to any rights.

Swift, meanwhile, was starting to seem like a potential liability. To challenge the administration, they were going to need a sophisticated legal strategy, and Swift was constantly conflating precedents and misquoting statutes. He talked too much and never seemed to say enough. And he was loud. Sundel was often shushing him, and John Podesta, President Clinton's former chief of staff, who now occupied the office next to Katyal's at Georgetown, complained about the noise. Katyal now had two small children at home, and his wife was working full-time as an internist at the VA hospital in Washington, D.C. In addition to his work on the commissions, he was busy writing law review articles and building a new house. He didn't have time for Swift's rhetorical field trips. For a while Katyal simply ignored him and focused on Sundel.

Then, one afternoon when the three of them were sitting in Katyal's office, talking about the president's decision to suspend the Geneva Conventions in the war on terror, Swift launched into one of his monologues. The words began to rumble forth; Katyal tuned him out. Gathering steam, Swift rose from his chair and pointed at his shirt. "Here's the thing civilians don't understand about the Geneva Conventions. If I'm captured on a battlefield, the thing that protects me from getting tortured is that I'm wearing this uniform! I don't want some emperor saying we don't have to give Geneva Conventions protections! The only people I trust to make that decision are the military, because they know how high the stakes are!"

Katyal perked up. Usually his eyes glazed over when Swift or Sundel mentioned the Geneva Conventions. He thought of them as a toothless international treaty, not an intimate part of America's military fabric. But Swift had just articulated the most compelling reason he could ever imagine to honor them: To do otherwise would put our own troops at risk.

FROM THE BEGINNING, Katyal stressed that the JAGs' best shot at justice for their eventual clients—their only hope, really—was to challenge the commissions in a civilian court. But that was going to require persuading a federal judge that he or she had the authority—the jurisdiction—to hear a lawsuit brought against the commissions, despite the fact that their eventual clients were being held on Guantánamo Bay, which the administration had reasoned was outside the reach of America's courts. There was also the plain text of the president's November 13 military order, which proclaimed that individuals subject to the order "shall not be privileged to seek any remedy or maintain any proceeding, directly or indirectly, or to have any such remedy or proceeding sought on the individual's behalf, in . . . any court of the United States, or any State thereof." By even agreeing to entertain an argument against the lawfulness of the commissions—let alone accept it—a judge would be contradicting the express wishes of the nation's commander in chief.

Just as the government had predicted, the detentions had not gone unchallenged. No sooner had the first planeload of prisoners touched down on Guantánamo Bay than lawyers started filing petitions for habeas corpus—literally, "you should have the body"—on their behalf.

The right to habeas corpus—the mother of all rights, as it has been called—requires the government either to make a convincing case for a prisoner's detention or else to release him. The concept was imported from monarchical England and has been part of America's legal fabric since the nation's founding. It was so important to the framers, in fact, that they placed strict, explicit limits on its suspension. Article I, Section 9 of the Constitution states: "The privilege of the Writ of Habeas Corpus shall not be suspended, unless when in Cases of Rebellion or Invasion the public Safety may require it."

The very first Congress voted the right to habeas into law in 1789, and the Supreme Court has repeatedly acknowledged its unique place in America's legal system. As the justices wrote in 1969, "There is no higher duty of a court, under our constitutional system, than the careful processing and adjudication of petitions for writs of habeas corpus, for it is in such proceedings that a person in custody charges that error, neglect, or evil has resulted in his unlawful confinement and that he is deprived of his freedom contrary to law."

The mammoth importance of habeas corpus in American law notwithstanding, the government's strategy to keep the detainees out of the civilian courts appeared airtight. Through the fall of 2003, every judge who had been asked to hear a habeas petition brought on behalf of a Guantánamo detainee had concluded that he or she lacked the power to do so because the right to habeas was unavailable to enemy aliens being held outside the United States.

The two most recent cases were *Al Odah v. United States* and *Rasul, et al. v. George Bush. Al Odah* concerned a group of Kuwaiti detainees, including twenty-four-year-old Fawzi al Odah who had been picked up in Afghanistan in late September 2001. After receiving a letter from his son via the International Committee of the Red Cross, al Odah's father, an American-trained pilot who had fought with the Kuwaiti Air Force in the First Gulf War, tracked down the families of eleven other Kuwaiti prisoners and hired a white-shoe American law firm to represent them. *Rasul* was brought on behalf of two Australians and two British citizens, among them Shafiq Rasul, who had traveled to Afghanistan in October 2001 from Tipton, a small town in Britain's western Midlands.

Both suits had been filed in federal district court in Washington, D.C., and were subsequently consolidated into one, known simply as *Rasul*, which Judge Colleen Kollar-Kotelly dismissed on July 30, 2002. "The court concludes that the military base at Guantánamo Bay,

Cuba, is outside the sovereign territory of the United States," she wrote. "Given that . . . writs of habeas corpus are not available to aliens held outside the sovereign territory of the United States, this court does not have jurisdiction" to hear the case.

In March 2003 the D.C. circuit court of appeals upheld Kollar-Kotelly's decision. "The Constitution does not entitle the detainees to due process," the three-judge appeals panel wrote in a unanimous opinion. "They cannot invoke the jurisdiction of our courts to test the constitutionality or the legality of restraints on their liberty."

That appeared to be the final word on the viability of a habeas claim from Guantánamo. The lawyers for *Rasul* and *al Odah* would no doubt ask the Supreme Court to review the decision, but Katyal figured the odds were slim that the Court would oblige. The lower courts had already spoken in a unified voice on the matter, and the justices almost always gave the president a wide berth during times of war. *Inter arma silent leges*, the old Latin proverb goes: In time of war, the laws are silent.

With the front door to the civilian courts—a habeas corpus petition—seemingly closed, Katyal set about looking for a side door. The JAGs' mailboxes quickly filled with e-mails from him—draft copies of hypothetical motions, petitions, and strategic brainstorms. In lieu of filing habeas petitions on behalf of their clients, Katyal suggested that the JAGs might be able to file suit against the government on their own behalf: "The argument could be made that you shouldn't be made to participate in an unconstitutional proceeding, that doing so contravenes your oath to uphold the Constitution." At the bottom of one of his e-mails, Katyal pasted the U.S. kidnapping statute, 18 USCS 1201: "It might be crazy (but maybe no more crazy than some of my other ideas)—but perhaps it could be argued that the clients have been unlawfully seized and held for trial."

ON THE MORNING of November 10, 2003, Katyal read on the Supreme Court blog, SCOTUSblog, that the justices had agreed to hear *Rasul*. Stunned, he quickly tapped out an e-mail to Swift and Sundel: "I still cannot believe cert has been granted, but wow. I'd like to urge you to begin thinking about filing a brief as amicus in this case. I will do it for free if you wish. I know that the barrier is still that you do not have clients. But you have been designated to serve as defense counsel for commissions that are being built on the same Naval Base as the one in which cert has been granted. Your clients, and you, have an obvious stake in how this case is decided."*

The matters that come before the Supreme Court are typically far-reaching, rippling well beyond the immediate record parties of any given case. Hence the amicus curiae—or "friend of the court"—brief, which gives other groups and individuals a chance to bring their points of view to the attention of the justices. At their worst, amicus briefs are little more than an indirect form of lobbying, a nuisance for overburdened justices who are already inundated with paperwork in the months preceding important oral arguments. But amicus briefs can also be illuminating. And they have on occasion been influential: an amicus brief filed by the ACLU provided a blueprint for the majority opinion in *Mapp v. Ohio*, a landmark 1961 case banning the use of illegally obtained evidence in criminal trials.

Katyal's goals were more modest. He wanted the JAGs to alert the justices to the existence of a distinctly different class of prisoners from Rasul, al Odah, and the hundreds of others who were simply being detained on Guantánamo until the end of hostilities. His hope was that the JAGs would bring the Court's attention to their eventual clients, the as yet unnamed defendants for the president's military commissions. They too would be dramatically affected by the justices' decision on whether or not the federal courts had jurisdiction over Guantánamo. Katyal's fear was that the Court might otherwise unknowingly slam the door to judicial review for *all* the detainees and, in so doing, block the JAGs from challenging the lawfulness of a judicial system that he considered unconstitutional.

Swift was immediately enthusiastic about the idea. Sundel said no. He wrote to Katyal:

---

* "Cert" is short for *certiorari*, a Latin word meaning "to be searched." The formal requests to the Supreme Court to review a case are known as petitions for certiorari, or "cert petitions." If the justices agree to hear the case, they have thus "granted cert."

I'd love to be involved in filing, but I just can't think of a way to justify direct involvement in the case at this stage. I understand your point about our potential clients being the same as some of the actual petitioners in the granted case, but the problem is that they're only potential clients for us—it's entirely possible (and in fact looking more and more likely) that we'll never represent any of them. My entire professional career I've worked with the understanding that a defense counsel has no stake in any case unless he represents a client with an interest, and I can't see a way around that now.

Katyal had just moved into his new house with Joanna and their two kids, and had not yet set up his home office. That night, after his children had gone to bed, he sat surrounded by unpacked boxes and reread the petitions filed by the lawyers for *Rasul* and *al Odah*. Katyal was dismayed. The lawyers were asking the Court to rule that all the prisoners on Guantánamo Bay were entitled to file habeas petitions in federal court—save for one discrete group, those who were selected for trial before military commissions. "It is one thing to hold that war criminals . . . cannot seek further review in a civilian court," the lawyers had written. "It is quite another to extend that holding to people who have never been charged or afforded any process."

The lawyers were actually *steering* the Court toward a ruling that would close off the federal courts to the defendants in the military commissions. Katyal immediately started typing another e-mail to Swift and Sundel explaining the situation:

In my mind, this not only makes your office's participation in the case more important, it makes it essential. The government is going to say that no one gets habeas rights. The lawyers for the Petitioner are going to say everyone gets it EXCEPT those designated for military commissions. Who will speak for your future clients? Who is going to say that it is precisely the reverse of what the detainees' lawyers say—that when the government has the ability to mete out process in various increments at Guantánamo through a military trial, but then manipulate the trial rules and geography to evade review by civilian courts, . . . such manipulation cannot suffice to deprive civilian courts of jurisdiction?

Sundel agreed to give the idea a little more thought. Even if he did come around, though, Katyal had others to convince; over the summer Gunn had hired three additional JAGs, an Army major, a Marine major, and an Air Force lieutenant colonel. Katyal asked Gunn if he could make a formal presentation to the entire team. Gunn agreed.

A few days later Katyal took the Metro to the JAGs' new offices in a nondescript building in Crystal City, Virginia. He knew that the amicus brief was going to be a tough sell. Gunn was naturally cautious, and while Katyal had only just met the new JAGs, he couldn't imagine that they would be as willing to risk insubordination as Swift and Sundel.

Katyal opened the meeting by laying out the positions that the two sides—the government and the lawyers for the detainees—had staked out in *Rasul* and *al Odah*. Then he described the amicus brief he thought the JAGs should file. Unlike the detainees' lawyers', it would argue that the president should have the authority to detain enemy combatants when he is waging war. But unlike the administration's, it would contend that as soon as the president sets out to evaluate a prisoner's guilt or innocence, his decisions must be subject to review by the civilian courts. Katyal emphasized that this position was consistent with America's wartime history: it was a long standing tradition for the courts to review the legality of military commissions.

"What about blowback?" Gunn asked, referring to the consequences of the JAGs' staking out a position critical of the government.

Katyal had already thought about this and come up with a possible solution. Almost all amicus briefs are filed in support of one of the two parties to the case. But an arcane Supreme Court rule permitted a brief to be filed on behalf of neither one. The brief Katyal was proposing would hardly be dispassionate in tone or perspective—in fact, it would take aim squarely at the government's claim that none of the Guantánamo detainees should have access to the federal courts—but it would nevertheless be officially neutral, because the JAGs disagreed with the claims being made by both sides. This, Katyal explained, would both help prevent the administration from shutting down the brief and limit the political fallout from its filing inside the military.

The JAGs agreed to go ahead with the brief. Swift didn't think they needed to seek clearance from above. "It's easier to ask for forgiveness than to ask for permission," he argued. He was outvoted, but the JAGs didn't quite *ask* for permission. They modeled their letter to the Defense Department on Colonel Royall's to FDR: they told their higher-ups that they intended to file an amicus brief—on behalf of neither party in the *Rasul* case—unless explicitly ordered not to. One of the new JAGs suggested that they copy Katyal on the letter. He would be serving as their counsel on the brief, and the administration would have a much more difficult time stopping them if it knew that someone outside the Pentagon was aware of their intentions and could leak the story to the media.

A week later the JAGs received a response from Paul Koffsky, a deputy general counsel for the Defense Department, withholding permission to file the brief until they had discussed the issue with their military ethics advisers. The JAGs did as Koffsky asked and then promptly wrote him back to let him know that none of their ethics advisers had raised a red flag. This time Koffsky didn't respond at all.

AS THE JAGS AWAITED further word from the Pentagon, Katyal started roughing out the brief. Swift and Sundel volunteered to pitch in. Sundel was developing the case that the Constitution vests in Congress—not the president—the power to define war crimes and that it had done so in 1996, when it passed the War Crimes Act. Swift covered the walls of his office with diagrams of the Supreme Court's six previous rulings on military commissions.

The goal was to demonstrate that the Court had never intended to prevent the federal courts from hearing challenges to the lawfulness of military commissions. Toward that end their strongest precedent was a Civil War–era case called *Ex parte Milligan*. Lambdin P. Milligan was an Indiana "copperhead," a northerner whose sympathies ran toward the South. In 1864 federal agents discovered that an underground group to which Milligan belonged was plotting to abduct the governor of Indiana and free several thousand Confederate prisoners, and Milligan and several of his cohorts were arrested for treason. Two years earlier President Lincoln had suspended habeas corpus and ordered that anyone guilty of helping the Confederate forces be subject to trial by military commission. Milligan and his co-conspirators were ideal candidates. They were charged, convicted, and sentenced to death by hanging.

Their only recourse was to challenge the military commission's jurisdiction in civilian court. When the case reached the Supreme Court in 1866, the justices ruled unanimously in Milligan's favor: even in times of war, as long as civil courts were open and functioning, as they in Milligan's home state of Indiana, defendants were entitled to a trial by a jury of their peers. "The Constitution of the United States is a law for rulers and people, equally in war and in peace, and covers with the shield of its protection all classes of men, at all times, and under all circumstances," the Court's majority opinion stated.

Arguing the *Quirin* case seventy-six years later, Kenneth Royall built his defense of the Nazi saboteurs on the back of *Milligan*. He was considerably less successful. In upholding the lawfulness of FDR's military commission, the *Quirin* Court went out of its way to distinguish the Nazi saboteurs from the copperheads. Milligan was a resident of Indiana—not one of the states in rebellion—and was therefore not subject to the laws of war, the justices held. For their part, the Nazi saboteurs were "unlawful belligerents" who had crossed enemy lines with hostile purposes and were therefore triable by military commission.

This distinction was clearly problematic for Katyal and the JAGs, whose clients would presumably be foreign fighters accused of violating the laws of war. But the *Quirin* decision was not all bad news. The Court had handed Roosevelt an almost total victory, but it had pointedly rejected at least one argument made by the government's lead lawyer, Attorney General Francis Biddle, that the right of habeas corpus was never intended to protect "armed invaders sent here by the enemy in time of war." In fact, reflecting later on his *Quirin* decision in a letter to a friend, Chief Justice Harlan Fiske Stone had commented: "I hope you noticed that the opinion flatly rejected (as unobtrusively as possible) the President's comment that no court should hear the plea of the saboteurs. That, I thought, was going pretty far."

The biggest obstacle for Katyal and the JAGs was *Eisentrager*. Katyal pulled the complete record of the case from the microfiche room at the Supreme Court library and studied the thousands of pages of briefs and trial transcripts. He quickly realized that it was going to be impossible to refute the central thrust of the Court's ruling—that enemy aliens had no right to America's courts—so instead Katyal looked for more subtle ways to undermine it.

Katyal's most important discovery was the fact that the Supreme Court had subsequently overruled one of the key precedents undergirding *Eisentrager*, the 1948 case *Ahrens v. Clark*. *Ahrens* involved a group of Germans who were being held on Ellis Island in advance of their deportation. They filed habeas petitions in district court in Washington, D.C., challenging their detentions but were rebuffed by the Supreme Court, which ruled that "the presence within the territorial jurisdiction of the District Court of the person detained is prerequisite to filing a petition for a writ of habeas corpus."

This holding had been overturned by the Court's decision in the 1973 case *Braden v. 30th Judicial Circuit Court of Kentucky*. Braden was serving time in an Alabama prison, but the state of Kentucky wanted to extradite him and prosecute him for crimes he'd been accused of committing there. Braden filed a habeas petition in Kentucky, challenging the legality of the extradition. Explicitly overruling its earlier decision in *Ahrens*, the Court determined that the Kentucky court could hear Braden's petition. "Contrary to *Ahrens*," it wrote, "the prisoner's presence within the territorial jurisdiction of the district court is not 'an invariable prerequisite' to the exercise of district court jurisdiction under the federal habeas statute."

Katyal reasoned that the demise of *Ahrens* made *Eisentrager* bad law.

KATYAL HAD NEVER BEFORE experienced much trouble juggling work and family. Joanna had heard all about his round-the-clock days at the Justice Department and had even gotten a taste of them during the thirty-six-day presidential election dispute in the fall of 2000, but the rhythm of their days as a family was relatively steady, if a bit of a high-wire act. Joanna was up at six every morning and out the door shortly after seven. Katyal would wake up when she left and make breakfast for Rem, who was now three, and Calder, who was six months. The babysitter arrived at nine to stay with Calder, and Katyal would drop Rem off at preschool on his way to Georgetown. At the end of the day he would pick up Rem and race home so the babysitter could leave by five-thirty. (The afternoon he made his presentation to Gunn and the JAGs, he was five minutes late, and she threatened to quit.) Joanna would come home at around six, and they'd have a family dinner before putting the kids to bed.

But with the amicus brief due at the beginning of January 2004, Katyal went into overdrive for the first time since having children. He managed to keep his daily schedule intact, but once the children were asleep he would retreat to his office to work on the brief until two or three in the morning.

By December 22, after five weeks of virtually constant work, Katyal had almost finished a draft, but Swift still hadn't delivered the section he'd promised. Katyal pressed him with good-natured e-mails—"Don't leave me hangin'!"—and Swift assured him that he was almost done and he wouldn't leave the office until he was finished. The section never came. By the following afternoon Katyal had run out of patience and circulated a thirty-eight-page draft among the JAGs without any input from Swift.

Katyal spent the next several days pruning the brief to get it under the thirty-page limit. Just when he thought he was there, he discovered that he'd used twelve-point Times Roman font, rather than thirteen-point Times Roman, as the Court's clerk required. Reformatting the brief added several pages to the document, forcing him to make still more edits.

The JAGs, meanwhile, had heard nothing further from the Pentagon. Word trickled down to them that their letter was being debated inside the White House and that Gonzales, the president's counsel, would be making the final call on the brief. Neither option—risking accusations of silencing the military lawyers or permitting them to take a public stand against their commander in chief—was particularly appealing to the administration. Koffsky finally wrote to the JAGs on December 30, 2003: White House Counsel Alberto Gonzales had instructed Haynes, the Pentagon's general counsel, to give them the go-ahead.

For the convenience of the justices, the Court has a color-coding system for amicus briefs. Those filed in support of neither party are to be printed in light green pamphlets. Katyal toyed with the idea of using brown instead—a prerogative reserved for representatives of the U.S. government—to make the brief more distinctive but decided that the justices might see this as grandstanding. Anyway, he was pretty sure that the six names on its cover, five of them JAG lawyers, would be enough to ensure that it was read.

Amicus briefs are delivered to the clerk's office at the Supreme Court and then distributed to designated in-boxes in the chambers of the nine justices. There they sit until a justice or clerk wants to take a look at them. Whoever read the JAGs' brief must surely have been struck by the opening line, a quotation from the Declaration of Independence in which the framers enumerated their charges against King George III, charges that included elevating the military above the civil power, trumping up offenses, and depriving colonists of the right to a trial by jury. "Those charges," the brief stated, "describe the United States' legal position in this case."

SIX

A Drowning Man

ON THE MORNING of December 16, 2003, a light blue manila folder stamped "For Official Use Only" arrived on Colonel Gunn's desk, hand-delivered from the Pentagon. It was not especially thick, about fifteen pages in all. On top was a target letter—a letter informing an attorney that one of his clients is about to be indicted—addressed to Gunn. It began: "On July 3, 2003, the President determined that Mr. Salim Ahmed Hamdan is subject to the Military Order of November 13, 2001. As a result . . . Mr. Hamdan shall, when tried, be tried for any and all offenses triable by military commission . . . and may be punished in accordance with the penalties provided under applicable law, including life imprisonment or death." It went on to mention some of the charges under consideration for Mr. Hamdan: attacking civilians and civilian objects, terrorism, and conspiracy.

Behind the target letter was a copy of a one-page order from the White House to Secretary Rumsfeld, signed by President Bush, directing him to subject Mr. Hamdan to his November 13, 2001, military order. It stated that the president had "reason to believe" that Mr. Hamdan is or was a member of al Qaeda; had engaged in, aided, or abetted, or conspired to commit, acts of international terrorism; and had knowingly harbored terrorists. The folder also contained several classified items intended to give Gunn a general sense of the government's case against Hamdan, including the report from a ten-page interrogation conducted with him by the FBI on Guantánamo Bay on July 10, 2002.

This was the second case that had arrived at the defense office in recent weeks. Not long before, David Hicks, an Australian convert to Islam who'd been captured in Afghanistan fighting with the Taliban, had been assigned to one of the other JAGs, Marine Maj. Michael Mori. Hicks's identity had been revealed months earlier, and he came with a legal entourage. Through backdoor negotiations with the Bush administration, the Australian government had arranged for him to be given an Australian lawyer, and a New York–based nonprofit, the Center for Constitutional Rights, was also aiding in his defense.

Gunn passed the folder along to Swift and asked him to write up a boilerplate assignment letter for whomever he decided to detail to the case. Swift studied the file's contents eagerly in his small, windowless office. The target letter authorized Gunn to detail a lawyer to Hamdan to "engage in pretrial negotiations with a view toward resolving the allegations against him." In other words, Swift surmised, the government was anticipating a guilty plea. This gibed with what he and the other JAGs had been hearing from the beginning: that the administration hoped to launch its historic war crimes trials with a few uncontested victories.

Swift hadn't been hanging around Washington for the last nine months to walk into the military commission courtroom and enter a guilty plea on behalf of his client. What's more, he recognized that pleading guilty—like Colonel Gunn's noble promises of a zealous defense—would only serve to validate a trial system that he believed was fatally flawed.

But as Swift read through the interrogation transcript, he wasn't persuaded that Hamdan wanted to make a deal. He spoke with none of the remorse that usually characterized guilty pleas, and in Swift's experience, people who didn't believe they had done anything wrong didn't like to admit to being guilty. Of course Swift's own motives might also have influenced his reading of the transcript: having spent so much time buried in oppressively theoretical legal issues, he was anxious to start defending a human being.

At the end of the day Swift went into Gunn's office to make his pitch for the case. Gunn was already planning to give it to him. He had always intended to assign two lawyers to contested cases and one to guilty pleas, and Gunn knew that Swift would be difficult to pair up.

He had seen some of the other JAGs roll their eyes as he held forth during staff meetings, his office was in a perpetual state of chaos, and his paralegal, a petty officer named Jason Kreinhop, had complained about Swift's irregular work habits.

Within hours of being assigned to the case, Swift was on the phone, taking one of the Pentagon's press people, Maj. John Smith, to task about the wording of the news release announcing his appointment. Swift objected in particular to a line in the release that characterized the commission trials as full and fair. "I don't want to use the opportunity of my detailing to stoke your propaganda, John," Swift said. "I don't think this is a fair process. In fact, I think it's an incredibly unfair process."

Later that night Swift called Katyal. He knew that there was no way he could challenge the commissions on his own. The legal issues were extraordinarily complex, and there would be a lot of briefs to produce, each requiring painstaking precision and the patience to write and rewrite, endlessly expanding arguments and then ruthlessly whittling them down, word by word, for clarity and concision, which Swift knew was not his forte.

By this point there was no shortage of lawyers who had volunteered their services to the defense team's office, a number of whom had handled more than their share of high-profile civil liberties and human rights cases. But Swift wanted Katyal, which meant selling him on Hamdan.

"I've got the guy," Swift told him over the phone.

"Who is he?" Katyal asked.

"Well, do you want the good news or the bad news first?" Swift said.

"The good news."

"The good news is that he never shot at anybody, he doesn't seem to have been part of any plot, and he's got no other lawyers."

"What's the bad news?" Katyal asked.

"He was bin Laden's driver."

Katyal told Swift he needed to mull it over for a few days. Having come this far, he felt a duty to follow through with his challenge to the commissions, and as a constitutional law expert with national security experience—not to mention a track record of hawkishness that would help insulate him from criticism—he considered himself uniquely qualified for the job. And yet he had always envisioned defending an anonymous recruit, a hapless foot soldier who'd been in the wrong place at the wrong time. He never imagined that his client might be someone with a direct link to bin Laden, which would certainly hurt their odds of finding traction in the civilian courts: no judge needed to be reminded of Justice Oliver Wendell Holmes's famous maxim about hard cases making bad law.

Katyal thought too about his career. He had tenure at Georgetown, but he was hoping for an appointment in the next Democratic administration, perhaps back in the Justice Department or on the National Security Council. His work at the Justice Department and on the 2000 election dispute had not gone unnoticed; more recently he had played a key strategy-shaping role in the landmark University of Michigan affirmative action case *Grutter v. Bollinger*. Katyal was known as a liberal who was tough-minded on criminal law issues, a pairing that gave him added political cachet in the post-9/11 era, and he was often introduced at Washington parties, only half-jokingly, as the future first Indian-American Supreme Court justice of the United States. If he signed on to this case, he would instead be introduced as the lawyer who had defended Osama bin Laden's driver.

Katyal asked his former constitutional law professor Akhil Amar for advice. Amar told him not to do it, that he was almost certain to lose and that it might actually be worse for his career if he won. "Your ticket is already punched," Amar said. "Just hang out at Georgetown, write some articles, and wait for the Democrats to take back the White House."

Joanna wasn't exactly thrilled with the idea either. They had two small children now, and she was anxious about the security of the world they would be growing up in; representing one of bin Laden's associates hardly sounded like noble work to her. When Katyal explained that all he would be doing was ensuring that Hamdan got a fair trial, she was at least partly persuaded, but she remained concerned about the implications for his career.

Katyal had been asked to help defend Hicks, but had declined in part because he didn't want to have to answer to the rest of Hicks's legal team. With Hamdan, at least, that wouldn't be a problem. It would just be himself and Swift. Working with Swift would obviously involve its share of frustrations, but by now Katyal had come to appreciate Swift's sporadic gift for cutting through the legal fog to articulate the profoundly American principles at the heart of their shared objection to the military commissions. This was going to be a fight over the law, but it was also going to be a battle for public opinion. The government would use every opportunity to remind the nation that we were at war with an enemy who deliberately targeted innocent civilians. He and Swift were going to have to combat that sort of rhetoric by convincing people that their challenge to the military commissions was not about our enemy. It was about us. In this respect, it was difficult to imagine a more powerful weapon than a blond-haired, barrel-chested Naval Academy graduate who loved nothing more than talking about duty and honor.

Katyal told Swift that if Hamdan would cooperate, he was in.

THE CENTERPIECE of the government's case against Hamdan was a seven-page interrogation report, known as a 302, written by the bureau's foremost expert on al Qaeda, a Lebanese-American FBI agent named Ali Soufan.

One of only a handful of agents who spoke perfect Arabic, Soufan had been handpicked for the al Qaeda squad in the wake of the 1998 embassy bombings by the FBI's head of counterterrorism, John O'Neill. In 2000, Soufan had been dispatched to Yemen to serve as the lead case agent on the *Cole* bombing. He was still there a year later, when the two hijacked commercial airplanes slammed into the World Trade Center.* Rather than return to New York, Soufan stayed in Yemen to investigate some leads. One took him to a Yemeni prison and to Abu Jandal—or Nasser al-Bahri—the man who had introduced Hamdan to jihad and subsequently been taken into custody after the *Cole* attack. Their interview lasted nearly two weeks and yielded an ex-

* O'Neill was among those killed in the 9/11 attacks.

traordinary amount of intelligence; among other things, al-Bahri confirmed the identities of every one of the 9/11 hijackers.

It was also the first time that the name Salim Hamdan had come to
the attention of the U.S. government. Having studied al Qaeda for
years, Soufan had accumulated dozens of names—some real, some
aliases of people he suspected of being operatives for the organization. During one of their many conversations, Soufan asked al-Bahri
if he'd ever heard of a man named Saqr al-Jedawi. Al-Bahri responded
instantly. "That's Salim Hamdan," he said. "Bin Laden's driver and my
brother-in-law."

His interest piqued, Soufan questioned al-Bahri a little further
about Hamdan, and al-Bahri told him the story of their arranged mar-
riages to Yemeni sisters. Soufan asked if Hamdan had sworn a *bayat*, or
oath of allegiance, to bin Laden. Al-Bahri said he had.

About a year and a half later, when Soufan learned that Hamdan was
in U.S. custody and on Guantánamo Bay, he got on the first plane that
he could to Cuba. Knowing the kind of proximity Hamdan had had to
bin Laden, Soufan figured he could be a huge intelligence asset.

During their first few meetings, Hamdan was intransigent and arrogant. He made fun of his previous interrogators' ignorance of al
Qaeda and insisted that he had already divulged everything he knew.
Soufan was sure he was lying. He told Hamdan about his lengthy interview with al-Bahri and mentioned a few details about al Qaeda to
display his knowledge of the organization. "If you're smart, you'll tell
me the truth about everything," Soufan said, "because I'm going to
know when you're lying."

Soufan and his partner, George Crouch, gradually built a relationship with Hamdan, exploiting the same void in the prisoner's life that
had led him to jihad—the orphan's yearning for connection. Whenever they visited Hamdan on Guantánamo they brought him food—
usually pizza or a Filet-O-Fish sandwich—as well as the American car
and truck magazines that he loved. Soufan once even arranged for
Hamdan to speak with his wife on a satellite phone.

Hamdan eventually started talking. He detailed his rise from un-
trained recruit to bin Laden's personal driver, and admitted to having

trained at al Qaeda–sponsored camps in Afghanistan and transporting weapons for bin Laden. He told Soufan and Crouch that he had helped evacuate bin Laden's compound in Afghanistan before the 1998 embassy attacks, and acknowledged that he had been returning to bin Laden at the time of his capture in November 2001. Hamdan offered useful information about al Qaeda as well. Among other things, he identified mug shots of other bodyguards who were being held on Guantánamo, told Soufan about the leaders of the *Cole* bombing, and helped fill in the map of bin Laden's post-9/11 whereabouts.

Soufan thought he had plenty of evidence to prosecute Hamdan in federal court, but he was eager to have him testify against more significant terrorists instead. After all, Hamdan knew all of the al Qaeda leadership and had even been with bin Laden and Zawahiri on September 11, when Khalid Sheikh Mohammed, the mastermind of the attacks, briefed them on the success of the operation.

Soufan wasn't sure, but he thought he might be able to persuade Hamdan to plead guilty and cooperate with the government in exchange for a lighter sentence. He had several conversations with David Kelley, the deputy U.S. Attorney in Manhattan, about the possibility of offering the detainee a deal. Kelley said he was talking to the Pentagon and Justice Department about working something out.

So it came as an unpleasant surprise to Soufan when, several months into his interrogation of Hamdan, the Bush administration designated him for trial before a military commission. Soufan's access to Hamdan was immediately cut off, and the FBI lost a crucial source of information, as well as a potential key witness in other al Qaeda trials.

THE DAY AFTER being assigned to the *Hamdan* case, Swift went to see the lead prosecutor, Lt. Comdr. Scott Lang, about what kind of deal the government had in mind.

Lang had joined the commissions in November 2002, a year after the president's military order. Shortly after moving into the Pentagon, he and his fellow prosecutors were presented with files on about six hundred detainees and told to choose the most suitable defendants. It was an inversion of how the process of meting out justice typically works. "Normally, you have the crime first and then you find the criminals," Lang later recalled. "When we showed up, they already had the criminals. We were tasked with finding the crimes."

Within a matter of months, Lang had zeroed in on Hamdan. In a sense, he was a surprising choice. He wasn't a high-ranking officer of al Qaeda, nor had he participated in any specific terrorist operations. But because the military commission system was brand-new, Lang thought it made sense to try some lower-ranking operatives first, in case anything went wrong. He also liked the fact that Hamdan had been in U.S. custody since his capture and hadn't been rendered to any foreign countries for interrogation, which might open the door for his defense attorney to raise questions about his treatment.

Hamdan's story certainly had narrative appeal. Many jihadis had never even met bin Laden, but Hamdan had admitted to working directly for him. Better still, unlike the cresting wave of jihadis who went to Afghanistan after 1999, once bin Laden had already established himself, Hamdan had been with him between 1996 and 2001, a stretch of time that spanned not just 9/11 but also the 1998 embassy attacks and the 2000 USS *Cole* bombing. If Hamdan didn't plead guilty, Lang figured he could turn his trial into a history of al Qaeda's long-standing jihad against America.

Building a case against Hamdan proved unexpectedly arduous. It took months to sift through the evidence from the field, primarily Afghanistan, all of which had been logged in to an enormous and poorly organized database. What's more, the FBI and CIA were anything but forthcoming with interrogation reports and the names of the agents who'd conducted the interviews. Requests that should have taken days wound up taking months.

Nevertheless, Lang's case gradually started coming together. In addition to Soufan's interrogation report, he had compelling corroborating evidence. There were photographs and videotapes of Hamdan standing beside bin Laden, including one taken at a news conference for the Pakistani media in Afghanistan in 1997 in which Hamdan is wearing military fatigues and clutching what looks like a semiautomatic weapon. There were incriminating documents too, such as a written request for Hamdan to deliver Pika machine-gun belts and magazines to al Qaeda fighters. In addition, there was photographic evidence of the surface-to-air missiles that had allegedly been found in the trunk of the car he was driving at the time of his capture: the U.S. Army major who took Hamdan into custody snapped pictures of the missiles before destroying them.

Lang eventually managed to speak with almost every officer and agent who had come into contact with Hamdan since his capture, including one intelligence agent who said that Hamdan admitted to feeling "uncontrollable enthusiasm" when he was in bin Laden's company. Once he was satisfied with his case, Lang passed Hamdan's file up the chain of command for approval. It went first to the Pentagon's adviser for the commissions, then to the deputy defense secretary, Paul D. Wolfowitz, and finally to the president himself.

A former cross-country runner, Lang was reed thin, with close-cropped blond hair. He had been in the Reserve Officer Training Corps as an undergraduate at Villanova and had gone on to become the navigator on a Norfolk-based destroyer before the Navy sent him to law school. Like Swift, he loved being in the courtroom, though Lang had stuck almost exclusively to prosecuting and had excelled, racking up one of the best conviction rates in the Navy.

Lang and Swift had known each other for years, ever since 1993, when Lang was an instructor at the Naval Justice School in Newport, Rhode Island, and Swift did a nine-week JAG training course there after law school. Lang's first impression had not been favorable. "Charlie Swift was the unanimous winner of the Spring Bud award," Lang remembered, "which goes to the student who's constantly springing up out of his seat to make pain-in-the-ass comments. In the three years I taught at Naval Justice, no one got more votes than Swift."

The moment Lang heard that Swift had been assigned to represent Hamdan, he was sure that the government had made a mistake. The JAG community is relatively small—there are about seven hundred Navy JAGs on active duty—and while he and Swift had never squared off in the courtroom, Lang was well aware of his tendency to showboat on behalf of his client. "I knew that Swift was going to go to the media and make Charlie Swift a major focus of the case," Lang recalled. "If the senior leadership of the JAG Corps didn't realize that, they made a major miscalculation."

For his part, Swift considered Lang uptight and ungenerous, too prone to divide the world into good and evil. "Lang would have hanged the innkeeper in the Lincoln conspiracy case," says Swift.

Their first meeting about the Hamdan case was brief. Lang told Swift he wasn't authorized to make a binding deal, but that he was thinking twenty years for full cooperation, including testifying at the military commissions of other detainees.

"What happens if we don't plead guilty?" Swift asked.

Lang wasn't surprised. The civilian lawyers at the Pentagon were confident that the JAGs on the defense team would all fall in line and push their clients to take pleas. Lang didn't agree. He was sure that Swift and the other JAGs were planning to fight.

SWIFT WAS EAGER to get down to Guantánamo to meet Hamdan, but before he could go, he needed a translator. His first choice was Anna Wuerth, a visiting professor of religion at the University of Richmond. ("I liked the idea of the jury watching my client whisper in the ear of a Western woman," Swift later recalled. "Would that fit your image of an Islamic terrorist?") But because Wuerth was a German national, she couldn't get the necessary security clearance for Guantánamo and instead recommended Charles Schmitz, a professor of geography and Arabic studies at Towson University in Baltimore. Swift called Schmitz in mid-January to introduce himself and gauge his interest.

It was limited, to say the least. Schmitz didn't know much about the military, but his impressions were not positive. As a student at the University of California at Santa Cruz and Berkeley in the late 1970s and early 1980s, he had been active in several left-wing student groups dedicated to supporting national liberation movements in Latin America. To his mind, the U.S. military trained the torturers of freedom fighters. If he needed another reason to be wary, Schmitz had read recently about the arrest of a civilian translator on Guantánamo Bay for espionage.

Swift proved to be a hard guy to shake, though, and Schmitz eventually agreed to at least hear his pitch in person. They made plans to meet at a Metro station in suburban Maryland, roughly halfway between them.

Swift was late, leaving Schmitz, a tall, ruggedly handsome man with shaggy, sand-colored hair, waiting warily on the outdoor platform in the bitter cold. Swift finally stepped off an arriving train thirty minutes after the appointed time. He had a meeting at the Pentagon later that afternoon and was wearing starched dress whites beneath a dark blue overcoat. He looked to Schmitz like an advertisement for the Navy, with his round officer's hat and earnest blue eyes. Swift pumped Schmitz's hand vigorously, apologized profusely for his tardiness, and launched into a monologue about how he was going to take down the military commission system and bring justice to Guantánamo Bay on behalf of *"Sah-LEEM."*

Fifteen minutes later, Swift was still talking and Schmitz was freezing. "Okay, I'll do it," he said, believing it was the only way to shut Swift up. Schmitz never actually thought he'd end up with the job; he had a lot of Arab friends and had written a number of scholarly articles critical of the U.S. government. How would he ever get the necessary security clearance?

Before they parted, Schmitz handed Swift an academic book on Yemeni history that he had brought for him. Swift asked Schmitz if he had any advice for him with respect to his client. "Well," Schmitz answered, "you could start by pronouncing his name correctly. It's not *Sah-LEEM,* it's *SAH-lem."*

A week later Schmitz got another call from Swift. His security clearance had been granted. They were going to Guantánamo.

IN THE PREDAWN DARKNESS of a raw, gray Friday morning in late January 2004, a taxi pulled up in front of the Hilton in Norfolk, Virginia, to take Swift, Schmitz, and Swift's paralegal, Jason Kreinhop, to Norfolk Naval Station to catch a military charter to Guantánamo Bay. The plane was about half full with military personnel, their families, and private military contractors. Swift and Schmitz took seats next to each other; Kreinhop opted to sit alone several rows behind them.

Schmitz had brought a book and was just settling in for a long flight of uninterrupted reading when Swift began to talk. After a few minutes it became clear that he wasn't interested in having a conversation so much as an audience, and the topic at hand was the battle of Gettysburg and how it applied to this great mission they were on. Full of hot purpose, Swift lectured Schmitz on the details of the battle, growing increasingly emotional as he arrived at the story of the fight for Little Round Top and his boyhood hero, Col. Joshua Lawrence Chamberlain.

"Here was this math teacher from Bowdoin College who had never been given a command," Swift began, his words ripe with incredulity. "He stands there at the top of Little Round Top and makes an audacious decision. It's four in the afternoon, and he's out of ammunition. He's outnumbered four to one. The South is getting ready for one last push, and he doesn't have the ammunition to fight it. So he orders his troops to fix their bayonets, says to his brother next to him, 'I want you to stay behind me because Mother will be sorely vexed if we both die today,' leads his charge down the hill, shatters the morale of the Southern troops and drives them back across the wheat field. He wins one of the first Congressional Medals of Honor for this, and then goes on to become governor of Maine. No one saw him coming, but at that moment in time he simply said, 'I will make a difference. I will change history.'"

As the story came to its conclusion, Schmitz noticed that Swift had moved himself to tears.

Guantánamo is just four hundred miles south of Miami, but because of a lengthy layover and a circuitous route to avoid Cuban airspace, it was eight hours before they finally touched down. Schmitz's book was still sitting unopened in his lap. Out on the tarmac, while their bags were being sniffed by German shepherds, Kreinhop gave Schmitz some unsolicited advice: "You've got to learn not to sit next to the commander, sir."

GUANTÁNAMO BAY NAVAL BASE is divided into two areas—windward and leeward—by the two-and-a-half-mile-wide bay for which it is named. The airport is on the leeward side; nearly everything else is a short ferry ride away on the windward side. There are housing sub-divisions, a few fast-food restaurants, a strip mall, a bowling alley, a drive-in movie theater, and a neglected nine-hole golf course. The overall effect is small-town America, if a sad and somewhat dated version of it. The whole base is about forty-five square miles, or roughly the size of the island of Manhattan.

After disembarking from the ferry, Swift and Schmitz made their way to the headquarters of the joint task force that runs the base. They happened to arrive in the midst of a drill to prepare for a terrorist attack. Roadblocks had been erected everywhere, and the female soldier charged with preparing their access badges was made up to look like a casualty, theatrics that were hardly necessary to make this place one of the strangest either of them had ever been. Swift soon found his footing, though. Asked to sign a statement ensuring that he wouldn't say anything to the media about what they saw on Guantá-namo, he insisted on amending the language to read that he wouldn't say anything "in violation of the National Security Act."

That evening he and Schmitz went to the Marine galley—even though it's officially a naval base, the joint task force that oversees Guantánamo includes all four armed services as well as the Coast Guard—which Swift had been told had decent food and a great view. It was surf and turf night, so they ate steak and lobster, followed by Ben & Jerry's Peace Pops, as they watched the sun drop down below the bay.

Thirty-six hours later they set out for Camp Delta in a rusty red van to meet Hamdan. From a distance, Swift could make out the plywood guard towers draped in American flags and, as they drew closer, the heavy chain-link fencing topped with concertina wire that ringed the camp. A four-by-eight-foot sign hung from the main entrance to Delta: HONOR BOUND TO DEFEND FREEDOM, the motto for the Joint Task Force–Guantánamo.

Swift wore a khaki uniform rather than his dress whites because he wanted to seem as accessible as possible. At the entrance gate, he declined to place a strip of black tape over his name tag, the custom among most soldiers and officers, who prefer to keep their identities hidden from the suspected terrorists inside.

For the past several weeks, ever since the president had designated him for trial by military commission, Hamdan had been in solitary confinement—or, as the Defense Department called it, precommission confinement—in a separate area inside Delta known as Camp Echo. The administration didn't want the other detainees to know that he had been assigned a lawyer or, worse, give him the chance to report to the rest of the prison population on the substance of their conversations.

Swift and Schmitz were led down a long dirt path toward a cluster of eight cinder block huts with corrugated tin roofs that faced inward on a square. The sky was a hard blue. It hadn't rained on Guantánamo in weeks, and they kicked up small clouds of dust as they walked. The guards unlocked the door to Echo 3, and Swift got his first look at Hamdan, a small, frail-looking man—five feet six inches, 130 pounds, he estimated—in a baggy orange jumpsuit. He had a shaved head and a long beard. And he was smiling. As Swift would later learn, Hamdan always smiled when he was nervous.

The hut was divided in two by a heavy metal grate. On one side was a metal bed and stainless steel toilet. On the other were two abutting folding tables and three white plastic chairs. Salim Hamdan sat at the opposite end of the tables, beneath a bank of bright fluorescent lights. His hands and feet were bound to a chain around his waist, his ankles fastened to an eyebolt in the floor. An old air-conditioning unit labored noisily against the stifling heat.

"I want him released from those chains," Swift said.

"We can't do that," one of the guards answered. After some debate, they agreed at least to unchain his hands. They asked Swift if he wanted one of them to remain in the cell, and Swift said no. They showed him the red panic button marked DURESS on the wall and left him alone with his client.

"I'm a military attorney, and I've been appointed to represent you," Swift began. "I can understand if you don't trust me right now. I work for the same people who are holding you here." He proceeded to detail his educational background and military rank, which an Arab culture expert had told Swift would impress Hamdan. They didn't seem to. Hamdan was polite but curt, insisting on a civilian lawyer. He wasn't any happier with Schmitz; he wanted an Arab translator. Swift asked for a chance to earn his trust.

Whether Hamdan really believed that Swift was his lawyer or, more likely, just another interrogator, he was eager to rant about his mistreatment at the hands of the Americans. He told Swift that during his first several weeks in Bagram, he had been stashed away in a dark cell in the basement of the prison when representatives from the International Committee of the Red Cross came through. He also claimed to have seen a fellow detainee beaten to death by a prison guard in Afghanistan. Swift scribbled furiously onto a yellow legal pad as Hamdan spoke.

About an hour into their two-and-a-half-hour meeting, Swift told Hamdan about the government's offer: twenty years for a guilty plea and full cooperation. "What do they say I've done?" Hamdan asked.

"They haven't charged you yet," Swift answered. "They sent me here to negotiate a guilty plea."

"How can I plead guilty if I don't know what I've done?" Hamdan asked.

After a long pause, Hamdan asked Swift if he thought he should take the deal. Swift gave him his advice: "These military commissions are presidential policy, and sooner or later the president is going to change. A different president may want to pursue a different foreign policy. If you plead guilty to something, no president is going to argue for your release. On the other hand, if you plead not guilty, there's a very real possibility that someone in the future may release you."

Swift then outlined for Hamdan the alternative to a guilty plea. He listed some of the rights under the Geneva Conventions and Uniform Code of Military Justice that he believed Hamdan was entitled to but had thus far been denied. It was unclear how much, if anything, Hamdan was grasping, yet Swift pressed on. "The only way to get you these rights is to sue the Bush administration," he said. "That's what I'd like to do. Sue President Bush."

Another long pause followed. "This lawsuit, will it make you rich?" Hamdan finally asked.

"No," Swift answered. "But it might make me famous."

Then he added, "It might make you famous too."

"I don't want to be famous," Hamdan replied. "I just want to get out of here."

That night Swift and Schmitz watched the Super Bowl on Armed Forces Television, poking fun at the military network's commercials, which promoted safe sex and the importance of maintaining strong, healthy bodies. The following day, they returned to Camp Echo. At the end of the meeting, Swift told Hamdan they'd be back soon and encouraged him to think about the government's offer in the interim.

"Do you believe we're here to help you?" Swift asked, standing up to leave.

"A drowning man will grab onto any hand that's extended to him," Hamdan replied.

SEVEN

The Lawsuit

THE AMERICAN JUDICIAL SYSTEM generally limits the filing of lawsuits to individuals with a personal stake in the litigation, but there are instances when litigants cannot themselves prosecute an action. They might be mentally incompetent, physically incapacitated, or incarcerated. In such instances, they can designate a third party to stand in for them via what's known as the next friend doctrine.

On Friday, three days after they'd returned to Virginia, Swift and Schmitz flew back to Guantánamo. In Swift's backpack was a copy of a one-paragraph next friend letter that Katyal had drafted authorizing them to file a petition for habeas corpus in federal court on Hamdan's behalf.

Swift deliberately kept Saturday's meeting with Hamdan informal, hoping to build up at least a little more trust before again taking up the matter of the lawsuit. On Sunday they brought Hamdan a Styrofoam container of jerk chicken, beans, and rice from a local Jamaican restaurant, which Schmitz figured he'd prefer to the Big Mac they'd brought him the day before. After Hamdan had finished eating, using his fingers, as is the Yemeni custom, Swift produced the next friend letter, and asked Schmitz to read it out loud. Hamdan agreed to sign it, but he wanted it translated into Arabic first. And he wanted it typed. "If you're a real lawyer," he told Swift, "you can get it typed."

Swift asked Hamdan to sign something else too, something not yet written. The initial target letter from the Pentagon had stated that Swift's access to Hamdan would continue as long as they were engaged in "pretrial negotiations." Swift was worried that the administration might cut him off from his client the moment it learned that he wasn't going to simply plead guilty. He wanted to get some sort of sworn statement from Hamdan attesting to his innocence, in the event that this was their last meeting.

That night, after spending the rest of the day going over Hamdan's story with him, Swift and Schmitz drove over to the Marines' Morale, Welfare, and Recreation Center to use the computers. It took a couple of hours for Schmitz to figure out how to install the software necessary to convert the keyboard into Arabic. Once he had done so, Schmitz quickly translated the next friend letter and then worked on the affidavit well past midnight, long after the rest of the service members had cleared out. Swift paced behind him, stepping outside from time to time to smoke a Dutch Masters cigar.

They returned to the rec center first thing in the morning to finish the affidavit and then drove over to Camp Echo to show it to Hamdan. He demanded some small changes and didn't want them handwritten in the margins, so Swift and Schmitz went back to the rec center one last time. Hamdan finally signed both documents that evening. Swift called Katyal with the good news, reaching him on vacation in northern California, in the midst of a run with his wife and a couple of her friends in the hills of Marin County.

The affidavit was three and a half pages long, single-spaced. It began with a very brief biographical sketch: "My name is Salem [*sic*] Ahmed Hamdan and I am a Yemeni citizen. I have been known by the name Saqr. I was born in the village of Khoreiba in the governate of Hadramawt in approximately 1969."

The affidavit proceeded chronologically, describing in broad strokes Hamdan's recruitment for jihad in 1996 by Nasser al-Bahri (though Hamdan, in an apparent effort to protect his brother-in-law, called him Ali al-Yafi). Hamdan asserted that he had started out as a driver on bin Laden's farm, ferrying Afghani workers back and forth to the local village, but that after about seven months he was asked to drive for bin Laden himself. He went on to tell the story of his capture, explaining that he was with bin Laden in Kabul in October 2001 when he heard that the Northern Alliance was about to attack Kandahar and returned home for his family. "I decided to borrow a car to drive my family to Pakistan," the affidavit read. "After I had taken my family to Pakistan, I tried to return to Afghanistan to return the car to its owner and to return to my house to sell my belongings to get money in order to return with my family to Yemen." Hamdan said that he was subsequently stopped by some Afghani warlords who were "looking for Arabs to sell to American forces." He tried to flee, but was captured.

The second half of the affidavit was devoted to Hamdan's treatment in U.S. custody. It read, in part:

While I was in Afghanistan, I helped and cooperated with the Americans in every way. Despite the fact that I cooperated with the Americans, I was physically abused. I have a bad back from work in Yemen. I told my investigators of this condition but was transported in positions that caused me physical agony in my back. I was dressed in only bright blue overalls in sub-freezing temperatures and was very cold. I was made to sit motionless on benches with other prisoners for days. When I did not know the answers to the investigator[']s questions, the soldiers would strike me with their fists and kick me with their feet, after the investigator left, before they took me back with the other prisoners. When I took them places I had driven Osama bin Laden, they would threaten me with death, torture or prison when I did not know the answers to their questions. One of their methods to threaten was to put a pistol on the table in front of me and show me the gun and ask, "What do you think?" . . .

In June 2002, I was flown to Guantánamo Bay, Cuba. In Guantánamo Bay, Cuba, I was put in a large prison with many other men. I was held in a single cell in a cellblock of 48 men. These cells were open to the air and I could talk to the other men. I was given 15 minutes a week of exercise in a[n] 8 meter by 7 meter fenced in area. A Muslim cleric would come and talk to people and I talked with [sic] and I could hear the calls to prayer. At Camp Delta, I was questioned by many people from the FBI and Arab police forces. They showed me pictures and asked me to identify the people. On two (2) occasions they allowed me to call my wife on a portable telephone and speak with her and to calm her. I had not heard from her since I left her in Pakistan and I was worried about her . . .

In December 2003, I was moved from Camp Delta, and put in a new cell, this cell was enclosed in a house, and from that time I have not been permitted to see the sun or hear other people outside the house or talk with other people. I am alone except for the guard in the house. They allow me exercise three times per week but only at night and not in the day. They gave me the Quran only but not other books . . . I have pains in my back and leg and I itch from lack of sunshine . . . I asked for books from the library, but was told it was closed.

LCDR Swift told me that the government letter demanded to know whether I would plead guilty to unspecified charges in exchange for a guaranteed sentence. LCDR Swift also told me that in addition to pleading guilty, that I would have to be a witness for the United States as part of the agreement. I do not believe I should plead guilty, because I do not believe I have committed any crime.

Being held in the cell where I am now is very hard, much harder than Camp Delta. One month is like a year here, and I have considered pleading guilty in order to get out of here. I believe that I am a civilian, I have never been a member of Al-Qaeda and I am not a terrorist and I believe I should have a civilian trial, but any trial is better than what I have now . . .

AS SOON AS he returned to Virginia, Swift drafted a request to speak with the media about Hamdan.

There was an unwritten prohibition in the JAG Corps against litigating your cases outside the courtroom. Swift had been dancing around this rule for much of his career, but from the start he and the other JAGs on the military commission defense team had been determined to not simply play the role of the loyal opposition. In order to zealously defend their clients, who were being tried inside a courtroom they considered to be rigged, they knew they were going to have to go on the offensive. That meant getting the media on their side.

The answer came back from the Pentagon a couple of days later. Swift was permitted to comment on his client's background and his mental condition and, more generally, to discuss the military commissions and the war on terror, but anything that pertained to Hamdan's capture, interrogations, or detention fell into the category of "sources and methods"—meaning that the disclosure of such information could jeopardize intelligence gathering—and was therefore off-limits for reasons of national security.

Swift's first interview appeared on the front page of *The Miami Herald* a few days later. DRIVER FOR BIN LADEN IN A GUANTÁNAMO CELL, the headline read. "He fully admits that he was an employee of Osama bin Laden," the *Herald*'s reporter, Carol Rosenberg, quoted Swift as saying about Hamdan, "but he adamantly denies that he was ever a member of al Qaeda or engaged in any terrorist attack. He worked for bin Laden solely for the purpose of supporting himself and his family."

Swift was instantly deluged with calls. Several other newspapers did their own Hamdan stories, and Swift was a repeat guest on both Fox News and CNN. He liked being on TV, but he quickly discovered that he'd underestimated the public's antipathy toward his client and soon started to second-guess his decision to describe Hamdan as bin Laden's driver, rather than a civilian employee whose responsibilities sometimes included driving. "Driver" suggested an intimacy that was going to be hard to overcome. "You claim . . . that he [Hamdan] was not affiliated with al Qaeda. How can you make that argument knowing the security detail that Osama bin Laden employed for anyone to get near him for the past 10 years?" CNN's Bill Hemmer asked skeptically. "You know when reporters went to meet him, oftentimes they were driven around for days with blindfolds over their eyes just to get access to him."

On February 12, 2004, Swift and Katyal took their first legal step on Hamdan's behalf. "Mr. Hamdan demands to be informed of the specific charges against him or to be released from pre-commission segregation into general detention," Swift wrote in a memo to John D. Altenburg, Jr., a retired Army general and former Green Beret who had recently been named appointing authority for the commissions, making him responsible for charging the defendants and appointing the members of the panels that would hear the cases.

Swift was asserting his client's right to a speedy trial under Article 10 of the Uniform Code of Military Justice, which states that when an individual is imprisoned prior to prosecution, either "immediate steps" must be taken to charge and try him or he must be released. Swift also established why he believed that his client was entitled to this right. The Uniform Code of Military Justice gives the president the authority to prescribe the rules for commissions, he wrote, but only if they are consistent with the UCMJ itself.

Eleven days later Swift heard back from Altenburg's legal adviser, Army Brig. Gen. Thomas Hemingway, about his speedy trial request. The response was three sentences long: "I am in receipt of your February 12, 2004, memorandum requesting a determination that Article 10, UCMJ, applies to the Department of Defense detention of Salem Ahmed Hamdan. The Department of Defense is detaining Mr. Hamdan as an unlawful enemy combatant. Article 10, UCMJ, does not apply to Mr. Hamdan's detention."

In American jurisprudence, bringing suit is supposed to be an act of last resort. The legal doctrine known as the exhaustion of remedies requires that litigants pursue all routes to having their grievances addressed before seeking relief from the courts. As there was no military commission yet in which Swift and Katyal could contest Hamdan's solitary confinement and the legitimacy of the system by which he would be tried, Swift had now officially exhausted his remedies. The only alternative was to sue his client's jailer, the U.S. government.

OVER THE COURSE of the fall, Katyal had spent countless hours researching where to bring their lawsuit against the dozens of military commissions. Suits launched from outside the United States are generally supposed to be filed in district court in Washington, D.C., yet given how poorly the two latest Guantánamo cases, *Rasul* and *al Odah*, had fared there, he was eager to find an alternative venue.

Katyal had considered the possibility of naming Maj. Gen. Geoffrey D. Miller, the commander of the Joint Task Force–Guantánamo, as the principal defendant, and filing the suit in the Fifth Circuit, which encompassed Miller's hometown in Texas. He had also run across a 1973 case, *Kinnell v. Warner*, involving an American service member at sea who had filed a habeas petition in the federal district court closest to his vessel. Commission defendants had presumably been transported from Afghanistan to Guantánamo Bay by military planes; perhaps their flight paths had taken them near a more favorable district?

Then, in the middle of December, when a federal appeals court issued a surprise ruling in the case of a Libyan prisoner named Salim Gherebi, a more attractive option presented itself.

Like the rest of the habeas corpus petitions brought on behalf of Guantánamo detainees, Gherebi's, which had been filed by his brother, a resident of San Diego, had started inauspiciously: a federal judge in Los Angeles threw out his petition, citing the by now familiar argument that Guantánamo Bay was outside American sovereignty. Gherebi appealed to the U.S. Court of Appeals for the Ninth Circuit, headquartered in San Francisco, with little hope of success. Not only had every prior ruling gone against the detainees, but the Supreme Court had already agreed to hear *Rasul*. With the justices about to issue the final word on whether the Guantánamo detainees should have access to the federal courts, it seemed extremely unlikely that the Ninth Circuit court of appeals would issue an independent ruling in *Gherebi*. Instead, the appeals court determined on December 18, 2003, that the United States had the equivalent of sovereign control over Guantánamo. Everyone being held there was entitled to habeas corpus rights.

No one expected the decision to stand for long. The Ninth Circuit court of appeals is known as the nation's most liberal circuit court, and the author of the opinion was its most liberal judge, Stephen Reinhardt—"the judge the Supreme Court loves to overturn," as *The*

Weekly Standard once described him. Still, for the moment, Reinhardt's ruling was the law of the land in the Ninth Circuit.

It was obviously the ideal place to bring suit against the military commissions, but litigants can't simply choose where they want to file complaints. Katyal and Swift needed a legitimate reason for why the Ninth Circuit had jurisdiction over Hamdan's petition. Thanks to an administrative quirk of the military, they had one. American service members are considered legal residents of wherever they last lived before joining up. So even though Swift had lived in Puerto Rico, Florida, and now Virginia, his official place of residence hadn't changed since he attended law school in Seattle. As Hamdan's next friend, he was entitled to file suit in Washington State, which, as luck would have it, is part of the Ninth Circuit.

Given the vulnerability of Judge Reinhardt's decision, Swift and Katyal had to move quickly, but the lawsuit needed to be compelling and thorough. Katyal enlisted four Yale law students to help him prepare it. Three of them, Nola Heller, Jonathan Kravis, and Stephen Fuzesi, had excelled in his first-year constitutional law class and were now in their final years of law school. The fourth, Stephen Vladeck, had been recommended to him by a former colleague at Yale.

"Happy holidays," Katyal's e-mail to the group in December 2003 began.

> I am writing to see if you are interested in a major pro bono effort that I am leading to take down the military tribunals . . . I have been working with the Pentagon's defense team (the military lawyers who would represent those indicted in the tribunals) for several months. They have asked me to prepare a constitutional challenge to the tribunals . . . The military lawyers may lose their jobs for filing this suit, which is why I need everything so hush-hush. We will be catching the US Govt completely off guard. I fully expect this case to be heard by the Ninth Circuit, and the Supreme Court. I know that all of you have exams, and so it's not the easiest thing in the world, even if the holidays weren't around. But if any of you are interested in helping, this case will be about as leanly staffed as it

gets, and so each of you would get the opportunity to draft parts of the brief and kick around strategy on one of the most serious constitutional issues we have ever faced in our lives.

IN EARLY FEBRUARY, Katyal and his student team were in the midst of drafting the lawsuit when he got a phone call from his sister, Sonia, in New York. She had just spoken with their father, and he had sounded confused. Katyal called his father himself and got the same impression. Their mother was at a family wedding in India, so Katyal asked a family friend in Chicago to take him to the emergency room. An X-ray turned up two lesions. The doctor said it could be a tropical disease, but Joanna thought it sounded more like cancer. Katyal was supposed to leave for Aspen in a few days to go skiing with a friend, but he canceled the trip and flew to Chicago first thing the next morning.

As a child, Katyal hadn't seen much of his father. Like many first-generation immigrants, he had been preoccupied with providing for his family and spent most of his time at work. When Katyal was thirteen years old, though, his father was fired from his job as a chemical engineer months before his pension was to vest. He hired a lawyer and sued his former employer for wrongful termination, but before the lawsuit had even gotten under way, his lawyer quit to work for the company's legal team. Katyal's father continued pro se, or without an attorney, and the federal judge assigned to the case thought there was enough merit to it to take the highly unusual step of ordering the court to pay for a new attorney. By this point, however, Katyal's father had lost his stomach for the suit. He agreed to a meager settlement and never worked as an engineer again, instead managing a handful of rental properties in Chicago.

For Katyal, the immediate effect of his father's firing was that the two started spending a lot more time together. Perhaps even more profoundly, though, the experience inspired him to study law. Growing up in an affluent suburb of Chicago, Katyal had several classmates whose fathers were corporate lawyers, but it had never before occurred to him that the law could be used not just to protect a company's fortunes but to redress wrongs.

The experience had the opposite effect on both of Katyal's parents, who emerged from it with a visceral hatred of lawyers. Having seen how roughly the company's lawyers had treated his father, aggressively deposing him and defending his firing with dubious claims, they concluded that the law was a dirty business. Years later, when Katyal told his parents that he wanted to go to law school, they tried everything, including bribing him with a used car, to persuade him to consider medical school instead.

By the time Katyal landed in Chicago, an MRI had confirmed that his father had an unusually aggressive form of brain cancer known as glioblastoma. Katyal's mother was already in transit from India but had missed her connecting flight, so it wasn't until late that night when she called him from New York that he was able to speak to her. Katyal had wanted to wait to tell her about the cancer in person, but when he heard her voice, the news spilled out. The following morning, he picked her up at the airport and they drove straight to Northwestern Memorial Hospital, where his father had already been prepped for surgery.

Katyal canceled all his classes and spent the next several weeks in Chicago with his mother and sister. His father underwent a second emergency surgery, and Katyal made arrangements for a new bathroom and bedroom to be built on the first floor of his parents' house for him because he would be returning from the hospital in a wheelchair and might not have the use of his legs. Joanna took a week off work and came to Chicago with Rem and Calder to help out and keep Katyal company.

Katyal was too worried about his father to give much thought to the lawsuit, though Swift was in touch almost every day, not to talk about the case but to see how he was doing. Katyal had called him from a hospital pay phone when he'd first gotten his father's diagnosis to let him know that the suit was going to be delayed and had been instantly struck by his compassion. Swift had just said he was sorry, but he spoke in a way that conveyed sincerity and deep concern. It was a very different side of Swift from the blustery trial lawyer whom Katyal had first been exposed to back in the summer.

Katyal finally left Chicago at the end of February 2004. His father was recovering, but the diagnosis was not good. The average post-surgery life expectancy for patients with glioblastoma was ten months.

BACK IN WASHINGTON, Katyal threw himself into his work. He had two weeks' worth of classes to make up, and he was also eager to get Hamdan's habeas corpus petition finished as soon as possible. Joanna, who had initially been ambivalent about his signing on to the case, now recognized it as a valuable distraction from his father's illness and encouraged him to spend as much time on the lawsuit as he needed.

Katyal and his Yale team had soon finished drafting the petition, but he had not anticipated how hard it was going to be to find a law firm in Seattle willing to file it, a requirement under the rules of Seattle federal court. In the midst of the search, Katyal received an e-mail from a former student of his at Georgetown named David East asking for his help getting a job as a federal prosecutor. "It's been a few years, and I know that you have had more than your share of students during your tenure," East wrote, "but I was hoping that you might remember me from your Clinton class and Crime and Punishment seminar." East went on to say that he was currently doing commercial litigation work for a Seattle-based law firm, Perkins Coie.

Katyal responded immediately: "It's very funny that you write at this moment, you may be in the right place at the right time. I may have a major, very high profile pro bono case that I will be bringing in Seattle in the next few weeks. I will need a local attorney to work with me. I imagine you will need the approval of the poo-bahs at your firm, as it is a very serious matter. But if you want to have some fun, far more fun than you'd have in govt, I may have the ticket."

East passed the request along to the firm's pro bono coordinator, Julia Parsons Clarke, who called Katyal to learn a little more about the case. The next day she followed up via e-mail with some additional questions. "Who would the defendants be?" Parsons Clarke asked.

"The suit," Katyal replied, "would be filed against the following: DONALD H. RUMSFELD, United States Secretary of Defense; PAUL WOLFOWITZ, United States Deputy Secretary of Defense; JOHN D. ALTENBURG, JR., Appointing Authority, Department of Defense; GEORGE W. BUSH, President of the United States."

Parsons Clarke brought the request to a fifty-year-old senior partner at the firm, Harry Schneider. Inside his large corner office, which overlooked Puget Sound and the snow-capped Olympic Mountains and was incongruously decorated with psychedelic rock concert posters, Schneider and Parson Clarke discussed the lawsuit in general terms.

Schneider, a 1979 graduate of the University of Chicago Law School with a round, pleasant face and an easygoing manner, was intrigued. He had handled some of Perkins Coie's biggest cases, including the divorce of the cellular phone pioneer Craig McCaw, but during his twenty-five years as a lawyer he had never filed a habeas corpus petition. On its face, Hamdan's situation certainly looked tailor-made for one; here was an individual being held by the president in solitary confinement without charges.

But Schneider had a lot of questions. Even if they were lucky enough to draw a judge who agreed with Judge Reinhardt's conclusion that Guantánamo was within the reach of the federal courts, could they really make a credible argument that the Ninth Circuit was an appropriate venue for Hamdan's lawsuit, given that it was thousands of miles away from Camp Echo and that Swift hadn't lived in Washington State in years? This sounded a lot like forum shopping, or trying to pick a court that would be sympathetic to your case, something judges invariably frowned upon. And what, exactly, were they asking the court to do? Lawsuits are more than just complaints. Litigants must urge the court to grant a particular remedy, and when it comes to habeas suits, the remedy is usually freedom. Were they really going to walk into a federal courtroom in Seattle and ask the judge to release a prisoner on Guantánamo Bay whom the president had deemed to be a terrorist?

Schneider arranged a conference call with Swift and Katyal to learn a bit more about the case. Their conversation further piqued his interest, but he was still a little wary. "Their attitude was: 'Nice to meet you. Let's file this thing tomorrow morning,'" Schneider later recalled. "I had never heard of this guy Commander Swift, and while I was sure David's old professor was a perfectly good guy, they were asking us to sue the president of the United States and his secretary of defense on behalf of Osama bin Laden's driver. I felt like we needed to do some due diligence."

Schneider enlisted the help of two of the firm's lawyers, Joseph McMillan and Charles Sipos. Neither of them had ever heard of military commissions, but together they retraced Katyal's steps, scrutinizing his legal analysis from every possible angle until they were comfortable it was sound. At the next weekly meeting of Perkins Coie's five-person senior management committee, Schneider said he wanted to take on the case. Large law firms are inherently risk-averse, and Schneider acknowledged that the suit could draw a lot of attention to the firm, some of it no doubt negative. No one objected.

After the meeting, Schneider told Katyal that his team wanted to rework the petition before filing it. Katyal said fine but urged him to move quickly: it was already March, and the *Rasul* case, which would determine whether or not the Guantánamo detainees even had habeas rights, was going to be argued before the Supreme Court in late April, with a ruling to follow before the summer that could very well overturn Judge Reinhardt's Guantánamo opinion and seal off the federal courts to Hamdan.

The Perkins lawyers were on unfamiliar terrain. McMillan, a forty-four-year-old former U.S. history professor at a community college in the Midwest, specialized in commercial litigation and intellectual property. He was used to conducting research by typing keywords into Westlaw, a legal database, and finding cases that supported his claims. But the courts had not been asked to grapple with the lawfulness of military commissions in more than fifty years; their sources of legal authority were necessarily going to be obscure. Sure enough, McMillan soon found himself poring over dusty tomes like Col. William Winthrop's 1886 book *Military Law and Precedents*.

Days passed, then weeks. Katyal and Swift grew impatient. In early April, Swift got on a plane to Seattle and took a taxi to the Washington

Mutual Tower. He rode the elevator to the forty-first floor and presented himself in Schneider's office. It did not take Schneider long to realize that Swift had no intention of leaving town until the petition had been filed. He gave Swift a passkey to the building and set him up in an empty office, making sure it was on a separate floor.

The Perkins lawyers thought Katyal's draft of the petition was too free-flowing and digressive, that it read more like a law review article than a legal action. (Katyal and his student team had, in fact, used his *Yale Law Journal* article as a guide.) McMillan wanted to impose some structure on the petition and dramatically cut back the number of arguments, theories, and historical references. "We felt things needed to be pared down, prioritized, and organized in ways that would be recognizable to a federal judge," McMillan remembered. "It all needed to be made much, much clearer and more straightforward."

Drafts started flying back and forth between the Perkins team and Katyal. Swift turned up in Schneider's or McMillan's office after each one, having extensively marked up his copy with suggestions. After a few days of this, McMillan told Schneider that if he could get Swift out of the building, they might be able to finish the petition. Schneider brought Swift home, unannounced and in uniform, for dinner. They grilled steaks on the back deck as Swift held forth to Schneider's children on Yemeni tribal culture and the abuse of presidential power.

The next morning, the documents were finally ready. The Perkins team had divided Katyal's initial draft into two separate documents, the petition and a memorandum of law. The petition contained just the facts of the case, the allegations, and the conclusions. The memorandum included all of the finer legal points, including a lengthy discussion of the relevant laws and Supreme Court precedents. This was an unusual move. Ordinarily, a litigant wouldn't provide so much detailed analysis until directed by the judge to "brief" the case, and whatever analysis was provided would be part of the petition itself. But this case raised a great many complicated legal issues, from the always esoteric question of the jurisdiction of the courts to the extent of the government's obligations to honor international treaties like the Geneva Conventions. Schneider and McMillan didn't want to bog down the petition. At the same time, they recognized the complexity of the issues and agreed that a judge would benefit from a road map of Katyal's thinking.

In addition to the petition and the memorandum of law, they were filing several exhibits under seal, in accordance with the Classified Information Procedures Act, which permits litigants in criminal cases to share with judges information that they think might be classified. These exhibits included Hamdan's affidavit and a statement from an expert witness, a professor of psychiatry at the University of Hawaii, testifying to the grave risk of mental impairment faced by Hamdan were he to remain in solitary confinement much longer. Swift argued against filing them under seal. He didn't think the affidavit and the psychiatrist's statement contained any classified information and wanted them to be available to the media as soon as the lawsuit was filed. But Katyal insisted that it was important to signal to the court that they intended to treat issues of national security with an abundance of caution.

The petition* was a relatively straightforward document, virtually free of footnotes and case law and accessible even to nonlawyers. Unlike most habeas petitions, which challenge the legality of an individual's detention, theirs was challenging Hamdan's pending military commision and the pretrial isolation that went with it. After a brief overview of the case, the petition went on to establish why the U.S. District Court for the Western District of Washington was the appropriate place for the suit and then to explain why the court possessed the necessary jurisdiction to hear a case from Guantánamo. A somewhat more detailed statement of the facts of the case came next, followed by a concise enumeration of Swift's accusations against the administration, the eight different ways in which the government's treatment of Hamdan violated the Geneva Conventions, the Constitu-

---

*The petition was actually two petitions, a request for a writ of habeas corpus and a request for a writ of mandamus. The right of mandamus—meaning "we command"—enables petitioners to ask a court to compel a government official to do something. It's an arcane judicial remedy that has fallen almost completely out of use since the nineteenth century, but Katyal thought it was perfectly suited to Hamdan's predicament. He was asking the court to compel the secretary of defense to give him something he was due, a fair trial. But Katyal's real motive was strategic: by fashioning Hamdan's lawsuit as a mandamus petition as well as a petition for habeas corpus, they could perhaps keep their case alive even if the Supreme Court ruled in *Rasul* that the Guantánamo detainees had no habeas rights.

tion, and the Uniform Code of Military Justice. It concluded with a prayer for relief, a list of actions that Swift was asking the court to take on Hamdan's behalf. These included declaring the military commissions unconstitutional and ordering the government to move Hamdan out of solitary confinement.

The accompanying seventy-four-page memorandum of law was a much different animal. A clear product of Katyal's omnivorous yet exacting legal mind, it marshaled no fewer than 113 precedents and 22 U.S. statutes, as well as numerous acts and treaties to buttress the argument that the administration's treatment of Hamdan was illegal and that the court possessed the power, and the responsibility, to honor Swift's petition and stop it: "This petition asks the federal court to do what the federal courts have done time and time again throughout our history—to stand as a bulwark against excessive unilateral overreaching by the Executive Branch . . . When the Constitution, laws, and treaties of the United States have been violated, it is up to the courts to restore the equilibrium that our Founders envisioned."

Two copies of the lawsuit left the Washington Mutual Tower via courier on the afternoon of April 6, 2004. One was headed for the office of John McKay, the U.S. Attorney for the Western District of Washington, the other for the clerk's office in the federal courthouse. Schneider told the messenger headed for the courthouse to call the instant they had a judge. When the messenger arrived with the suit, the court clerk spun a large lottery wheel used to ensure that judges are randomly assigned. The arrow landed on the name of Robert S. Lasnik.

Schneider phoned Katyal with the good news. Judge Lasnik was a Clinton appointee, the son of a New York City schoolteacher and a social worker. Schneider told Katyal that he and McMillan had both argued before him many times and found him to be unfailingly thoughtful and engaged. Now all they could do was await the government's response.

EIGHT

Tugging the Lion's Tail

ON APRIL 23, two and a half weeks after Hamdan's petition was filed, the government responded. An assistant U.S. Attorney for the Western District of Washington filed papers signed by the office of the solicitor general—which represents the United States before the Supreme Court and almost never appears in a lower court—asking Judge Lasnik to hold off on hearing *Swift v. Rumsfeld* until the justices had issued their ruling in *Rasul*.

The government's strategy was obvious: if the justices found that the federal courts had no jurisdiction over Guantánamo Bay, then Lasnik would likely have no choice but to dismiss the case before the proceedings had even gotten under way. Hamdan's lawsuit would be dead on arrival.

Having attended the oral argument in *Rasul* at the Supreme Court a couple of weeks earlier, Katyal was not optimistic about the detainees' chances. Speaking on their behalf had been a retired federal judge named John Gibbons. A Republican nominated to the bench by President Nixon and a Navy veteran, Gibbons certainly seemed like an unassailable choice. But he had been awful.

Arguing before the Supreme Court is like running a football downfield. It requires stiff-arming defenders—or fighting off tough questions from hostile justices—as well as reading blocks, or picking up on helpful hints from sympathetic ones. Justice Stevens opened a big seam for Gibbons, all but telling him, several times and in several different ways, that the key precedent for *Eisentrager, Ahrens v. Clark* had been overturned. But Gibbons had refused to charge through the hole, never once mentioning the Court's ruling in *Braden*, which had made it clear that a prisoner did not need to be within the territorial jurisdiction of a particular court to file a habeas petition there. Returning to his criminal law class afterward, Katyal told his students that it was the worst performance he had ever seen.

Lying awake in his hotel room in downtown Seattle the night before he was to contest the government's motion to postpone the proceedings in *Swift v. Rumsfeld*, Katyal was worried that he might not do much better. He had flown in earlier that day for a status conference with Judge Lasnik, assuming that the argument was still a couple of weeks off. But when the government's lawyer asked Lasnik to schedule it as soon as possible, the judge suggested the following morning. The government's lawyer said fine, and Katyal had gone along as well.

It would be only the fourth time Katyal had ever appeared in court: he had argued a drug case in the D.C. circuit court of appeals for the Justice Department, a speeding ticket in college, and a tenant eviction in an extracurricular legal clinic in law school. Walking into Judge Lasnik's courtroom that afternoon, he had needed to be told which side of the room the petitioner was supposed to stand on. It had not helped his nerves any to discover moments later that the government had dispatched Gregory Garre, an assistant solicitor general and a veteran Supreme Court advocate, to argue its case. Katyal had been hoping for an anonymous and inexperienced local assistant U.S. Attorney.

After a restless night, Katyal met Swift in the hotel lobby in the morning and they walked over to the U.S. courthouse for the hearing. Garre spoke first, urging Judge Lasnik to set aside the case for now: "The government's position at this point in the case is simple and straightforward. We would ask that the court simply hold this case in abeyance for the approximately sixty-day period until the Supreme Court is expected to hand down its decisions in the *Rasul* and *Al Odah* cases."

Fifteen minutes later, it was Katyal's turn. He stressed the danger of delaying Hamdan's case any further: his time in solitary was causing irreparable psychological damage, and every extra day there could undermine his ability to defend himself at trial. Katyal had written out his entire argument the night before, but tried not to read it. He spoke quickly, too quickly—the legacy of his years as a debater. Every fifteen seconds or so, he glanced down anxiously at his notes to make sure he hadn't skipped over something.

At the Perkins Coie offices the previous afternoon, Schneider had told Katyal that their one advantage over the government was that they at least had *evidence* to bolster their claim that Hamdan's confinement was eroding his mental faculties—his affidavit and the psychiatrist's statement. Katyal hammered the point: "Let's turn to what the government's evidence is, since, of course, they bear the burden of proof in moving for a stay. And you look and you look, and the evidence is missing entirely. They have offered no evidence at all to this court on the issue of irreparable harm."

The argument lasted one hour. Lasnik closed the proceedings with an encomium to America's independent judiciary—"it's what separates this country from other very powerful, very rich, and very militarily strong countries." Katyal took this as a good sign. Still, he knew they faced an uphill battle. A federal judge was not likely to tackle an issue that the Supreme Court was already in the process of deciding.

Sure enough, a few days later Lasnik granted the government its stay. "Given that the Supreme Court is certain to shed light upon, if not resolve, a fundamental jurisdictional question present here"—whether aliens detained on Guantánamo Bay as enemy combatants may seek recourse in federal court—"the Court finds that Respondents have established good cause to stay the proceedings," he wrote.

Swift and Katyal had lost their first motion, but it wasn't all bad news. Schneider sent an upbeat e-mail to the group, pointing out that Lasnik had described their case as one of "monumental significance" and acknowledged that there was "credible evidence" that the conditions of Hamdan's imprisonment were causing him harm. Best of all, Schneider wrote, was a footnote at the end of the eight-page decision. Lasnik noted that the old federal courthouse, a relic of the Depression era's Work Projects Administration, was about to be replaced and that the arguments in

Swift v. Rumsfeld in September would be among the first to be heard in the new courthouse. The old courthouse, Lasnik wrote, had been the ignominious setting for several trumped-up cases brought against Japanese-Americans in the wake of Pearl Harbor—"constant reminders of how our country and our courts must always remain true to the core principles embodied in our United States Constitution, even in the aftermath of devastating attacks on our people and even in times of war."

FOLLOWING LASNIK'S RULING, Katyal returned to his classes and family and waited impatiently for the Supreme Court to issue a decision in *Rasul*.

Swift, meanwhile, was busy preparing for Hamdan's as yet unscheduled military commission trial. He was also closing on a new house, a modest single-story home in Falls Church, Virginia. Swift had stumbled onto the "For Sale" sign one Sunday afternoon in May, after pulling his car off the road during a cell phone conversation with a producer from ABC. Debbie had just gotten a new job with Chautauqua Airlines and would be making more money, so Swift figured they would have some extra income and could use the tax break available to first-time homeowners. She was going to be based out of LaGuardia but would have nearly two weeks off each month to spend in the D.C. area. Why not buy a house? Swift met the asking price—$460,000—on the spot. The seller agreed to pay all the closing costs if he waived the inspection. Debbie was annoyed that she hadn't gotten to see the house first, but Swift insisted that it was too good a deal to pass up.

Along with the rest of the country, Swift had also become consumed with the widening scandal over Abu Ghraib. He had been in the basement of his grandmother's house in Virginia, getting organized for a trip to Guantánamo, when CBS aired the first photographs from the prison on the night of April 28, 2004. Swift wasn't exactly surprised by what he saw: the now infamous images of U.S. soldiers abusing Iraqi detainees. Almost a year earlier he'd read an interview in a newsmagazine with an unnamed senior intelligence officer in Iraq who had told the reporter that the gloves were now off, which Swift figured was another way of saying that coercive methods were being introduced into interrogations at the prison. What's more, rumors of the abuse at Abu Ghraib had been circulating inside the military for months. "It's incredibly difficult to restrain soldiers on a battlefield," Swift said at the time. "From the time of the Visigoths, villages poured boiling oil on enemy soldiers. Why is rape part of war? Because war is bestial. Think of it, you're out there on the battlefield and they are trying to kill you and they are going to try every day. You are scared out of your mind, and to kill other human beings, it is necessary to do what a psychopath does: dehumanize people. Restraining your army requires discipline, it really does. That's what the Naval Academy teaches."

Seeing the images from Abu Ghraib, Swift remembered that Maj. Gen. Geoffrey Miller, the commander of Guantánamo Bay, had been dispatched to the prison to overhaul its intelligence-gathering operations. He had learned about Miller's approach to intelligence gathering during a PowerPoint presentation on one of his first visits to Guantánamo. Miller's system—Total Force Intelligence, it was called—was built around the concept of prison guards working hand in hand with interrogators. Miller's logic was easy to follow: if everyone who came into contact with the detainees was focused foremost on intelligence gathering, it would be a lot easier to put pressure on the detainees to cooperate.

To Swift, though, prison guards and intelligence officers served very different, even contradictory, functions. The job of the guards was to provide a safe environment for the detainees; the job of the interrogators was to extract information from them. Combining the two might make sense strategically, but it was an invitation to mistreatment. Watching the PowerPoint presentation, Swift had been reminded of what his father used to say to him and his two younger brothers when they were hitting one another in the back of the car: "If you boys keep that up, somebody's going to get hurt."

The Abu Ghraib scandal stoked the media's interest in Hamdan; Swift was inundated with calls from reporters and producers inquiring about his client's treatment. He wrote up another media request to discuss the subject. It was again denied, but the *Seattle Post-Intelligencer* asked Judge Lasnik to unseal Hamdan's affidavit, and Perkins Coie was confident that it would be only a matter of time before Lasnik, a proponent of judicial transparency, granted the newspaper's request.

For weeks, Swift and his JAG colleagues talked about little other than Abu Ghraib and its potential impact on the commissions. "One thing is for sure," Gunn told his defense team. "You folks have an audience now."

IN THE MIDST of the ongoing fallout from Abu Ghraib, an extraordinary series of memos was leaked to the media suggesting that the roots of the scandal ran much deeper than a few poorly disciplined soldiers or a controversial intelligence-gathering system.

The memos, beginning in early 2002, concerned the president's recent decision to exclude detainees from rights granted in the Geneva Conventions, an international treaty ensuring humane treatment of individuals captured on the battlefield, and what that would mean as far as interrogations went.

The decision itself was anchored in a legal opinion again authored by John Yoo and one of his colleagues, Robert Delahunty. Because al Qaeda was a violent militia group rather than a nation-state, they had determined it "ineligible to be a signatory to any treaty."

The question of the Taliban was more complicated, as it had been the ruling regime in Afghanistan, which had ratified the Geneva Conventions decades ago. Still, as Yoo and Delahunty saw it, the Taliban had been more a militia or faction than a government. On the basis of their analysis, the president issued a "group status determination" covering everyone on Guantánamo Bay. They all were "unlawful enemy combatants"—as opposed to legitimate prisoners of war—and were thus not entitled to the protections of the Geneva Conventions, including, most significantly, the provision known as Common Article 3, which sets a minimum baseline for the treatment of all captured combatants, prohibiting not only cruel treatment and torture, but also trial by any court that doesn't afford the judicial rights "recognized as indispensable by all civilized peoples."

Secretary of State Powell had opposed the president's decision to suspend the Geneva Conventions in the conflict in Afghanistan, writing that declaring the conventions inapplicable "will reverse over a century of U.S. policy and practice" and "undermine public support among critical allies."

By contrast, the White House counsel, Alberto Gonzales, had advised the president to hold his ground. "As you have said, the war against terrorism is a new kind of war," he wrote in a January 25 memo to the president posted on *Newsweek*'s website on May 19, 2004. "The nature of the new war places high premium on other factors, such as the ability to quickly obtain information from captured terrorists and their sponsors in order to avoid further atrocities against American civilians, and the need to try terrorists for war crimes such as wantonly killing civilians. In my judgment, this new paradigm renders obsolete Geneva's strict limitations on questioning of enemy prisoners and renders quaint some of its provisions . . ."

In addition to preserving what Gonzales referred to as "flexibility" when it came to intelligence gathering, he pointed out in his memo that by suspending Geneva Conventions protections, the president would be protecting U.S. officials against the possibility of being charged in domestic courts with war crimes. His memo cited a 1996 U.S. statute, the War Crimes Act, which criminalized all breaches of Common Article 3. As Gonzales saw it, if the Geneva Conventions weren't applicable, then neither was the War Crimes Act.

But the most controversial memos were the ones that went on to explore exactly how much muscle intelligence officers could flex when they interrogated detainees now that the Geneva Conventions had been set aside. Assistant Attorney General Jay S. Bybee, one of John Yoo's colleagues at the Office of Legal Counsel, provided some guidelines in an August 2002 memo to Gonzales, made public by *The Washington Post* on June 8, 2004.

Bybee was asked to weigh in on a separate U.S. criminal statute governing the standards of conduct for interrogations, a law designed to implement the Convention Against Torture and Other Cruel, Inhuman or Degrading Treatment or Punishment, a UN convention that had been ratified by the United States in 1992 and subsequently enshrined into law by Congress in 1998. He concluded that the statute covered only "extreme acts." As Bybee put it, "Where the pain is physical, it must be of an intensity akin to that which accompanies serious physical injury such as death or organ failure. Severe mental pain requires suffering not just at the moment of infliction but it also requires lasting psychological harm." Having narrowly defined what constitutes torture under the statute, Bybee went on to argue that the whole issue could well be academic, as it might be considered unconstitutional to apply the anti-torture statute to interrogations authorized by the commander in chief.*

The public's response to Abu Ghraib was largely one of horror and disgust, but it was directed for the most part at individuals. The subsequent disclosure of these memos curdled those sentiments into a national sense of outrage. "U.S. soldiers violated their training because they got the wrong message, from their commanders, the Pentagon and the White House," *USA Today* editorialized on June 10. "The result is a scandal that aids the enemy, endangers U.S. soldiers and insults the nation's most basic standards of decency."

FOR HIS PART, Swift focused instinctively on what the leaked memoranda and the torture they sanctioned revealed about the military commissions.

In civilian trials and courts-martial, prosecutors are obligated to share all of their evidence, even exculpatory evidence, with the defense. But in the military commissions designed by the White House, the prosecutor himself would be privy only to evidence provided to him by the CIA or FBI. So if the accused's statements were coerced by physical or emotional torture, neither the prosecution nor the defense would necessarily know anything about it. What's more, in civil trials and courts-martial a defense lawyer can subpoena an interrogator to find out how a statement or confession was obtained. But because the military commissions were going to allow hearsay evidence

---

*It was later revealed that Yoo had written the memo for Bybee.

in lieu of testimony, an edited summary of the interrogation could serve as evidence and the interrogator himself was not obligated to appear in court.

Finally, federal and military trials precluded the use of evidence obtained through unconstitutional means. Both the Fifth Amendment's protection against forced self-incrimination and its guarantee of due process make it illegal for the federal government to use coerced testimony in a criminal trial. The rules for the military commissions contained no such provisions.

All along, the government claimed that the commissions had been designed to suit the exigencies of war, but in the wake of the leaked memos, it occurred to Swift that they may very well have been designed to permit the use of statements obtained through torture.

Katyal didn't necessarily agree. As he saw it, the commissions were first and foremost about consolidating presidential power. Nevertheless, he volunteered to draft a letter for the JAGs to the Senate Armed Services Committee urging it to take a fresh look at the planned military commissions in light of the recently revealed memos. In it, he pointed out the very real possibility that statements obtained under torture would be introduced as evidence in the trials: "On behalf of our clients," the JAGs' letter read, "we implore your committee to consider not only the abuses connected to the detainees in Iraq, Afghanistan and Guantánamo, but to consider the military commission system created for the express purpose of insulating military and civilian interrogators from criminal sanction and utilizing evidence obtained through unlawful methods for trial."

Katyal didn't think there was much chance the Republican Congress would ever take on the president over the commissions, but he was hopeful that the leaked memos might give the Supreme Court pause as it weighed whether to grant the Guantánamo detainees access to the U.S. courts. The very day CBS aired the first images of torture at Abu Ghraib, the deputy solicitor general in the Bush administration had argued a case before the Supreme Court concerning the indefinite detention of an American citizen in the war on terror. He had urged the justices to "trust the executive" on matters of military judgment and noted that the government was well aware that coerced confessions were often unreliable. When Justice Ruth Bader Ginsburg pointed out to him that the presidents of some countries do engage in "mild torture" for the purposes of extracting information from prisoners, the government's lawyer had answered quickly and definitively: "Well, our executive doesn't."

The leaked torture memos had revealed otherwise. To Katyal's mind, it was one thing for the administration to stake out aggressive legal positions concerning the president's wartime powers; it was quite another for it to do so without any public debate in a series of memos that had never been intended to see the light of day. The Supreme Court's tendency to defer to the wartime president notwithstanding, there had to be *some* public accountability.

IN THE 1950s two American psychiatrists, Lawrence Hinkle and Harold Wolff, undertook a study of the psychological effects of isolation for the Department of Defense, which was concerned at the time about how American POWs were being treated in Korea. "The prisoner becomes increasingly dejected and dependent," the psychiatrists wrote. "He gradually gives up all spontaneous activity within his cell and ceases to care about personal appearance and actions. Finally, he sits and stares with a vacant expression, perhaps endlessly twisting a button on his coat. He allows himself to become dirty and disheveled . . . Ultimately, he seems to lose many of the restraints of ordinary behavior. He may soil himself; he weeps; he mutters."

Swift and Schmitz witnessed this firsthand with Hamdan. Since their first trip to Guantánamo four months earlier, in January 2004, they had been coming every few weeks, spending a few long days with Hamdan each time. In the beginning he had been surly, yet alert and engaged, but the intervening period had taken its toll. By the end of February his gaze had become detached, and he was alternately angry, sullen, and weepy. The act of speaking became increasingly foreign; with each visit, it took him longer to start talking.

In March, Hamdan went on a weeklong hunger strike to protest the conditions of his imprisonment. He didn't get along with the guards but was even more distressed to learn in April that they were going to be replaced by a twenty-four-hour video surveillance camera, which would reduce his human contact even further. Swift tried unsuccessfully to prevent the installation of the camera. "Mr. Hamdan reports that during short periods of time when guards have been absent from his cell he has experienced bouts of acute anxiety and is extremely fearful of complete isolation from any human contact for extended periods of time," he wrote in a memo to the base commander.

After more than four months in solitary, Hamdan's precarious emotional state caused enough concern inside the camp to warrant a visit from a psychiatric team of Navy officers. (Hamdan told Swift the visit was prompted by a remark he had made to a guard to the effect of "Don't be surprised if you find me dead in my cell.") Among the questions that the team asked Hamdan, presumably to help it assess the risk of his killing himself, was whether he'd been beaten as a child. Hamdan said yes, as a young teenager in Mukalla, when he was working at a grocery store and got an order wrong. When asked directly by the psychiatric team if he had contemplated suicide, Hamdan answered: "Look at the conditions I live in. Of course I've thought of suicide."

Swift wasn't sure whether to protest additional psychiatric visits from the military. Hamdan clearly needed the therapy—and the human contact that came with it—but Swift was concerned about the lack of doctor-patient confidentiality. What was to prevent Hamdan's statements to the psychiatrists from being used against him in his military commission? Swift asked that two independent therapists be able to see Hamdan instead. When his request was denied, he fired off an angry memo forbidding future psychiatric visits with his client if he wasn't present.

Not that his client necessarily wanted Swift there. Their relationship had deteriorated dramatically after the first few meetings. Hamdan had initially been caught up in the flurry of activity surrounding the preparations for the lawsuit. He had his doubts about Swift and understood almost nothing about the legal issues underpinning his case, but he seemed to feel that at least *something* was happening that might potentially change his situation. Hamdan had been impatient for the suit to be filed, and when it finally was, Swift brought a copy down to Guantánamo to show him.

"I win this and I get out?" Hamdan asked.

"Well, not exactly," Swift answered.

It hadn't helped matters that Swift had failed to deliver on most of Hamdan's requests. With the exception of the Bible, some children's stories, and a handful of car and truck magazines, almost everything Swift had brought down for him—Islamic holy texts, Yemeni history books, an Arab-language survey of the American political system— was stamped REFUSED BY JTF–GUANTÁNAMO BAY by the military censors. Newspapers were out too, as were any discussions of events taking place in the outside world.

Swift managed to win a few small victories for his client, including permission to exercise outside forty-five minutes every day rather than forty-five minutes every other night. But such victories only produced more demands. Hamdan had repeatedly told Swift that he was useless, a waste of his time, that he would never be able to understand him because he wasn't a Muslim. He also refused to answer many of Swift's questions. "That's not important," he snapped when Swift asked about his relationship with bin Laden. At the same time, Hamdan knew that Swift and Schmitz were all that he had. He would invariably brighten at least a little bit over the course of each of their visits and then become angry and despairing as their departure approached.

The unambiguous relationships that Swift typically had with his clients had always been a haven for him. Their roles were clear, and the ends noble. Swift worked zealously for them, and they in return believed in and depended on him. But he was no hero to Hamdan, and his client's distrust and truculence sapped his usually clear sense of pride and purpose.

Nothing about Guantánamo was easy for Swift, beginning with the administrative hassles of just getting down there and back. He and Schmitz inevitably turned up at Norfolk Naval Station before dawn to catch the weekly military charter to the base, only to be told that there was a problem with their travel orders. On the way back, the charter left Guantánamo in the late afternoon and went only as far as Jacksonville, so they had to spend the night at a hotel before flying on to Virginia.

On the base itself, Swift had to deal with a culture that viewed the presence of lawyers as a necessary evil at best. The priority of the joint military task force that ran Guantánamo was to maintain a secure environment in which to hold and interrogate prisoners, not to provide them with due process. As a result, there were very few formal procedures concerning attorney-client visits. This had its advantages. Swift and Schmitz could stay with Hamdan until midnight and were able to bring him snacks—nuts, chocolate, coffee—that he was allowed to keep in his cell. But it also had its disadvantages. The ad hoc rules that governed Swift's visits with his client were constantly under revision by Guantánamo's authorities. There were two ways to deal with this: try to make allies on the base and engage in the subtle art of gentle persuasion, or turn everything into a showdown. Swift opted for the latter.

When on Guantánamo, Swift fought tirelessly to defend his client's rights and to protect the sanctity of their attorney-client relationship. But he was also looking for opportunities to goad the administration into doing something he could use against them—to tug at the lion's tail, as Sundel liked to say. "Let's see what we can fuck with next"—a line borrowed from Eddie Murphy in the film *48 Hours*—was Swift's credo. "Charlie was always setting traps for the government," Schmitz later recalled, "and the government would almost always duly fall into them."

On one early trip to Guantánamo, Swift was informed that there was a new policy on the base: all of his bags, even those containing the notes from his conversations with his client, would now be subject to search. This was a meaningless edict, and Swift could have easily ignored it. Luggage was searched not at the airport but at a separate hangar on the other side of the island. No tags were placed on the bags after they were searched, so it was essentially a voluntary system. Swift had never before bothered to stop by the security hangar before leaving the island, but once the new policy went into effect, he told Schmitz that he wanted to.

Sure enough, a team of Marines tried to search Swift's bags, including the one containing his laptop and case files. Swift refused to give up the bag, explaining that the contents were protected by attorney-client privilege. The Marines insisted, and Swift quickly escalated the dispute. "Let's be clear about this, Captain, just so that there's no misunderstanding," Swift said, his voice rising. "This is an unlawful search, and I am not voluntarily submitting to it. You have a gun; you are putting a gun on me and seizing my bag. When I talk to CNN in Florida tonight, that's exactly what I'm going to tell them."

A Marine colonel came over to intervene, and Swift repeated his claim. The colonel started shouting at him. "You can yell at me all you want, sir," Swift said. "It doesn't change the reality. I'm just telling you what the situation is, sir. Your men are putting a gun on me and unlawfully seizing my bag, sir." In the end, the Marine colonel backed down and let Swift go.

Swift got a rush from these kinds of confrontations. For Schmitz, who had a firsthand view of all of Swift's disputes on Guantánamo, "they were a little scary," he remembered. "I was always standing behind Charlie, and he was always going on the attack, making as much trouble as possible."

Despite his initial apprehension, Schmitz had quickly warmed to Swift. He was impressed by his tenaciousness, and like everyone who got close to Swift, Schmitz had learned that there were ways to tune him out when necessary. From time to time, he would protect Swift from himself during their visits with Hamdan by liberally translating a self-aggrandizing comment that he suspected would not go over well with an Arab man.

As for his feelings about Hamdan, Schmitz had fought back tears after their first meeting and had only come to feel more sympathetic toward him since then. Schmitz had lived in Sana for a year on a Fulbright scholarship and had a sense of the society and culture Hamdan came from—both the kind of poverty and limitations that he had tried to escape and the insular nature of life in Yemen.

If Schmitz wanted the best outcome for Hamdan, though, he didn't feel personally responsible for ensuring it. So while Swift often felt thwarted by his client, Schmitz, who wasn't pushing for tangible progress, felt mostly compassion for him. It also didn't hurt that Hamdan targeted his anger and resentment at his lawyer, not his translator.

The work was nevertheless both exhausting and stressful for Schmitz. He had never translated before, and there weren't Arabic words for many of the legal terms that Swift used. To help him unwind after their grueling days at Camp Echo, he carted bottles of gin and vermouth back and forth with him to Guantánamo.

In the late spring, Swift finally managed to break through to his client. For months Hamdan had been pressing him to get in touch with his wife and in-laws in Sana, but there were no street addresses in Yemen, and the phone number Hamdan had given him didn't work. The Yemeni government was no help, and while the International Committee of the Red Cross knew the family's whereabouts, it was unwilling to disclose them; the organization was wary of running afoul of the administration and further restricting its already limited access to Guantánamo Bay.

In May, Amnesty International hosted a human rights conference in Yemen. Swift persuaded the Red Cross to invite Hamdan's family and asked Clive Stafford Smith, a civil liberties lawyer who was going to be in attendance, to be on the lookout for them. Hamdan's brother-in-law Muhammad al-Qala turned up on the last day of the conference and gave Stafford Smith his cell phone number and several photographs, including one of Hamdan's two-year-old daughter, whom Hamdan had never met.

On Swift's next trip to Guantánamo, Hamdan was characteristically morose when he and Schmitz first entered his cell. Swift put the photos of his family on the table between them, and Hamdan began to weep.

ON JUNE 28, 2004, exactly two months after the first photos from Abu Ghraib had been made public, the Supreme Court finally handed down its decision in *Rasul*. Katyal was in his office when snippets of the Court's ruling first started appearing on the Supreme Court blog, SCOTUSblog. The early reports were sketchy—SCOTUSblog's reporter was racing in and out of the courthouse to file updates via BlackBerry—but it looked as if the detainees had won, six to three.

The first complete opinion Katyal managed to get his hands on was the dissent. It was written by Justice Scalia, and it was scathing. "The Commander in Chief and his subordinates had every reason to expect that the internment of combatants at Guantánamo Bay would not have the consequence of bringing the cumbersome machinery of our domestic courts into military affairs," Scalia said. The consequences of the Court's decision would be "breathtaking," he wrote, conjuring images of military officers being pulled off the battlefield during wartime to testify in federal court against enemy aliens. "This is an irresponsible overturning of settled law in a matter of extreme importance to our forces currently in the field," he concluded.

Katyal took Scalia's outrage as a positive sign. It almost certainly meant that the majority opinion, written by Justice Stevens, was unambiguous.

It was. The Court had rejected the government's contention that Guantánamo Bay Naval Base was part of Cuba, concluding instead that because the American government exercised "exclusive jurisdiction and control" over Guantánamo, it was for all intents and purposes part of the sovereign United States. What's more, the justices ruled that the government's favorite precedent, *Eisentrager*, had already been overturned by *Braden*: a prisoner did not necessarily need to be present in a court's jurisdiction to claim habeas corpus rights.

The decision came as a huge blow to the administration. The government's entire detention operation on Guantánamo Bay had been built on the premise that enemy aliens being held there would not be able to contest their imprisonment in U.S. courts. The justices had decisively rejected this assumption. The doors to the federal courthouse were now open to the prisoners on Guantánamo Bay, Hamdan included.

Katyal and Swift were thrilled; their challenge to the military commissions could go forward. But the elation faded quickly. *Rasul* was immediately followed by another, more worrisome decision from the justices. The case concerned Jose Padilla, a former gang member and convert to Islam who had been arrested for allegedly conspiring with al Qaeda to detonate a dirty bomb in the United States. Katyal had been following the case closely but didn't expect it to have much of a bearing on Hamdan's fate. Not only was Padilla an American citizen, but he had been picked up in May 2002 in the United States, at Chicago's O'Hare International Airport, and had since been held exclusively on U.S. soil, first in New York, then in a Navy brig in Charleston, South Carolina.

The problem for Katyal and Swift wasn't that the justices had ruled unfavorably in the Padilla case. It was that they had decided not to rule on it at all, instead kicking the case back to the lower courts on a technicality. Their stated reason: Padilla had brought his complaint in the wrong place; he needed to sue in South Carolina, where he was currently being held, not in New York, the place of residence of his "next friend" and lawyer.

It was terrible news. Following the Court's line of reasoning, Hamdan's habeas corpus petition belonged in Washington, D.C., where lawsuits originating from outside the United States were supposed to be filed. *Swift v. Rumsfeld* was almost certainly going to be taken out of Judge Lasnik's sympathetic hands.

NINE

"Oh, I Doubt That Seriously, Sir"

THE IMPACT of *Rasul* was immediate and dramatic. Before the Supreme Court's decision, the president had been in no real hurry to begin the military commissions. The administration had assumed that it could hold all of the detainees indefinitely and without charges, so what was the rush? But *Rasul* had radically shifted the landscape. Now that the U.S. courts were open to the detainees, the government was suddenly eager to get the commissions going so that the system would be up and running by the time a federal judge considered Swift and Katyal's challenge to it.

The day after the ruling—and more than two and a half years after the president's November 13, 2001, military order authorizing the commissions—the Pentagon named a presiding officer for the trials, Army colonel Peter Brownback, a decorated combat soldier in Vietnam and retired military judge. Days later, the Pentagon charged the first defendant, the Australian David Hicks, with conspiracy to commit war crimes, attempted murder, and aiding the enemy.

Hamdan couldn't be far behind. Swift could be going to trial in a matter of weeks. He needed to start getting ready; that meant going to Yemen.

Swift had been looking forward to making an evidence-gathering trip to Hamdan's homeland ever since being assigned to represent him. He had been boning up on the country's history and culture for months and was anticipating some good war stories. "With twenty million people and sixty million firearms, basically in the form of AK-47s,

Yemen really is the Wild, Wild West," Swift said shortly before he left, "and I have the challenge of going and investigating a guy who's supposed to be in al Qaeda and not getting killed."

In July 2004, Swift packed a suitcase with a couple of new blazers, some pants, and a pair of leather shoes from Men's Wearhouse, and he and Schmitz set out for Sana, a sixteen-hour trip with layovers in Frankfurt and Cairo.

By now Swift had a general sense of the government's evidence against his client—and of how he was going to rebut it. The government would surely be relying heavily on Soufan's interrogation report, which included all of Hamdan's most incriminating statements. Swift planned to argue that everything his client had told the FBI agent was unreliable, that by this point in his incarceration, Hamdan would have said anything if he thought it might help get him off Guantánamo sooner. Swift intended to dismiss the videotape of Hamdan in fatigues at the Pakistani news conference as a bin Laden publicity stunt, proving nothing more than the fact that his client had been around and willing to pose for the cameras. As for the two missiles that had allegedly been found in the trunk of the car Hamdan was driving when he was captured, Swift was going to underscore that it was a borrowed vehicle. His client had never intended to return to the battlefield in Afghanistan; rather, he was planning to meet up with his wife and daughter in Pakistan after returning the car.

Yet even if Swift managed to cast doubt on the veracity of the evidence against Hamdan, he still had to deal with his client's prolonged intimacy with bin Laden. Swift himself had publicly acknowledged that Hamdan had been a driver for the most wanted terrorist in the world for the better part of five years. How was he going to persuade a jury of military officers that the same man was nevertheless innocent?

This was partly a legal question: Where does criminal liability end? Swift and his JAG colleagues had debated the issue ad nauseam, often using Al Capone's driver as their hypothetical. "He knows from reading the *Chicago Tribune* that Al's a big-time criminal, a hoodlum, and a murderer," as Swift put it. "He drops Al off at warehouses and drives around with a pistol for his own protection, but does that make him a criminal?"

But Swift knew he had to move beyond this legal question and build a plausible counternarrative of Hamdan's life, one that made him out to be, at worst, a marginal figure in al Qaeda. Swift hoped that meeting Hamdan's family and seeing their home in Yemen would help him paint a picture of him that would contradict the government's.

The trip got off to an inauspicious start. Schmitz, who had last been to Yemen in the mid-1990s, was disappointed to find that the American Embassy had booked them at the Sheraton, a well-guarded Western hotel conspicuously devoid of local character. Diluting the experience even further was the fact that the hotel was filled with FBI agents who had come to observe the trial of several of the terrorists who had been involved in the *Cole* bombing.

Swift spent their first night in Yemen bent over the toilet in his hotel room after eating something that didn't agree with him at a local fish restaurant. The following day, still feeling weak and queasy, he and Schmitz checked in at the embassy and received a lecture on how to stay safe in Yemen before setting off to track down Hamdan's family.

Hamdan's wife and their two daughters, then five and three, lived in a cramped two-story stone house down a narrow alley in central Sana that they shared with Um Fatima's mother and brother, Muhammad al-Qala, as well as his wife and children. Since Um Fatima's father's death—he had died the same day Um Fatima received her first letter from Hamdan in U.S. custody in Afghanistan—al-Qala, a sergeant in the Yemeni Army, had assumed the role of family patriarch. He invited Swift and Schmitz over for lunch.

The men ate seated on the floor downstairs, picking up pieces of roast lamb with their fingers and dipping flatbread in a meat stew spiced with fenugreek, a Yemeni specialty known as salta. When they finished, they repaired to a second-story sitting room lined with shiny, floral-patterned blue floor cushions. Al-Qala, a stocky man with a dark mustache, full lips, and glassy, expressionless eyes, pruned large stalks of khat as they spoke, the bulge in his cheek swelling as the afternoon wore on. Schmitz, who had brought his own bag of khat to the house, chewed too; Swift abstained.

After a little while Hamdan's wife, Um Fatima, joined them in a full-length black covering that revealed only her eyes. Swift gave her a set of Guantánamo Bay–issue prayer beads from her husband, and she became so overcome with emotion that she had to leave the room. When she returned, they talked about Hamdan. Um Fatima seemed to understand very little about why he was being held. What could a superpower like the United States possibly want with Salim?

Despite the fact that Hamdan was one of more than one hundred Yemeni prisoners who had been held on Guantánamo for more than two years, there was surprisingly little public outcry over the detentions in Yemen. (Imagine if this many Americans had been imprisoned without charges in a foreign country for that long.) This was by design. Most of the Yemeni newspapers are state-run, and the rest are under intense pressure to toe the government line; the last thing Yemen's president, Ali Abdullah Saleh, wanted to do was call attention to the plight of the detainees and, in so doing, further inflame anti-American sentiments in his country. He was already having a hard enough time convincing the United States that Yemen wasn't a haven for al Qaeda without thousands of protesters taking to the streets to denounce America. As a result, families like Hamdan's were left largely in the dark.

Swift and Schmitz followed more or less the same ritual for most of their stay. They would arrive at al-Qala's home for lunch and, after eating, move upstairs with al-Qala to chew khat and talk. Um Fatima and the children would drift in and out throughout the day. Schmitz told Swift that they were going to break the family financially—Arab hospitality would compel al-Qala to feed them as long as they were in Yemen—so they gave him six hundred dollars from their per diem expenses and said it was a donation from a humanitarian organization. Al-Qala also insisted on showing them around Sana. One afternoon he took them on a tour of the Old City. Another day they brought a picnic to an ancient village in the mountains outside the city. After lunch, al-Qala pulled a couple of AK-47s out of his trunk and gave them to Swift and Schmitz to fire. Swift checked in at the embassy every day, but said little about what he was up to.

About ten days into their two-week trip, al-Qala told Swift and Schmitz to come to the house the following day in the late afternoon rather than at their usual time. A couple of hours after they arrived, just as the sun was setting, a tall, rangy man with a receding hairline and neatly trimmed beard appeared in the living room. He looked different from the smattering of men who had passed through al-Qala's home over the course of their visit. His white robe was crisper and cleaner, with no blazer over it, and he wore a red-checked head scarf in the Saudi style. Al-Qala introduced him as Nasser al-Bahri.

Swift could hardly contain himself. After months of questioning, Hamdan had only recently told Swift that al-Bahri, his brother-in-law, was the man who had recruited him for jihad. Hamdan assumed he was still in prison in Yemen. Shortly before Swift and Schmitz left for Sana, though, Schmitz had read in an Arabic newspaper that al-Bahri had just been released. Swift was eager to meet him and had been pestering al-Qala to arrange an introduction for days but had all but given up hope by this point.

Al-Bahri owed his freedom to a government-sponsored program called the Committee on Thoughtful Dialogue, Yemen's creative solution to the sticky situation in which it found itself following 9/11. At the time, the United States was pressing Yemen's president to purge his country of extremists or else face a military strike. Saleh knew this would be impossible; his own *government* was rife with Islamic extremists, and he had spent decades nurturing and exploiting his country's culture of jihad. Extraditing Islamic radicals, or even putting them in jail for more than a couple of years, would provoke a national outcry. So Saleh created the dialogue program. It's a simple process: A respected jurist and cleric leads imprisoned extremists through a series of questions about their beliefs, using the Koran or the hadith, a collection of the Prophet Muhammad's teachings, to persuade them that they have been misled and that Islam does not in fact condone acts of terrorism. Those participants who vow not to take part in future acts of terrorism on Yemeni soil are granted presidential pardons and liberated. Al-Bahri graduated from the program, signed the pledge, and became a free man. Though he was not permitted to leave Yemen, the Yemeni government set him up with a taxicab to drive and helped pay his way through graduate school in business to discourage him from returning to jihad.

Swift took to al-Bahri right away. He had a pious air about him—he didn't chew khat or smoke, and because of diabetes, he didn't eat sweets—but his presence was not forbidding. On the contrary, he was courteous and relaxed. Like Swift, he was endlessly discursive, the sort of person who answered every question with a story. Swift felt a peculiar sense of kinship with al-Bahri, who also viewed himself as an outsider in his military—al Qaeda.

Al-Bahri told Swift about his path to jihad. It had started when he was a teenager in Jidda in the early 1990s, a time of great unrest in Saudi Arabia. Saddam Hussein's troops had just invaded Kuwait, and the United States had sent half a million soldiers into Saudi Arabia to protect it. A number of Saudi clerics were railing against the presence of American GIs on Muslim holy land. Many of these clerics were imprisoned for their rabble-rousing, which to their followers only confirmed their warnings of America's corrosive influence in the Muslim world. A new generation of jihadis was born, and al-Bahri was among them.

After several years as an itinerant holy warrior, al-Bahri had found a powerful new sense of purpose in bin Laden and al Qaeda. And yet despite his exalted status in the organization—as one of bin Laden's most trusted bodyguards, he carried two special bullets in his gun to kill the sheikh if they were ever facing capture—al-Bahri told Swift that he quickly became disillusioned with it. He didn't doubt al Qaeda's mission, but he did disapprove of its indiscriminate recruiting tactics. Most of the young men flooding into Afghanistan at the turn of the twenty-first century were only superficially committed to the cause. To al-Bahri, it seemed as though al Qaeda's rise to prominence had transformed jihad from a genuine religious mission to a cattle call for any and all Muslims.

According to al-Bahri, Hamdan was one of these enthusiastic but ineffectual jihadis. He said that by the time they found their way to bin Laden, it was clear that Hamdan lacked both the zeal of a holy warrior and the religious grounding or inclination to grasp the ideology undergirding the movement. Having grown up in Saudi Arabia, Islam's holiest land, al-Bahri had responded personally when he heard bin Laden's pledge to drive the Americans from the Arabian Peninsula.

But he told Swift that Hamdan wasn't interested in the sheikh's preachings. Nevertheless, al-Bahri said, he had come to like Hamdan—he characterized him as cheerful and naive, almost childlike—and wanted him to stay. So he suggested to bin Laden that he keep him on as a driver and mechanic.

Swift was thrilled. He had found the perfect foil, the hardened jihadi and senior al Qaeda operative who explained his client's proximity to bin Laden. Hamdan had been entrusted with driving for bin Laden because al-Bahri had vouched for him.

The theatrics of a trial never far from his mind, Swift had visions of summoning al-Bahri to Guantánamo Bay (on the government's dime) to testify at Hamdan's military commission. Swift needed a backup plan, though. It took them a couple of days, but he and Schmitz eventually managed to find a video camera at the embassy. On their last day in Yemen they taped a ninety-minute interview with al-Bahri. Swift couldn't wait to spring it on Lang.

Back home in Virginia in early August, Swift was exhilarated. His counternarrative was coming into focus: Hamdan was an uneducated, orphaned Muslim who had stumbled into jihad, found a proxy father figure in al-Bahri, and then took a job working for bin Laden because it paid a lot better than driving a *dabab* in Yemen.

The goal had always been to prevent Hamdan's military commission from taking place, but there was now a part of Swift, a large part even, that wanted a shot at getting him acquitted. "Salim is not a warrior, never was," he said at the time. "He's not a martyr, he's not political. He has been about self-preservation since day one." Swift's mind was already racing ahead to the two of them stepping off the airplane together in Sana. "I get him home and I'll never be able to buy anything in Yemen again."

ON JULY 13, 2004, two and a half years after his capture, Hamdan was formally charged with conspiracy. The charge sheet read:

Salem Ahmed Hamdan, in Afghanistan, Pakistan, Yemen and other countries, from on or about February 1996 to on or about November 24, 2001, willfully and knowingly joined an

131

enterprise of persons who shared a common criminal purpose and conspired and agreed with Usama bin Laden, Saif al Adel, Dr. Ayman al Zawahiri (a/k/a "the Doctor"), Muhammad Atef (a/k/a Abu Hafs al Masri), and other members and associates of the al Qaida organization, known and unknown, to commit the following offenses triable by military commission: attacking civilians; attacking civilian objects; murder by an unprivileged belligerent; destruction of property by an unprivileged belligerent; and terrorism.

The charge sheet went on to enumerate some more specific allegations. While Hamdan wasn't accused of being a member of al Qaeda per se, the government claimed that he had delivered weapons and ammunition to al Qaeda members and associates, including Saif al-Adel, the head of the organization's security committee; chauffeured bin Laden around Afghanistan to keep him safe following the September 11 attacks and al Qaeda's 1998 attacks on the two U.S. embassies in East Africa; driven bin Laden to various al Qaeda training camps to rally the troops to conduct "martyr missions" against Americans; and received weapons training at an al Qaeda–sponsored camp called al-Farouq. The government, no doubt annoyed that Hamdan had refused to plead guilty, was seeking a life sentence, with no opportunity for parole.

Colonel Brownback, the judge for the commissions, was anxious to get the trials under way. In mid-July he summoned the defense team to a meeting with the prosecutors to go over the procedures. Swift was still in Yemen, but Sundel went and brought along a tape recorder. By this point he and the other JAGs had done some research into Brownback and didn't like what they saw. Not only was he close to John Altenburg, the retired Army general who was supervising the commissions for the Pentagon, but Brownback had a poor record on defendants' rights. Most infamously, he had presided over the 1996 court-martial of William Kreutzer, Jr., an Army sergeant at Fort Bragg who was sentenced to death for opening fire on his own brigade. The verdict had been overturned by an Army appeals court on the ground that Brownback had erred in denying Kreutzer's attorneys' request for a mitigation expert, a mental health expert who specializes in presenting mitigating evidence from the defendant's personal history in death penalty trials.

The JAGs' doubts about Brownback were quickly confirmed when in one of his first statements to the assembled lawyers, the judge announced that there would be no promise of speedy trials for the detainees. Because speedy trials are guaranteed by Article 10 of the Uniform Code of Military Justice, every military commission defense lawyer intended to insist on them for their clients, just as Swift and Katyal already had.

The lead prosecutor, Army colonel Robert L. Swann, instantly recognized that Brownback had just opened himself up to charges of judicial bias. "Sir," Swann said, "I wouldn't even be commenting on that in light of the fact that I think Mr. Katyal and Lieutenant Commander Swift believe Article 10 applies to these proceedings, so we ought to stay away from that issue."

About fifteen minutes later, Swann noticed Sundel's tape recorder. "Is that running?" he asked. Sundel answered that it was.

Furious, Brownback ordered him to shut it off.

"Are you telling me this session is off the record?" Sundel asked.

"Yes, it is," Brownback answered.

"Then we aren't going to participate."

Brownback ordered Sundel to turn the tape recorder back on. Once he had, Brownback announced that the meeting was over. Then he forbade Sundel from distributing the tape to anybody without his permission.

HAMDAN'S ARRAIGNMENT and first precommission hearing was scheduled for August 24, 2004. For Swift, who was still riding the high of his trip to Yemen, the moment couldn't arrive soon enough.

It was a voir dire hearing, Swift's chance to go after Brownback, who would serve as both the judge and a member of the jury, and the other five military officers who had been appointed to Hamdan's commission panel. Swift studied their juror questionnaires on his flight down to Guantánamo as he contemplated his broader strategy for the hearing.

The big question was how aggressively to go after Brownback and the prospective jurors—or, as Swift put it, whether to burn down the courtroom. There would be plenty of reporters there, and he didn't want to miss an opportunity to show the public that the deck was stacked against his client. What's more, he knew that any exchange that helped underscore the flaws with the trial system would come in handy in their federal lawsuit against the commissions. And yet this was the same judge and jury that would soon be assessing his argument for Hamdan's innocence. "Once you start burning the place down, you can't throw water on it," Swift said at the time. "You do not publicly embarrass someone and not make an enemy. If you start sticking it to these guys and you don't manage to get them thrown off the jury, do you think they're going to forget?"

Swift woke up early the next morning, dressed in his Navy whites, and made his way to the military commission courthouse, a T-shaped building on a bluff overlooking the bay. The government had spent half a million dollars preparing the courtroom, a former dental clinic, for this day, trying to give an otherwise brightly lit, modern facility with air-conditioning units protruding from its walls a sense of grandeur befitting the occasion of the nation's first war crimes trials in more than fifty years. The courtroom was framed by blue velvet curtains and carpeted in crimson. Behind the dark-paneled bench for Brownback and the jurors stood a row of flags, one for America, the others for the various armed services. There was an interpreter's booth off to the side and a small gallery for the press and human rights observers.

Security was tight. Teams of bomb-sniffing dogs swept the courtroom, and the seventy reporters who had come to cover the event were brought to the courthouse by military escorts. They had been warned when they arrived on Guantánamo a couple of days earlier that the government was reserving the right to seize their notebooks for redacting. There were no cameras allowed inside the courtroom, and the sketch artist was ordered not to portray the faces of any of the commission participants.

At 10:00 a.m. sharp, the rumbling of conversation inside the courtroom halted as Hamdan was led through a side door by two soldiers. He was shackle-free and wore a long white robe beneath a black-and-tan-checked sports coat, which Swift had brought back from Yemen for him. He had shaved his unruly beard but retained a thin mustache.

Hamdan paused briefly at the threshold to remove a white patterned head scarf and drape it over his shoulders, and then stepped into the courtroom and took his seat next to Swift. A few seconds later he turned around and glanced at the crowded gallery of reporters and observers. He smiled uncomfortably, clearly overwhelmed by the sight that had greeted him.

At 10:06, Brownback leaned forward in his red leather chair and called the hearing to order. After a few procedural issues had been resolved, Swift rose to speak. He was uncharacteristically jittery, having not argued before a court in almost a year and a half. He began tremulously but was soon overtaken by the familiar surge of nervous energy that he always felt when he stood inside a courtroom.

"Sir, I would like to start by clarifying your membership in the Virginia bar," Swift said, launching his attack on Brownback's qualifications because his law license had lapsed. After pursuing this line of questioning for a while, Swift shifted directions and raised the possibility that Brownback might, in fact, be *over*qualified; as the only lawyer on the jury and a former military judge, he could potentially exert improper influence over the rest of the commission members.

Brownback struggled to be patient, but Swift's persistent and often meandering questioning quickly wore him down. He soon became testy, barking at Swift to get to his point and chiding him for misrepresenting the rules of the commission and for taking quotes out of context: "Commander Swift, if you are going to read something, let's read it all."*

As the morning continued, Swift grilled Brownback about his re-

---

*The *New York Times* reporter covering the hearing described the dynamic thus: "Most of the time, he [Brownback] seemed as if he wanted to lunge across the tables that separated him from Commander Swift and grab him by the neck just above the defense lawyer's white dress uniform."

lationship with Altenburg and brought up his contentious meeting with Sundel, asking pointedly if he had expressed an opinion about detainees' rights to a speedy trial.

"No, I didn't," Brownback answered.

"I wasn't at that meeting, but I was told that you did," Swift replied.

Before the court broke for lunch, Swift formally asked Brownback to step down from the case. Visibly annoyed, Brownback refused but agreed to forward the matter to General Altenburg, the appointing authority for the military commissions, for his consideration. In the meantime, he said, Hamdan's trial would continue.

The hearing resumed, and Swift started interrogating the other jurors. One, an Army lieutenant colonel, admitted to not knowing America's obligations under the Geneva Conventions. Another, a Marine colonel who had commanded a reservist and New York City firefighter who died on 9/11, said that he had attended the reservist's funeral and visited Ground Zero a few weeks after the attacks. "Were you angry, sir?" Swift asked, in an effort to raise doubts about the colonel's impartiality. Two of the other panel members were intelligence officers who had been involved in operations in Afghanistan in the aftermath of 9/11. One had been in Afghanistan when Hamdan was captured; the other had been responsible for arranging the transfer of suspected al Qaeda and Taliban prisoners to Guantánamo Bay. Swift questioned their suitability to serve as jurors as well.

A number of Swift's queries required the disclosure of classified information, so in the late afternoon Brownback asked the audience and the defendant to leave the courtroom so that Swift could continue his examination of the jurors. Impatient to bring the hearing to a conclusion, Brownback asked Swift how long he thought he was going to need, thirty minutes?

"Oh, I doubt that seriously, sir," Swift answered.

"An hour?" Brownback asked.

"For each one?"

"No, for all of them," Brownback replied.

"For all five of them, sir?" Swift asked incredulously.

At that point Swift raised another objection. He didn't want his client removed from the courtroom with the rest of the audience. At the very least, Swift said he wanted an independent classifying authority—an individual with the power to classify or declassify material—to rule on whether or not Hamdan could be present for the entirety of his voir dire. "Nothing is more fundamental in my client's faith in the process," Swift said. "To exclude him at this point without even trying to include him is not in keeping with the full and fair trial as dictated by the president, sir."

"Your request is denied, Commander Swift," Brownback replied, matter-of-factly.

It was evening before the hearing was finally wrapping up. Swift lodged formal challenges against four of the five jurors, in addition to Brownback. Just as Brownback was adjourning the hearing, Swift stopped him. "Sir, I have one administrative note not requiring the other members that I would like to take up with yourself."

"Yes, Commander?" Brownback asked warily, after excusing the rest of the jurors.

Swift proceeded to tell Brownback he had just learned that there was a tape of the meeting at which he had made his disputed comments about whether detainees should have speedy trial rights. Swift wanted to have it entered into evidence so that General Altenburg would take it into account when he made his ruling on whether or not to relieve Brownback of his duties.

It was difficult to tell whether Brownback was legitimately stunned by the disclosure, annoyed by this bit of gamesmanship, or simply at his wit's end with Swift, but for whatever reason, he buried his face in his hands and sat in silence for ninety seconds. He finally looked up and said that the tape had been made without his permission but that Swift could go ahead and forward it to Altenburg.

Swift emerged from the cool, windowless courtroom into the hot Guantánamo night in high spirits. "It would seem to me that there must be someone in the officer corps we can pull who was not an intelligence officer in Afghanistan, was not involved in detainee operations, and did not go to the 9/11 site afterwards," he told reporters.

His aggressive questioning of Brownback dominated all of the media coverage of the hearing, including a front-page story in the next day's *Washington Post*, headlined BIN LADEN AIDE IS CHARGED AT FIRST TRIBUNAL; DEFENSE LAWYER CALLS PROCESS UNFAIR.

BACK IN VIRGINIA, Swift and Debbie drove up to Annapolis on a Friday evening in late September 2004 for Swift's twentieth reunion at the Naval Academy.

While Swift had been away in Yemen, Debbie had started her first job as a commercial pilot and had been struggling to juggle the demands of work with those of organizing their new home. Swift had left when virtually everything was still in boxes, and while he was gone, the dual air-conditioning and heating system broke down, requiring thousands of dollars' worth of repairs. Swift wasn't there to blame for waiving the inspection, so Debbie was left to fume alone, and she did. She was accustomed to Swift's disappearing into his cases, and they both traveled for work, but he had never gone this deep for this long, and it felt much more isolating to her now that they weren't living on a naval base where they always had a built-in network of friends. Also, his spur-of-the-moment purchase of the house still rankled. She knew that it wasn't completely within his control— his ADD made him prone to impulsive decisions—but at times she resented being the person left to live with the consequences while he ricocheted around from cause to cause.

Nevertheless, when Swift came back from Yemen and then Guantánamo so excited and full of such grand, patriotic visions, it was easy to forgive him. Plus, Debbie was looking forward to the reunion. Annapolis, a quaint colonial town of Georgian mansions, was always gorgeous in the fall, and this was her crowd. She had grown up in the shadow of the academy, sailing on the Chesapeake and dating midshipmen.

A big white tent had been set up on the campus for the Class of 1984 cookout. Swift and Debbie milled around, reconnecting with his old classmates and their wives. Many of them had read about Swift's exploits in the papers or seen him on TV and teased him about being famous. Many more were surprised that Swift had become a lawyer in the first place. ("Chuck always struck me as more of a blue-collar kind of guy," one of his old roommates later recalled.) What seemed the same about him was that he was, as another classmate put it, "still tilting at windmills."

Swift of course couldn't get enough. Charlie "N.T." Swift, who had barely managed to graduate, was now being singled out for being a celebrity. Somehow he had become a person of note, and he'd done it on his own terms—defending a suspected terrorist, of all things, and suing his commander in chief. At the end of the night, on their way to Debbie's aunt's house, just a couple of miles from campus, Swift and Debbie vowed to spend more time in Annapolis.

The next morning they woke up early for the Navy-Vanderbilt football game. It was an Indian summer day, warm and cloudless. The fall foliage was peaking, and the Chesapeake was already crowded with boats. Swift had been a Navy season ticket holder since moving back to the area but had not yet made it to a game. The pregame pageantry was just as it had been when he was a midshipman: all of the academy's brigades marched onto the field and stood at attention, then cheered themselves hoarse and ran up into the stands; a few minutes before kickoff, an F-18 buzzed the stadium.

The game was a blowout, so at halftime Swift wandered out to his company's tailgate party in the parking lot. On his way there, he noticed an old classmate with whom he had gone through plebe summer. Swift was a little nervous to see him coming his way. He was a hard-charging Marine colonel now and a good bet to make general. Swift figured he might not approve of what he was doing. He was wrong. "The rule of law is what I fight for," he told Swift. "Don't stop."

TEN

"Judge Assigned—We Won the Lottery"

KATYAL HAD SPENT THE SUMMER of 2004 shuttling back and forth to Chicago. His father had recovered from surgery but was no longer the same person. His mobility was limited, his speech was slurred, and his comprehension was poor; he knew his son's name but couldn't always remember that he was a lawyer. Still, Katyal's father wasn't despondent. He was aware that he wasn't well, but he thought he was going to get better. He didn't seem to understand that he had a terminal disease.

The management of his thirty-five rental units had fallen to Katyal and his sister, Sonia, a law professor at Fordham. When Katyal's father first got sick, Sonia, who didn't have any children, had been annoyed at her brother for not pulling his weight. Katyal felt guilty and was also haunted by a childhood memory: when his father had sued his ex-employer for wrongful termination, he had sought out Katyal's help, but Katyal had been too busy with his high school debate team. He didn't want to make the same mistake again, so in July, when one of his father's tenants took him to small-claims court over a rent dispute, Katyal argued the case himself (and won). His extended absences from home put additional pressure on Joanna, who had to pick up his share of the child care while continuing to work full-time. When she was feeling especially overwhelmed one weekend in July, Katyal's boss, the dean of Georgetown's law school, sent his thirteen-year-old son over to help her out.

In addition to caring for his father, Katyal was doing everything he

140

could to push the *Hamdan* lawsuit forward. With the government now aggressively moving ahead with the military commissions, he and Swift were racing the clock. They needed to convince a federal judge that the commissions were illegal before their client found himself convicted by one.

Judge Lasnik had indeed decided to grant the government's request to move *Swift v. Rumsfeld* to Washington, D.C., but before doing so, he gave Katyal and Swift a parting gift: he didn't rule on the government's transfer request until *after* the government had filed its brief defending the lawfulness of the military commissions, which ensured that the case wouldn't be stalled in transition from Seattle to Washington, D.C.

The government's brief was due on Friday, August 6. Katyal couldn't wait to read it. Until now the administration hadn't been forced to grapple with the substance of any of the claims from Guantánamo. It had simply argued that the federal courts lacked the power to hear the cases. But the Supreme Court's decision in *Rasul* had effectively killed that argument. The government was going to need a new strategy.

It was close to midnight when Katyal finally received an e-mail alert notifying him that the brief had been filed. It was sixty pages, much longer than he'd expected. As he printed it out and started reading, his heart sank. It was powerful, smart, and rigorous, and it featured an undeniably persuasive answer to their challenge to the commissions, one that he had somehow overlooked.

In short, the government argued that just because a court has the jurisdiction to hear a case doesn't mean it has to. The federal courts possess an awesome power, the power to overturn actions undertaken by either branch of the federal government, and there is a school of thought that believes the courts should exercise this power with extreme care, that they should practice what's known as judicial restraint. Boiled down to its essence, judicial restraint is a matter of abstaining and deferring—to the president, Congress, or another court. And that's precisely what the government was asking the federal court to do with respect to *Swift v. Rumsfeld*. "Petitioner asks this Court to intercede in the midst of an ongoing military process designed to determine whether Hamdan has committed violations of the laws of war and other offenses triable by military commission," the brief began. "The Court should reject this invitation."

The government centered its argument on *Councilman v. Schlesinger*, a 1975 case brought by the Army captain Bruce Councilman against the secretary of defense James R. Schlesinger. Councilman was going to be court-martialed for possessing and selling marijuana when he tried to stop the proceedings in civilian court by arguing that the charges were not service-related and that a military court therefore lacked the jurisdiction to hear them. The case rose to the Supreme Court, which denied Councilman's claim on the ground that it was inappropriate for a federal court to intervene in an ongoing military trial.

The government now urged the district court to apply the same logic to Swift and Katyal's challenge to Hamdan's military commission:

> The principles that led the *Councilman* Court to reject federal court intervention in ongoing military proceedings apply with even greater force here, where the President in his capacity as Commander in Chief . . . established the military commissions challenged herein upon finding that they are "necessary" for "the effective conduct of military operations and prevention of terrorist attacks" . . . The Executive Branch, not this court, bears the responsibility for protecting the nation from foreign attack . . .

If a civilian court *is* going to hear a legal challenge to Hamdan's commission, the government's brief continued, it should at least do so *after* his military trial.

Katyal knew the government had just presented their new judge with a very tempting option in a case that represented a direct challenge to the president's authority: the judge could simply rule that he had decided not to rule.

Katyal got started immediately on the reply brief. There had been some changes to the legal team in the preceding months. His Yale stu-

dents had graduated in June but had handpicked their successors before leaving. For its part, Perkins Coie had enthusiastically agreed to
stay on as pro bono counsel after the case was transferred and had
brought aboard a sixty-year-old veteran partner in Perkins Coie's D.C.
office, Benjamin Sharp, to anchor the effort.

Katyal roughed out different sections of the brief and e-mailed
them to his Yale students to tear apart. Once he had rebuilt them, he
would send them on to McMillan, Sharp, and the rest of the Perkins
lawyers for their proposed edits. Because he was constantly traveling
back and forth to Chicago, Katyal bought a BlackBerry to keep the
process running as efficiently as possible.

The reply brief gradually started to take shape over the course of
July and August, even as it grew to epic proportions. The thrust of
Katyal's answer to the government's abstention argument was that it
was disingenuous: the government was saying that Hamdan could
challenge his commission after a verdict had been rendered, but in
fact the president's military order explicitly precluded such challenges, leaving Secretary Rumsfeld's handpicked appeals panel as
Hamdan's only recourse. More generally, Katyal argued that abstention might very well be appropriate in the context of civilian courts or
court-martial trials—legal systems in which the procedures had been
carefully vetted by Congress—but not in the context of the president's
unilaterally authorized military commissions.

To bolster his case that the court should hear Hamdan's challenge
now, Katyal flung the government's favorite precedent for the military
commissions back at it. The trial of the Nazi saboteurs had actually
been halted in midstream, he pointed out, so that Colonel Royall's
challenge could be argued and decided by the Supreme Court. "In
Quirin," Katyal wrote, "the parties recognized that it would be inappropriate, even during a World War, to have a commission pronounce
guilt when a legal cloud of uncertainty existed over the proceedings."
In addition, Katyal discovered a report undertaken by the Defense
Department when President Nixon was considering using military
commissions in Vietnam, concluding that it would actually *benefit* the
government for the federal courts to rule on the lawfulness of the
commissions *before* the trials got started.

BY THE MIDDLE OF SEPTEMBER 2004, while the Pentagon was considering Swift's challenges to the composition of Hamdan's military commission panel on Guantánamo, Katyal was cutting the brief, trying to reduce it from well over one hundred pages to just under seventy. It wasn't due until the end of the month, but he was racing to finalize it by the night of September 27, when Katyal's parents would be flying in from Chicago so that Katyal could take his father to see the cancer specialist at Duke University who was overseeing his postoperative treatment. This was going to be their third trip to Duke, and the previous two had been exhausting. Duke was a long drive from D.C., five hours each way. Both times the doctor had done an MRI the moment they arrived, leaving them to wait nervously for the results. The news had been good—his father's tumor wasn't growing—and the doctor was as optimistic as he could realistically be, but the trips were nevertheless physically and emotionally taxing.

Katyal circulated what was his twenty-sixth draft of the brief to McMillan and the rest of the Perkins team on September 22 and waited impatiently for a response.

The Perkins lawyers felt it needed a lot of work. They again thought that Katyal was trying to do too much. The brief was too dense and contained too many arguments, each one of which was overadorned with detail.

With the help of Schneider, Sharp, and Charles Sipos, the young associate who had been helping out on the case, McMillan spent several days overhauling the draft. Six days later, he sent Katyal a new, shorter version. "While the quality and the depth of the scholarship on the issues addressed are obvious to everyone, there is a major concern that we are simply burying the Court in too much detail, and that in doing so we are really doing a disservice to our cause," McMillan wrote Katyal.

Katyal was beside himself. It was now the morning of the twenty-eighth, hours before he had to leave for North Carolina. What's more, the new draft seemed to him to betray a fundamental misunderstanding of the nature of their case. "They wanted to treat this like a commercial dispute, where both sides argue that the other one is wrong," Katyal later recalled. "They didn't get that this was a frontal attack on the president's prerogatives and that we were asking an unelected court, in a time of armed conflict, to stop the president from doing something."

Katyal did his best to contain his frustration as he tapped out an e-mail urging McMillan to leave the brief as it was:

> For whatever it is worth, here's why the brief looks the way it does . . . This case involves 11 dramatically different issues of constitutional law, international law, military law and criminal law. Unlike a commercial matter, it is inherently complicated. If there are some minor places where you think your edits make the argument STRONGER, instead of simply more streamlined, then please insert them into the version . . . and I will review . . . But please do not cut this version down for the sake of making it shorter.

McMillan was taken aback by Katyal's e-mail. While he had been eager to get involved in the *Hamdan* case, it had hardly been easy for him to make time for the brief. Not only did he have four children at home, but as a partner at Perkins he was under intense pressure to bill hours, and pro bono cases didn't count. He had worked with strong-willed lawyers before—he considered himself one—but he had rarely, if ever, encountered anyone this unwilling to cede any ground. Substantively, McMillan was convinced that his extensive revisions had dramatically improved the brief. The rest of the Perkins team felt just as strongly. Sharp, in particular, was adamant that all of Katyal's obscure historical citations and abstract theoretical arguments were blunting the force of their more persuasive legal claims. But the unfortunate reality was that Perkins had no leverage with which to force him to accept its edits; the next friend letter that Katyal drafted and Hamdan signed had designated Katyal, not Perkins Coie, to serve as Swift's lawyer in Hamdan's habeas suit.

McMillan sent Katyal a conciliatory e-mail, suggesting only a handful of minor changes before filing the brief with the federal district

145

court on September 30, 2004. "This case challenges an unprecedented and dangerous expansion of Executive Branch authority
cloaked in the exercise of the President's war powers," the brief began.
"Far from the battlefield and remote from any zone of military occupation, the President has unilaterally created a military commission,
justified by a so-called 'war on terrorism.'"

ON SEPTEMBER 2, *Swift v. Rumsfeld* was assigned to a new judge in
the U.S. District Court for the District of Columbia, James Robertson.
Katyal liked what he knew about him: he was a Clinton appointee who
had worked for the Lawyers' Committee for Civil Rights in Mississippi. A quick Westlaw search of Robertson's opinions revealed that
he had decided a number of high-profile cases, including Ken Starr's
1998 tax fraud case against the Clintons' friend Webster Hubbell,
which Katyal took as another good sign. It suggested he wouldn't be
intimidated by the stakes of their suit. Katyal called a few friends who
argued regularly in the D.C. district court. All of them raved about
Robertson. "Judge assigned—we won the lottery," Katyal wrote in the
subject line of his e-mail informing Swift and the Perkins team.

Katyal had attached Judge Robertson's résumé to the e-mail. Reading Robertson's bio, Swift was drawn to one line in particular: the judge
had done a five-year tour in the Navy. "In honor of Judge Robertson's
naval background, allow me a naval analogy," Swift wrote Katyal and
the rest of the team. "The wind has most definitely shifted and it is the
government that finds itself against the lee shore. The key is to keep
them there and not let them tack outside of us—(paraphrasing Nelson
at the battle of the Nile)."

Now that they had been assigned to a judge they liked, the challenge was going to be to keep him.

The district court in Washington, D.C., had been flooded with
Guantánamo-related cases in the wake of *Rasul* and had appointed a
special judge, Joyce Hens Green, to figure out how to deal with them
all. No one knew exactly what she planned to do, but Katyal was pretty
sure she would wind up consolidating the individual cases into a sin-

gle class action–style lawsuit, and he didn't want *Hamdan* to be lumped in with them. The new suits were still being filed, so in terms of timing, being merged into a larger case would set them back months, maybe longer. With Hamdan still in solitary confinement and the government now aggressively pushing his military commission forward—the final pretrial hearings would be taking place in the courtroom on Guantánamo in a matter of weeks—every day was precious. What's more, Katyal had no desire to file joint briefs and share argument time with another legal team.

Robertson scheduled their first status hearing for the afternoon of September 14. The team met a few days beforehand at the D.C. offices of Perkins Coie to strategize. The game plan was simple: distinguish *Hamdan* from the rest of the Guantánamo cases. Sharp wanted to act as the team's lead lawyer. Katyal was a little surprised but didn't object. He recognized that he owed Perkins Coie a big debt for all of the help they were providing.

At the hearing, Robertson wasted no time flashing his military credentials, referring to Swift, who was wearing his dark blue Navy uniform, as Mr. Swift, as is the custom among senior Navy officers, rather than Commander Swift: "I spent five years in the Navy calling people with two and a half stripes Mr. Smith, so I'll call you that, and you and I will know what that means and everyone else will think that I'm dissing you but I'm not."

The hearing was largely procedural. The only real issue discussed was whether the case could go forward or if, as the government had argued, Swift lacked the standing to bring suit on Hamdan's behalf because the *Rasul* decision had empowered Hamdan to bring suit himself. It was a complicated legal question, but it was, at bottom, a technicality. Robertson proposed a practical solution for dealing with it: take Swift out of the caption and rename the case. Katyal initially resisted the idea. "We happen to think, as a matter of procedural nicety and squareness with the case law, that what we're doing as next friend is appropriate," he said in the hearing. Robertson, clearly a little frustrated with Katyal's obstinance, gave him a lesson in what he called judicial realism. He could spend weeks writing an opinion on the question of standing, he said, or they could simply rename the case and move on. Katyal now consented to the new title, *Hamdan v. Rumsfeld, et al.*

Then came the moment Katyal had feared. Robertson said he planned to turn the case over to his colleague Judge Green, who would decide whether or not to consolidate it with the rest of the Guantánamo cases.

The instant Robertson adjourned the hearing, Katyal walked over to talk to one of the government's lawyers, David Salmons, an assistant solicitor general whom he knew from the 2000 Florida recount case, and gingerly raised the possibility of writing a joint letter to Robertson asking him to keep the case and schedule oral arguments for as soon as possible. Playing to Salmons's interests, he casually mentioned that the question of abstention—the matter of whether or not a court should even hear a challenge to Hamdan's commission before it had run its course—was too complex to be given its due if the case was merged with the other detainee lawsuits.

Katyal knew it was a long shot. He figured the government would much prefer to delay the case and mute the issues it raised by burying them in the growing stack of Guantánamo lawsuits. Still, it was worth a try.

To Katyal's surprise, Salmons agreed. His only condition was that the letter state specifically that abstention be among the issues discussed at the argument.

Salmons drafted the letter that evening. Katyal suggested a few changes, and they sent it off to Judge Robertson, who consented to keep the case. Oral arguments were scheduled for one o'clock on the afternoon of October 25, 2004.

SWIFT HAD AGREED to a clear divison of authority when he first lobbied Katyal to help him defend Hamdan: Katyal would be the lead lawyer in their federal challenge to the commissions, and Swift would be the lead lawyer in the military commission itself.

With their first federal court argument approaching, though, Swift was feeling the pull of the spotlight. His self-confidence was surging after his performance at Hamdan's voir dire on Guantánamo, and the fact that his challenges to the makeup of the jury had been surprisingly successful further emboldened him. (Altenburg, the general who was overseeing the commissions, had struck three of the proposed panelists, and although Brownback was staying, the chief prosecutor for the commissions, Colonel Swann, had urged him to "closely evaluate" his impartiality.) While Swift recognized that Katyal was a formidable legal thinker and writer, he considered himself a much more persuasive, not to mention experienced, courtroom lawyer.

Until now there hadn't been any contested territory between the two lawyers: Katyal plotted the legal strategy and wrote the briefs (with support from Perkins Coie and his Yale students), while Swift talked to the media, handled the commission proceedings, and dealt with Hamdan himself. But when it came time for Swift, Katyal, and the Perkins team to decide who was going to argue their case before Judge Robertson, all that changed.

Sharp, a veteran Washington litigator, made it clear that he wanted to speak for the team, a suggestion that outraged Katyal. After all of the hours Katyal had devoted to the case, he was not about to be a spectator now, particularly because he wasn't convinced that Sharp had yet mastered all the relevant issues.

Still, Katyal wasn't quite sure how to handle the situation. He had no shortage of confidence in his abilities as a legal thinker, but as a courtroom litigator he was unsure of himself. He was also wary of alienating Perkins Coie. Their recent argument over the brief notwithstanding, he had come to rely on the firm's input, McMillan's in particular. While their styles of lawyering clearly clashed—McMillan was invariably inclined to simplify arguments, Katyal to add ever more layers of complexity to them—Katyal considered the tension healthy. He appreciated McMillan's dogged willingness to debate the narrowest legal point endlessly with him, and the very knowledge that McMillan would be scrutinizing his briefs made Katyal focus that much more intently on them.

After seething in silence for a couple of weeks, Katyal told Sharp during a strategy meeting in D.C. in mid-October that he intended to deliver the argument himself. Anticipating some fallout from this announcement, Katyal had conferred with Swift beforehand. Swift had assured Katyal that he would back him, and they had even mapped out exactly what Swift would say when the moment arrived.

But when Katyal made the announcement, Swift departed dramatically from the script and instead proposed dividing the argument between himself and Sharp, leaving Katyal out entirely.

Katyal angrily confronted Swift after the meeting. Swift backpedaled, telling Katyal that he was ultimately going to support him; he just wanted to give Perkins the impression that he was on its side. Katyal didn't buy it. "Maybe you and Perkins should just handle the case without me," Katyal told him bitterly.

A couple of days later, when his fury had subsided, Katyal came up with a new plan. They would divide the seventy-five-minute argument three ways among himself, Swift, and McMillan. Sharp was hardly happy with the solution—"Neal had almost no courtroom experience whatever, which made all of us a little nervous," he later recalled—but by including McMillan in the argument, Katyal had neutralized his ability to object.

Swift was pleased to have a speaking role. He also had a plan to improve Katyal's courtroom presence. At the Naval Justice School many years earlier, Swift had taken a trial advocacy seminar with a man named Joshua Karton. A former actor—his screen credits include *Doogie Howser, M.D.* and *Beverly Hills, 90210*—Karton had recently made the transition into trial consulting. In addition to training young JAGs, he taught at Gerry Spence's Trial Lawyers College, a ranch-cum–teaching institute in Wyoming where lawyers are led through a curriculum that includes dancing with members of a local Indian tribe and acting out difficult personal situations. ("I would rather have a skilled nurse represent me than a young lawyer," Spence once said. "Why? Because nurses, at least, have learned how to listen—how to love.") In addition to dispensing Mr. Spence's wisdom, Karton had developed his own system for what he called "transforming courtroom presentation into persuasion."

"You've got to meet this guy," Swift told Katyal. "He's one of the world's foremost trial experts."

Katyal was buried in work. In addition to everything he was doing on the lawsuit, the new semester had just started at Georgetown. He was also in the midst of two projects for the Democratic presidential candidate John Kerry, analyzing the effects of the possible changes to the composition of the Supreme Court in a second Bush term and helping the campaign define its approach to terrorism. Not wanting to offend Swift, though, Katyal agreed to spend a few hours with Karton.

Karton, for his part, couldn't have been happier to oblige. He had always been fond of Swift—"My first thought was Billy Budd," Karton says, describing their first encounter at the Naval Justice School—and had prepped him, free of charge, for a number of his court-martial cases over the years.

Karton flew in from Los Angeles on a Friday afternoon in October, and he and Swift spent the weekend at Swift's house in Virginia crafting what Karton called strategy messages in which they would boil down the essence of the case to ten words or less. They were due at Katyal's office at Georgetown at nine o'clock on Monday morning, but they left Swift's house late and then proceeded to get lost. Swift called several times from the car to apologize.

When they finally arrived more than two hours late, Katyal was annoyed. He was also distracted. For the past few days he'd been pushing Kerry's domestic policy adviser to persuade Kerry to come out against the military commissions. When Swift and Karton turned up in Katyal's office, he had just learned that Kerry had agreed to do so.

Katyal was instantly turned off by the sight of Karton, a Falstaff-like figure in a billowy white silk shirt, and further put off by his slow, deliberate manner of speaking. Karton and Swift shared some of the products of their brainstorming sessions. Katyal took copious notes on what he believed was ridiculous faux analysis—"Hamdan was the boy whose parents didn't pick him up after school. Do we want to send him to detention?"—to create the illusion that he was listening.

Karton, sensing Katyal's irritation but apparently warming to his role of guidance counselor, continued to press gently ahead. "Neal," he said, his eyes discomfitingly locked on Katyal's, "just practice your oral argument with me. Just once."

Katyal reached for his legal pad, but Karton stopped him. "Don't you use that," he said, his eyes still fixed hard on Katyal's. "Just tell me what you want to say to the judge."

At that point Katyal started his argument from memory, only to be stopped again by Karton, who was reaching across the table. "Do it holding my hand," he said.

Katyal rolled his eyes but reluctantly took the extended palm in his. To his surprise, he found himself speaking differently. He was no longer delivering a lecture; he was having an almost casual conversation.

"It's not you *at* them," Karton told him. "It's you *with* them."

Under Karton's tutelage, Katyal soon found himself standing in the law school's faculty lounge with a student on either side of him, holding their hands as he spoke. Katyal felt ridiculous, but he had to admit that it was having its intended effect. At the end of the day, he apologized to Swift for his skepticism.

IT TOOK SWIFT the better part of ten months, but by the fall of 2004 he and Hamdan were finally starting to develop a relationship. In the late spring Swift had gotten permission to wear civilian clothes during their visits, which seemed to put Hamdan at ease. Swift had also taken to showing him news clippings about their lawsuit, sensing correctly that they would help reassure Hamdan that Swift really was his lawyer. Even though all newspapers and magazines, like everything else Swift brought down for Hamdan, were supposed to be cleared by censors and would almost certainly have been rejected, Swift decided that Hamdan had a right to see them because they had a direct bearing on his case, and simply carried them with him into Camp Echo.

But the real turning point was Swift and Schmitz's trip to Yemen. Hamdan had gotten a vicarious thrill from the planning and had been eager to hear all of the details once they returned. They spent days recapping the trip, telling Hamdan where they had gone and what they had eaten and describing his young daughters. They also brought him back a suitcase full of stuff—Yemeni coffee, nuts, dried fruit, spices, new pictures of his family.

In early October, Swift learned the hard way just how far he had come with Hamdan. The precipitating event was his CSRT, or combatant status review tribunal.

The tribunals were a central feature of the government's post-*Rasul* effort to prove that it was giving prisoners some form of judicial process. Detainees who chose to participate were invited to contest their designation as enemy combatants before a panel of three military officers inside a double-wide trailer in Camp Delta.

Swift considered the CSRTs a sham. Not only were they effectively closed to the public, but detainees were neither presented with actual charges nor permitted to see the evidence against them. Nevertheless, Swift asked to be present for Hamdan's. His request was promptly denied. No lawyers were allowed at the CSRTs. Detainees were instead assigned "personal representatives" to guide them through the proceedings.

Another idea occurred to Swift. Now that he had interviewed al-Bahri, Swift figured that he possessed relevant and exculpatory information. Hamdan could call *him* as a witness. Keen to have Swift at the hearing, Hamdan eagerly agreed to give it a try.

Swift fashioned a witness request. He assumed the government would dismiss it out of hand; dozens of CSRTs had already been conducted, and the government had yet to grant a single request for a witness who was not being detained on Guantánamo.

To Swift's surprise, Hamdan's personal representative called a few weeks later to say his request was being considered. Swift heard nothing further until twenty-four hours before Hamdan's CSRT, when he was informed that the request had been granted. He scrambled to get the hearing pushed back but was unsuccessful. Swift briefly considered trying to race down to Guantánamo, but Schmitz wasn't sure he could make it; plus, Debbie was flying, and Swift had no one to take care of their dog on such short notice.

Swift decided not to go. The hearings were basically a rubber stamp—only one of the first one hundred-plus detainees to appear had been released—and anyway, he had already accomplished his main goal, which was to annoy the Pentagon with his requests to be present. Swift notified Hamdan's personal representative that he wouldn't be coming and faxed him a letter to give to Hamdan explaining what had happened and instructing him not to say anything at the hearing because his testimony could be used against him at a later date.

Hamdan's CSRT went forward as planned the following day. At the opening of the hearing, Hamdan's personal representative mistakenly gave the head of the panel Swift's letter to Hamdan advising him not to testify, which was intended to be a privileged communication between lawyer and client. By the time Hamdan realized what was going on, the letter had already mistakenly been read into evidence at the hearing.

Things deteriorated even further from there. When Hamdan was asked if he wanted to make a statement, he told the panel he was confused: Swift had told him not to speak, but his personal representative had encouraged him to tell his story. Could his personal representative advise him more specifically on what to say? Hamdan asked.

The head of the tribunal explained that Hamdan's personal representative wasn't his attorney and therefore couldn't give him advice. So Hamdan decided to keep his remarks brief. He told the panel that all the accusations against him were lies and then apologized for not having any additional evidence to present. The hearing was over in a matter of minutes.

When Swift came down a few days later, Hamdan was furious. "Where were you?" he asked. "Why did you leave me?"

Hamdan had vented at Swift before, but this time his anger had a much different quality. He wasn't lashing out; he was expressing betrayal. Swift was stunned. He tried to explain that the hearings were a joke, the verdicts a foregone conclusion, that at least the military commissions, with all of their flaws, were trying to pass themselves off as legitimate courts. The distinction was meaningless to Hamdan. Swift felt profoundly guilty. "I will do everything in my power, everything a man can do, never to abandon you again," Swift told Hamdan at the end of the day.

"I had represented close to two hundred people in my career," Swift later recalled, "but I had never before felt like I did at the end of that day. I was bonded."

ELEVEN

An Indefinite Recess

INSIDE the E. Barrett Prettyman Courthouse for the District of Columbia on the afternoon of October 25, 2004, Judge James Robertson, a sturdy-looking man with white hair and black-framed glasses, rapped his gavel and opened the proceedings in Civil Action No. 04-1519, *Salim Hamdan v. Donald Rumsfeld, et al.* The long wooden pews that made up the courtroom's small gallery were less than one-quarter full, occupied by a few newspaper reporters, Gunn, Sundel, a couple of members of Katyal's Yale team, and a handful of his law students from Georgetown.

Speaking in a commanding yet casual voice, Robertson set the scene with a brief overview: "This case is called *Hamdan v. Rumsfeld*. It's *Hamdan* now. It used to be *Swift v. Rumsfeld*. It deals with a man who was captured and detained in Afghanistan in November 2001, transferred to Guantánamo Bay sometime in 2002. After that time, the president of the United States issued a finding that he has reason to believe that Mr. Hamdan is or was a member of al Qaeda or that he harbored or aided and abetted or conspired with those who were. That made Mr. Hamdan subject to trial by military commission, and he was transferred in December of 2003 to a subset of what is at Guantánamo Bay called Camp Echo, and there he was held in isolation. Lieutenant Commander Swift, whom we will refer to in Navy fashion as Mr. Swift, was appointed counsel for Hamdan in December of 2003 and brought an action, a petition for mandamus and/or habeas corpus in the District of Washington in April of 2004. The case was transferred here in early September, after the Ninth Circuit concluded that the Supreme Court's ruling in *Padilla* required habeas cases to be sent to this court. More recently, a conspiracy charge was filed against Hamdan before the military commission."

Robertson proceeded to sketch out the broad outlines of the two sides' respective arguments. He first cited Hamdan's claims: that he'd been denied the right to a speedy trial, in violation of the Uniform Code of Military Justice; that his detention in solitary confinement in Camp Echo was unlawful under the Geneva Conventions; and that the military commission was itself unconstitutional. The judge then gave a summary of the government's motion to dismiss. "I think I must put, first and foremost or front and center, the government's argument on abstention," Robertson said, "which is an argument that I may not resolve the issues that Hamdan has brought to this Court, that I must await the outcome of the military process."

When the judge was finished, Jonathan Marcus, a tall and slender assistant solicitor general, rose to speak. Before even starting in on his argument, Marcus said he wanted to be sure that Robertson knew Hamdan had been transferred out of solitary confinement.

This had happened only a few days earlier. Swift and Katyal had obviously welcomed the news, though its timing smacked to them of legal gamesmanship: the administration was plainly trying to undercut the urgency of their lawsuit—and, in so doing, bolster its claim that the court should stand aside and let Hamdan's military commission proceed.

Robertson too seemed a bit suspicious about the timing of Hamdan's transfer, and asked Marcus for some more details about it.

Marcus explained that the move had been under consideration for some time and had been done for "logistical and operational reasons."

"Not legal reasons?" Robertson asked.

"No, not legal reasons," Marcus answered firmly, if unconvincingly.

It was a long seventy-five minutes for the assistant solicitor general. The first portion of his formal argument, abstention, went fine, but as soon as he moved on to the merits of the case, Robertson began peppering him with questions. Robertson seemed especially skeptical of Marcus's assertion that Hamdan was not entitled to Geneva

Conventions protections because the president had determined that the conventions didn't apply to America's conflict with al Qaeda. But how, the judge wanted to know, had the president decided that Hamdan was al Qaeda? "What was the basis of that finding—just the president's determination?"

"That's correct," Marcus said. "But moving on . . ."

Robertson wasn't ready to move on. "You've got to be certain that he's al Qaeda before you can put him in the pigeonhole that the president has established for al Qaeda people. And my question is, how can you be certain—and on the basis of what evidence—that he's al Qaeda?"

Marcus mentioned Hamdan's recent combatant status review tribunal, which he said had determined that Hamdan was either a member of or affiliated with al Qaeda. Robertson still seemed unconvinced. The back-and-forth over the Geneva Conventions continued for several more minutes, with Robertson prodding Marcus and Marcus stammering like an unnerved law student. Katyal scribbled nine words on his legal pad and slid it in front of Swift: "We are going to win this case on Geneva."

When Marcus finally returned to his seat, Katyal rebutted the government's case for abstention. McMillan, a slight, intense-looking man with a dark beard, followed, tackling the most theoretical of the government's arguments about the Geneva Conventions: that because the conventions were not enshrined in a U.S. statute, they could not be enforced in U.S. courts.

Now Swift rose from the counsel's table in his dark Navy dress uniform. Katyal was worried. A few days earlier they had done a dry run of the oral argument in the moot courtroom at Georgetown. Swift had been terrible, confusing dates, muddying issues, and becoming overly emotional. Even worse, he had prefaced many of his answers with the phrase "The thing you need to understand is . . ." Katyal had cringed every time. Federal judges don't *need* to understand anything! Katyal had recruited five moot judges for the panel, all distinguished lawyers or law professors. After the session, every one of them had urged Katyal to cut Swift out of the argument.

Swift stood at the podium and focused his gaze on Robertson.

Both Katyal and McMillan had dutifully framed their remarks by enumerating the legal issues they intended to address in their allotted time. Swift opened with a sweeping observation: that if the history of America's military commissions had taught us anything, it was that for the trials to be viewed as legitimate, they must champion the rights of the accused. "The civilian architects of Mr. Hamdan's commission have ignored history, and they've selectively read the Uniform Code of Military Justice and the Geneva Conventions with an eye to escaping their mandates rather than following them," he said.

From here Swift launched into a story that he believed nicely summed up the weakness of the government's position. It was more a moral critique than a legal one. During World War II, Swift said, the German Army gave prisoner of war protection to U.S., British, and French troops, but not to Russian troops, because they had not gotten around to signing the 1929 Geneva Conventions. "So the German argument was, 'Well, the Russians aren't POWs. That means they're not people. That means I can move you into a concentration camp. That means I can gas you. That means I can work you to death in slave labor and summarily execute you, and I haven't committed a violation against the laws of war because you aren't a POW.'"

This was Swift's setup for introducing the specific provision of the Geneva Conventions most germane to Hamdan's situation. The conventions had been revised and expanded in 1949, in the aftermath of World War II. As the Russian story illustrates, there was a major loophole in the existing language, as it covered only soldiers fighting for nations that were signatories to the treaty. The drafters of the 1949 conventions set out to close this loophole by adding Common Article 3, which established minimum standards for the detention and trial of a much broader class of prisoners—standards, Swift said, that Hamdan's treatment had failed to live up to.

Swift had brought a legal pad to the podium with him but never once bothered to glance at it. He was passionate yet restrained, confident yet respectful. His uniform gave him an undeniable moral force, and his emphasis on the human dimension of their legal arguments gave them fresh urgency and resonance. Katyal was impressed.

Later, during the final round of rebuttal, Swift even bailed Katyal out when Robertson hit him with a series of questions about military law that he couldn't answer. Swift was practically jumping out of his chair, so Sharp nudged him—"Get up there," he whispered—and Swift eagerly returned to the podium.

"I'm surprised you didn't feel the tug at your coat, professor," Robertson said at the sight of Swift suddenly looming behind his co-counsel.

Swift ably handled Robertson's queries and took the opportunity to tick off some of the due process deficiencies with Hamdan's commission. Swift explained that the rules permitted the government to present evidence that his client would never see; indeed, he noted, Hamdan could be excluded from portions of his own trial. "They make a big deal out of the fact that I can be there, but anybody who's practiced trial law, especially criminal law, knows that where you get your cross-examination questions from is turning to your client and saying, 'Did that really happen? Is that what happened?' I'm not permitted to do that."

Robertson sat up straight in his chair and narrowed his eyes. "Are you telling me he won't even be able to come to his own trial?"

"That's correct, sir," Swift replied. "He already has been excluded from voir dire."

AFTER THE ARGUMENT, Katyal rushed back to Georgetown to teach a class. Swift was starving, having had nothing but coffee since the previous night. He was still riding the adrenaline high from the argument as he devoured a basketful of bread and a soft-shell crab sandwich, washed down with more coffee, in a restaurant near the courthouse. "Today that's what I live for," he said. "That's what I do good. I may not be the academic Neal is, but give me an audience and an afternoon, and anything can happen."

It was anyone's guess when Robertson was going to rule. Swift liked their chances but was by no means ready to declare victory. "Here's the reality of this lawsuit," Swift said. "We're gazing down the barrel of 1600 Pennsylvania Avenue, looking eye to eye with the president of the United States, and nobody's comfortable. Even when you're a judge with lifetime tenure, the idea of staring down the ruler of the free world is enough to make most people blink."

WITH THEIR LAWSUIT against Hamdan's military commission formally submitted, Swift and Katyal turned their attention back to the commission itself. The final pretrial hearings were scheduled to get under way on Guantánamo in just two weeks, and they were still finishing their motions protesting the various rules and procedures.

Katyal had not been present for the voir dire hearing in August but had since volunteered to serve as Swift's co-counsel for the commission. He thought it was important to raise all the same challenges to the president's war crimes trials in Hamdan's commission that they were raising in federal court, and if they were going to be arguing about the unlawfulness of the commissions at the commission itself, Katyal wanted to be there. Happy for the help, Swift enthusiastically agreed.

Katyal and his Yale team had since taken over the writing of many of the motions. They were filing twenty-two in all, not including their replies to the government's. There were no page limits, and Katyal saw no reason not to make each one as detailed and comprehensive as possible. Many exceeded fifteen pages and were heavily footnoted and filled with obscure case citations. Swift's name still appeared on every one, but Lang could hardly fail to notice Katyal's handiwork. "I felt pretty confident responding to Swift's motions," he would recall, "but when Katyal came on, I thought, Whoa, I'm going to have to put a team on this."

Katyal's personal favorite was what he called their reverse abstention motion: just as the government's lawyers had argued that Robertson should refrain from hearing their lawsuit until after Hamdan's military commission had issued its verdict, so Katyal argued that Hamdan's military commission should not be convened until after the federal courts had ruled on whether it was lawful.

Swift flew down to Guantánamo via Fort Lauderdale a week before the hearing on Tuesday, November 2, 2004—election day. Kerry had been closing the gap in recent weeks, and President Bush's second term, a virtual certainty just a few months earlier, appeared to be in jeopardy. Swift and Katyal had more than a casual interest in the outcome, given that Kerry had vowed to abolish the commissions. Kerry was ahead in the early exit polls when Swift left Norfolk, but by the time Swift touched down on Guantánamo the following afternoon, Kerry had conceded.

Swift went straight to the military commission building. The hearings for the detainee David Hicks had just adjourned for the day. Lang was also serving as the lead prosecutor in the Hicks case, and he and Swift had a testy exchange in the lawyers' lounge.

Things were already tense between the two JAGs. Not only had Lang been put off by all of Swift's preening in the media, he was annoyed at him for waiting until a couple of days earlier to tell him about the al-Bahri video, which Swift and Katyal planned to introduce into evidence at the hearings, and for rejecting every one of his attempts to resolve even the most mundane logistical issues outside the courtroom. This was very much part of Swift's strategy. "If he had asked me to agree to take four quarters in exchange for a dollar, I would have said, 'No, I prefer paper money, and furthermore, I think you're trying to weigh me down, Scott,'" Swift later recalled. "You spin somebody up, and they make mistakes."

Lang told Swift that the Hicks hearings were going smoothly and that the jurors were being fair-minded. "He said, 'You're not going to get any traction on this or that,'" Swift remembered.

Lang's comments irritated Swift. "I'm getting tired of this," he said. "You're telling me that the panel is being fair, but that I'm not going to get any traction? These trials are a joke, and you know they're a joke, Scott."

"I won't have you denigrating this process," Lang shot back.

IN THE MORNING, Swift and Schmitz went to see Hamdan. He was now living in a wing of Camp Delta with the rest of the detainees who had been designated for commissions, though his meetings with Swift would still be held at Camp Echo, where the cells were better suited to attorney-client visits.

Swift noticed right away that Hamdan was wearing a new jumpsuit, tan instead of orange, one of the perks of his new cell assignment. Under the prison's color-coded system, orange was reserved for the most dangerous and least compliant detainees, a classification automatically bestowed on anyone living at Camp Echo.

Hamdan was hardly happy to be back at Camp Echo, even if it was just for a few hours. He was also irked at Swift and Schmitz for bringing him breakfast, a steak Egg McMuffin and a milk shake, during Ramadan, and annoyed that the English-speaking Hicks was getting preferential treatment in their cellblock. Still, he seemed more stable and better able to focus now that he was out of solitary.

Katyal came a few days later with one of the students from his Yale team, Danielle Tarantolo. Their trip had been filled with headaches. Tarantolo's father dropped her off at Katyal's house at one in the morning, and they set off for Norfolk Naval Station, a four-hour drive from D.C. They arrived at a little bit before five in the morning only to be told that their travel orders weren't valid because they had only a faxed copy.

Katyal's nerves were already frayed. He had been vetting job candidates for the Georgetown faculty the night before and had managed only a brief nap before the long drive to Norfolk. He and Tarantolo were told to get out of the car and were questioned separately by the military police. Katyal eventually managed to persuade them to contact their commanding officer. Several calls and more than an hour later, Katyal and Tarantolo were escorted to the terminal, where more problems awaited them. Swift had reserved their tickets and had assured Katyal that they could use credit cards. They couldn't. Katyal needed $760 in cash. With their flight now about to take off, he took out as much cash as he could from a nearby ATM and convinced the ticket agent to allow him to pay the $80 difference with a check.

They were finally standing on Guantánamo's hot tarmac in the early afternoon, though it was almost sundown before they had been through all of their requisite security checks. Katyal dropped his bags at the BOQ—bachelor officers' quarters—and drove over to Camp Echo with Swift and Schmitz to meet Hamdan for the first time. He was a little taken aback when they greeted Hamdan by kissing him on both cheeks, but decided to follow their lead. Hamdan offered Katyal a date, the traditional snack for breaking the Ramadan fast, and some raisins that Swift and Schmitz had brought back from Yemen for him.

A few minutes later Hamdan told Swift to leave the cell so he could be alone with Katyal. Once he was gone, Hamdan asked Katyal why he was defending him. The question took Katyal by surprise. He pondered it for about half a minute before answering: "My father came to America from India with eight dollars in his pocket because of this country's commitment to equality and its respect for individual's rights. There is no nation on earth that would have given me, the son of immigrants, the opportunities I've had—the education, the chance to work at the Supreme Court and in the Clinton administration. These military commissions are a betrayal of that vision of America."

Hamdan seemed genuinely moved. They talked for a little while longer. Katyal tried to explain the three tiers of the federal legal system to Hamdan with stick figures on a legal pad. He drew one figure on the bottom tier denoting the single judge who heard cases at the district court level, three in the middle for the three-judge panels on the court of appeals, and nine on the top for the nine U.S. Supreme Court justices.

LIKE MOST MORNINGS on Guantánamo, Monday, November 8, 2004, dawned sunny and still. But by noon the sky over the yellow military commission building had darkened. Whitecaps rolled across the sea below, and the American flag stationed outside the courthouse's entrance was flapping noisily in the breeze. Security for the commission was again tight. Helicopters hovered overhead; sharpshooters peered over the roof.

For his part, Katyal was locked inside a supply closet. He had gone in to grab a couple of legal pads and practice his arguments one final time and then couldn't get out. He finally knocked the doorjamb loose and hustled down to the courtroom a few minutes before Brownback called the hearings to order.

The courtroom looked to Katyal like a Hollywood set. All of the details gave the room a superficial sense of grandeur, but it was obvious that the construction had been done in haste. A seal from one of the service branches had come loose from the wall and fallen to the floor.

The gallery was only sparsely populated. Having covered Hamdan's voir dire in August, most of the major news organizations had decided to wait for the commission itself, particularly because these hearings were likely to drag on for days, even weeks. No formal timetable had been set, but between Katyal's exhaustiveness and Swift's long-windedness, the small press pool was fearing the worst.

Swift rose to make their first motion shortly after one o'clock. It was a doozy. Katyal had come up with it only a couple of days earlier at Camp Echo. He had been doodling mindlessly, pretending to take notes while Swift and Hamdan talked, when the germ for the argument occurred to him. Altenburg had said he was not planning to replace the three officers that he had struck from Hamdan's panel at Swift's request. It would therefore be a three-man jury. The voting rules for the commissions required a two-thirds majority to convict. So instead of needing to win four of five votes for a conviction, the prosecution would now need to win only two of three. Put another way, by striking the three jurors, Altenburg had reduced the prosecution's burden from carrying 80 percent of the votes to 66 percent of the votes.

Swift laid out this argument to the commission, building toward the priceless climax: he withdrew his challenge to the removed jurors and asked that they be reinstated.

Brownback shook his head in disbelief—the hearings were scarcely thirty minutes old, and he was already exasperated with Swift—but before he could respond, a Marine sergeant came into the courtroom and handed him a yellow Post-it note. Brownback banged his gavel, announced that the court was in recess, and disappeared.

Katyal turned to Swift. "What just happened?" he asked.

"I gave a damn good argument, that's what," Swift answered, his face still flush, his heart pounding.

For the next minute or two everyone just stood around, puzzled. In the gallery, stunned silence gradually gave way to idle speculation. Had there been a bomb threat? A terrorist attack?

Katyal glanced over at the prosecution's table and noticed that

Lang was reading something intently. He nudged Swift and suggested that he go over and ask Lang if he knew what was going on.

Swift went over—"What's happening, Scott?"—but Lang ignored him. A couple of minutes later Lang got out of his chair and approached Katyal, who was now standing beside the defense table, with a stack of papers. "You're going to want to see this," he said. "You just won your federal case."

It was Judge Robertson's opinion. Katyal read it on his feet, with Swift peering over his shoulder. He quickly skimmed through the first five pages, the background of the case, before arriving at the first subheading, "Abstention is neither required nor appropriate."

They had cleared the first hurdle. Katyal read on to subheading number two: "No proper determination has been made that Hamdan is an offender triable by military tribunal under the law of war." It was their Geneva Conventions argument, that the administration had unlawfully stripped Hamdan of his Geneva Conventions protections. According to Robertson, the president's unilateral finding that Hamdan was affiliated with al Qaeda was not enough. Under the Geneva Conventions, only a "competent tribunal" could make such a determination. "The president," Robertson wrote, putting an even finer point on it, "is not a tribunal."

"We won," Katyal told Swift. He turned around and repeated those words to the press gallery before returning to the opinion.

What Katyal read next came as a complete surprise. Robertson had determined that the commissions themselves were unlawful for another reason too, one that hadn't even appeared in the lawsuit or their subsequent briefs. Robertson had instead seized on his exchange with Swift at the end of the oral argument and had even quoted Swift in his opinion: the commissions were illegal, the judge declared, because they permitted the government to exclude defendants from portions of their own trial in direct contravention of the Uniform Code of Military Justice.

Brownback returned to the courtroom and called the proceedings to order. "I came back to state on the record that we are going to have an indefinite recess," he said. "That is all the business I am taking care of. Commission is in recess."

Hamdan and his defense team reconvened in an empty room next to the courtroom. Hamdan could tell that something big was going on, though he wasn't sure exactly what. He said something to Schmitz, and the two of them started laughing hysterically. Schmitz translated: "Swift has been down here twenty times, and nothing has ever happened. Katyal comes down once, and look."

Outside, it was now pouring. Swift and Katyal drove through booming thunder and a lashing tropical rainstorm to the nearby media center. After a short press conference, they picked up a bottle of Cook's Champagne from the Navy Exchange and toasted their victory at the BOQ with Schmitz and Tarantolo. (Swift drank coffee.)

Later that night they returned to Echo to see Hamdan. By now the government had already responded to Robertson's ruling. "By conferring protected status under the Geneva Conventions on members of al Qaeda," a Justice Department spokesman had said in Washington, "the Judge has put terrorism on the same legal footing as legitimate methods of waging war." The White House vowed to file a quick appeal.

Katyal, a vegetarian, heated up a stack of prepackaged meatless meals that he had brought with him to Guantánamo and gave them to Hamdan, who was still caught up in the drama of the day. He had never believed Swift when he'd told him that a judge could issue a decision that directly contradicted the wishes of the president.

Katyal wanted to make sure that Hamdan hadn't misunderstood Robertson's ruling. He explained that it didn't mean he was going to be released but that something big had indeed happened: his military commission had been indefinitely halted, and he was going to be moved back into the general population at Camp Delta in compliance with the Geneva Conventions, which prohibited treating Hamdan differently from the other detainees.

A WEEK LATER, *Esquire* magazine honored Swift at its annual "Best & the Brightest" dinner in Manhattan. The event had been in the works for a couple of months, but Swift's stature had now changed. To the liberal media, already thrilled to have found a man in uniform who shared their growing antipathy for the Bush administration, he was no longer just the military officer making a principled stand for the rule of law. He was now the Navy JAG who had successfully sued his commander in chief. ("It's one thing to be on a crusade," as Swift later put it. "It's another for Don Quixote to come home with the dragon.")

Swift spoke briefly about the case and took his seat at the head table with the actor Bill Murray, the film producer Barry Sonnenfeld, and the *NBC Nightly News* anchor Brian Williams. Sonnenfeld was complaining about Bush's reelection and threatening to move to Canada. Swift told him to cheer up. "I've got the toughest job in this room, and I'm an optimist," Swift said.

"I guess I'm just a pessimist," Sonnenfeld replied.

Swift started laughing. "Are you kidding?" he said, gesturing at Sonnenfeld's wrist. "You've got to be the most optimistic guy in the world if you're wearing that watch"—a Breitling pilot's watch with a built-in radio transmitter that can send an emergency distress signal to search parties. "You're betting that you're going to survive a plane crash!"

The whole table cracked up. "I can see why the president doesn't like you," Sonnenfeld joked.

TWELVE

"We're Going to Crush You"

THE *HAMDAN* DECISION provoked an angry backlash among conservatives. On Friday, November 13, four days after the opinion had been handed down, Attorney General John Ashcroft delivered the keynote address to the annual convention of the Federalist Society in the ballroom of Washington, D.C.'s Mayflower Hotel. Rather than celebrate Bush's recent victory and revel in its implications for conservative legal causes, Ashcroft girded the roomful of lawyers for battle:

> We are confronted by a profoundly disturbing trend in our national political life, and that is the growing tendency of the judicial branch to inject itself into the areas of executive action that were originally assigned to the discretion of the president in the Constitution. These encroachments include some of the most fundamental aspects of the president's conduct in the war on terrorism . . . The danger I see is that the intrusive judicial oversight and second-guessing of presidential determinations in these critical areas can put at risk the very security of our nation in a time of war.

Ashcroft hadn't mentioned him by name, but it was obvious to everyone in the room that he was talking about Judge James Robertson.

The government filed its appeal with the D.C. circuit court of appeals a week after Robertson's decision, requesting an expedited review of the ruling. *Hamdan* was now entering hostile territory. The D.C. circuit court is perhaps the most conservative court in the country: seven of its ten judges were Republican appointees likely to side with the president on matters of executive authority.

The composition of the court was only part of the problem, though. Courts are bound by the relevant precedents in their circuit, and there were a number of rulings on the books in the D.C. circuit court of appeals that undercut critical claims in the lawsuit. The most troublesome of them all was *Tel-Oren v. Libyan Arab Republic*, which threatened to completely eviscerate Katyal and Swift's Geneva Conventions arguments.

On its face, *Tel-Oren* bore little resemblance to *Hamdan*. The case concerned a 1978 terrorist incident in Israel in which thirteen heavily armed members of the Palestine Liberation Organization had hijacked a bus on the highway between Haifa and Tel Aviv. On their way toward Tel Aviv, the terrorists shot at several passing cars and tortured and killed some of their own hostages. They eventually ran into a police barricade and during the ensuing shoot-out blew up the bus with grenades. In the end, thirty-four people had been killed, and more than seventy-five injured. The wounded and the families of the victims, some of whom were citizens of the United States, sued Libya and the PLO for monetary damages in Washington, D.C., claiming that their human rights had been violated. Specifically, they charged that the terrorists had violated a number of different treaties, including several provisions of the Geneva Conventions designed to govern the treatment of civilians during times of war.

A three-judge panel on the D.C. circuit court of appeals unanimously dismissed the suit. Each judge wrote his own opinion. The most influential, and the one most relevant to *Hamdan*, was issued by Judge Robert Bork. The thrust of his analysis was that treaties were compacts between nations, not individuals. It was therefore up to the respective governments to determine how they should be implemented. The mere violation of an international treaty did not give individuals the right to sue in U.S. court.

For the twenty years since then, Bork's *Tel-Oren* opinion had been the bulwark of a legal movement built around the idea of preserving American sovereignty in an age of globalization (not to mention the bane of the international human rights community, which viewed the decision as an enduring obstacle to its efforts to create a global community with universal rights). Its implications for *Hamdan* were clear: if the Geneva Conventions' application to an individual could not be enforced in a U.S. court, Swift and Katyal didn't have much of a lawsuit.

WITH THE ODDS stacked so heavily against them in the court of appeals, Katyal decided their best strategy was to ask the Supreme Court to hear *Hamdan* now. It was an unorthodox move. The justices have the authority to take a case that has not first been heard by a federal court of appeals—if, as the Court's rules state, "the case is of such imperative public importance as to justify deviation from normal appellate practice and to require immediate attention from this Court"— but it is an exceedingly rare occurrence. The Court has granted just a handful of such petitions since World War II.

Just about everyone advised Katyal against going this route, including Tom Goldstein, an old friend from his college debating days who was now a specialist in Supreme Court litigation. Goldstein told Katyal that he had only one opportunity to make a first impression on the justices. Did he really want this to be it?

At Perkins Coie, Sharp, who had clerked for Justice Harry Blackmun and argued at the Supreme Court, thought the idea was idiotic— not just a waste of time but the height of arrogance. He warned Katyal that it would backfire. The Supreme Court has an abiding respect for judicial protocol; to ask it to reach down and effectively snatch the case out of the hands of the court of appeals would destroy their credibility with the justices.

Katyal insisted on going forward with it anyway. He drafted the petition in a few days and filed it with the Supreme Court during the third week in November 2004. It stressed both the significance and urgency of their claims. "Mr. Hamdan, as well as the entire government of the United States, those affected by the government's actions, the lower courts, and the world community, stand to benefit from clear guidance as to how the United States may wage the legal war on terror in the future," Katyal wrote. "Similarly, our country has a pressing need to know that those implicated in that war are being treated in the way the Constitution, our statutes, and the laws of war demand."

A few days after they filed the petition, *Hamdan* was assigned to a three-judge panel in the D.C. circuit court of appeals. It was every bit as inauspicious as Katyal had feared. All three were Republican appointees. The senior members were Judge Stephen F. Williams (Reagan) and Judge Arthur R. Randolph (the first President Bush). The panel's junior member, Judge John G. Roberts, had been appointed to the bench by George W. Bush. Katyal knew Roberts well, having worked for him at the D.C. law firm of Hogan & Hartson the summer after graduating from law school. While Katyal liked and respected Roberts—he had even written a letter to the Senate Judiciary Committee on his behalf when President Bush nominated him to the D.C. circuit court of appeals—he hardly expected them to see eye to eye on *Hamdan*.

The moment their panel was assigned, Katyal asked two members of his Yale team to research every relevant decision under the three judges' names. Surely, there had to be *some* promising avenues to pursue. The students sent back a forty-page memo that only confirmed Katyal's fears. Among other things, both Randolph and Roberts had recently signed opinions holding that foreigners in the United States involuntarily, such as Hamdan, were not entitled to any constitutional rights, including the right of habeas corpus.

WHILE THEY WERE WAITING to hear back about their request for a hearing at the Supreme Court, Katyal got to work on their brief for the court of appeals.

Robertson's ruling was aggressive, not to mention a little lean on supporting case law. It was, in other words, the kind of decision that was especially vulnerable on appeal. The government had already battered Robertson's opinion in its own brief to the court of appeals, attacking not only the particulars of the decision but the very fact that he had ruled in the case at all:

> The district court's deeply flawed opinion constitutes an extraordinary intrusion into the Executive's power to conduct military operations to defend the United States. In a case where the district court should simply have abstained, it instead engaged in a wide-ranging analysis of enemy status and international treaties ... The resulting opinion erroneously interprets United States and international law in ways that would give enemy combatants unprecedented access to the United States courts.

This would be the *Hamdan* team's longest, most complex brief yet. There was a fourteen-thousand-word limit for their response, and Katyal intended to use them all. Nearly half of these words would be devoted to defending Robertson's decision to rule on the case. Judicial restraint is a core value among conservative judges, and Katyal was deeply concerned that the panel would be persuaded by the government's argument for abstention.

As far as the specifics of the ruling were concerned, Katyal's principal worry was Robertson's holding, inspired by Swift's argument, that Hamdan couldn't be excluded from his own trial. For all the hours Katyal had spent developing the many claims of their lawsuit, this one had never crossed his mind. He had no idea if there was any case law to support it. The Yale team quickly found a handful of strong precedents, most notably *Crawford v. Washington*, a 2004 case in which the Supreme Court had reversed the murder conviction of a man accused of stabbing an acquaintance because a lower court had permitted the use of hearsay evidence in his trial and thus denied the defendant his fundamental right to confront his accusers. It was ideal fodder for their brief, particularly because the opinion's author was the Court's most conservative justice, Antonin Scalia.

It proved much harder to find an answer to *Tel-Oren* and the government's argument that the Geneva Conventions didn't give Hamdan any rights in American courts. Katyal wound up reaching all the way back to an 1804 case, *Murray v. The Schooner Charming Betsy*, in which the Supreme Court had ruled that federal statutes must be interpreted so that they are consistent with international law. The Court's logic in the case was intuitive: Congress, the body that makes the laws, would never deliberately set aside America's international obligations. In its *Hamdan* brief, the government had argued that when Congress gave the president permission to respond to the September 11 attacks with military force, it had implicitly authorized him to convene military commissions, which were part of his war-making powers. Even if this was true—and Katyal didn't agree that it was—Congress certainly had not given him the right to violate an international treaty like the Geneva Conventions.

Katyal now had twelve law students from Yale working with him, in addition to four from Georgetown and a full-time research assistant, Joshua Friedman, a recent graduate of Duke University. Katyal divided them into groups and asked each one to draft a different portion of the brief by December 10, 2004. Once Katyal had read their sections, he set them aside and then drafted his own version, a technique he had learned from Justice Breyer, who valued input from his clerks but preferred to write all his opinions from scratch.

Perkins Coie, meanwhile, had decided to take a different approach this time. The firm drafted its own version of the brief in the hope that Katyal would be more inclined to adopt its language and legal arguments if they were presented to him as a separate document instead of grafted onto his own draft.

The court's deadline for the brief could not have been worse: December 29, a few days after what Katyal feared would be his father's last Christmas, which his family was going to spend at an uncle's house in rural Pennsylvania with only dial-up Internet access. Katyal finished the bulk of the writing by December 15, but the brief was way too long, 23,000 words. Katyal turned his attention to cutting. On December 24 he stitched the brief's nine sections together and circulated a 16,500-word draft to the team.

The Perkins team was again displeased. Some of their material had been incorporated; much hadn't. The firm was impressed by the originality of Katyal's arguments and the dizzying array of legal authorities he had cited—the diaries of George Washington, nineteenth-century treatises on military law, and the 1956 edition of the *U.S. Army Field Manual*, to name just a few—but it thought the brief was unwieldy and undisciplined. Sharp, in particular, was concerned that Katyal was staking out unnecessarily aggressive legal positions. "Neal was hell-bent on turning this case into a major constitutional confrontation," Sharp remembered. He made his unhappiness known to Katyal, who pointedly defended his draft.

Sharp was losing patience with Katyal. He had been brought into the *Hamdan* case for his experience, yet Katyal was too arrogant to listen to his advice. And unfortunately from Sharp's perspective, that's all it was: advice. As the lead counsel in the case, Katyal had custody of all of the working drafts and final say over the finished product. Sharp had tried in the past to persuade Swift to lean on Katyal, but his attempts had gone nowhere. Swift liked Sharp and thought it useful to have someone on the team who wasn't intimidated by Katyal, but to Sharp's unending frustation, Swift ultimately always sided with Katyal.

McMillan too was worried about the brief, but he was even more concerned about Sharp's rising irritation with Katyal. If things continued the way they were going, Perkins was almost certain to withdraw from the case. In fact, Sharp had already mentioned the possibility. Katyal's obstinance notwithstanding, McMillan had come to admire his tenacity and creativity as a lawyer. Moreover, he believed that the stakes of *Hamdan* made it imperative that Perkins continue with the case, even if that meant fighting countless more losing battles with Katyal for every minor victory. "We were talking about the powers of the president, the constitutional order of the United States of America, and whether or not the nation is obligated to follow international law," McMillan later recollected. "We had to somehow hold it together and do whatever we could to craft the best legal arguments possible."

McMillan diplomatically suggested to Sharp that he take a step back on the case and pass all of his comments to Katyal through him. Sharp, at his wit's end with Katyal anyway, agreed.

Katyal, meanwhile, was at his uncle's house in Pennsylvania, trimming and sharpening the brief. He rarely left his room, even excusing himself early from Christmas dinner. When he wasn't writing or editing, he was trying to persuade McMillan that the brief's unusual level of detail wasn't inappropriate given the nature of the case and the intellectual heft of their audience: three erudite appellate judges and their nine elite law clerks.

On the evening of December 27, Katyal drove back to Washington to finalize the brief. It was seventy-two pages long—13,991 words—and opened with an assault on the government's description of Judge Robertson's ruling:

> Correctly characterized, the decision below is not "extraordinary," "unprecedented" or "counterintuitive." The District Court did not "overrule" the President, other than in the sense that any federal court might do so in determining that Executive action did not comply with the laws and treaties of the United States . . . Although this case undoubtedly raises issues of national and international importance, the court below did not unduly restrict the powers of the Executive as recognized by the courts; it simply did not acquiesce to claims for a substantial broadening of those powers at the expense of traditional functions reposed in the Judicial Branch and Congress.

TEN DAYS AFTER the *Hamdan* team filed the brief, the Supreme Court denied their request to hear the case. *Hamdan's* fate was in the hands of three Republican appointees in one of America's most conservative circuits. Oral argument was scheduled for March 8, 2005.

Swift wanted to deliver a portion of it. Katyal didn't think the forum played to Swift's strengths. Appellate court arguments typically value rigor over rhetoric. Appellate judges have relatively light caseloads and usually bring into the courtroom a nuanced understanding of the issues at hand. Their questions are often precisely focused, and they expect counsel's answers to be both subtle and on point. The worst mistake an advocate can make in the court of appeals is overstatement;

the slightest whiff of bombast can be enough to unleash the wrath of most appellate judges. Still, given how good Swift had been in front of Robertson, Katyal didn't think it would be fair to take the bat out of his hands. He agreed to divide the half hour argument between them. He would take twenty minutes, and Swift would have ten.

It quickly became apparent to Katyal how determined the administration was to erase its embarrassing defeat before Judge Robertson. Peter Keisler, a rising star in the Justice Department who had cofounded the Federalist Society while in law school twenty years earlier and would soon be nominated to serve as a judge on the D.C. circuit court of appeals himself, was going to be arguing for the government.* "Neal, we're going to crush you—crush you," Michael Dreeben, a deputy solicitor general and adjunct law professor at Georgetown, told Katyal at a faculty lunch in January.

IMPROBABLY, life on Guantánamo had gotten worse for both Swift and Hamdan.

Swift had made plenty of enemies on the base over the course of the past year, but he had never before had any problems with its military lawyers. He had spent idle hours hanging out in the staff judge advocate's office—the equivalent of the base's legal offices—and had even gone scuba diving with Guantánamo's number two JAG. They fought constantly over the policies governing Swift's visits with Hamdan, but unlike many of the guards and commanders, his fellow military lawyers understood that Swift wasn't just being a pain in the ass; he was advocating for his client.

Robertson's ruling had made short work of this goodwill. The very next morning, Swift had gone over to the staff judge advocate's office to ask about its plans for moving Hamdan in with the rest of the prison population and had been greeted with a coldness bordering on hostility.

---

* Still awaiting his confirmation, Keisler served as acting attorney general following Alberto Gonzales's resignation in 2007.

"Any questions should be referred to the office of the U.S. Attorney or the solicitor general," a Navy JAG whom Swift had known for years told him.

"What's up?" Swift asked, taken aback. "Are you not going to tell me anything?"

"If you have any questions, you can refer them to the office of the U.S. Attorney or the solicitor general," the JAG repeated.

Swift asked about some letters from Hamdan's family. Over the summer he had arranged for Hamdan's mail to get expedited review by government censors. Instead of months, it now took just a few weeks to get the letters redacted.

"Hamdan is just one of several hundred detainees," the JAG told Swift.

"Until then it was just Charlie being Charlie," Swift would recall. "Now we weren't just guys doing their jobs. We were on opposite sides of a huge lawsuit."

Broader changes were afoot on Guantánamo as well. Swift and his JAG colleagues were no longer the only lawyers on the base. Following the Supreme Court's decision in *Rasul*, the government had started granting detainees access to civilian counsel, and an ever-expanding roster of pro bono attorneys—human rights lawyers as well as representatives from white-shoe law firms—were now coming down in droves to meet with existing clients and sign up new ones; the Guantánano Bay Bar Association, they called themselves.

Swift was happy for the company, but their presence created complications for him. In the past he had been able to take advantage of the lack of formal procedures governing attorney-client visits. But more lawyers meant more rules. Swift once again had to wear his uniform inside Camp Delta, so the military could distinguish him from the civilian attorneys. He and Schmitz had always been able to visit with Hamdan as late as they wanted. Now the hours of their meetings were narrowly circumscribed.

In order to prevent detainees from relaying messages through their lawyers, Guantánamo's senior judge advocate general had also determined that anything a detainee said to his attorney was poten-

tially classified. In December 2004, Swift's notes were seized for review by a classifying authority. Swift hit the roof. "It was the stupidest
thing I had ever heard," he remembered. "What's in someone's head
can't be classified. If the government acknowledges that it happened,
then it might be classified, but until the government acknowledges it,
it's merely an allegation, and allegations are not classified." (The government eventually backed down and exempted the military defense
lawyers from this procedure, though the determination itself remained in effect.)

As for Hamdan, per Judge Robertson's order, the government had
moved him into the main part of Camp Delta a week after the ruling.
The only problem was that every cell around him was empty. For all
intents and purposes, Hamdan was back in solitary confinement. He
once again began to despair and took out his frustration on Swift, who
had repeatedly assured him—despite Hamdan's considerable skepticism—that if the court sided with them, the government would have
no choice but to obey the judge's ruling.

Swift notified a reporter from *The Boston Globe* about Hamdan's
treatment and then fired off an angry letter to the Justice Department,
complaining that the government had violated Robertson's order that
Hamdan be integrated into the prison's general population. Hamdan's
new quarters, Swift wrote, were "calculated to prevent him from
speaking to or having contact with any other detainees." This de facto
isolation, he continued, "has again had severe mental and emotional
consequences for him, the very same consequences that our psychol-
ogists have continually warned about." Swift was not being hyper-
bolic; in January, after a guard saw Hamdan tearing up a picture of his
children, he was stripped down to his underwear and placed on a
twenty-four-hour-a-day suicide watch.

The government denied that it had violated the judge's orders but
decided to move Hamdan anyway—"for operational and intelligence
reasons," according to the Justice Department. He now had neighbors, but all were Chinese-speaking detainees from East Turkistan.
Swift again complained, and in February 2005 Hamdan was finally
transferred into a regular cellblock with other Arab prisoners.

This created a whole new round of problems. It didn't take long for Hamdan's new neighbors to notice that he was getting special treatment. Back at Camp Echo, Swift had persuaded the guards to let his client keep a footlocker in his cell that Swift and Schmitz replenished with comfort items such as car and truck magazines, snacks, and toiletries. Hamdan had been toting this footlocker around with him ever since. Now his new neighbors told their lawyers that they too wanted footlockers. Their lawyers in turn complained to the leadership of Camp Delta. The upshot was that Swift was informed that his client would have to abide by the same rules as the rest of the detainees: he could no longer keep anything in his cell that hadn't been issued by the government.

Swift knew how important Hamdan's footlocker was to him. Hamdan was beginning to understand the significance of his case, but he was still far more concerned with his day-to-day life on Guantánamo. With his trial on hold, he was more focused than ever on his treatment. Aside from staying out of solitary confinement, nothing mattered more to Hamdan than his comfort items. Getting his client permission to keep things in his cell had gone a long way toward helping Swift earn his trust. He had no doubt that Hamdan would blame him when those same items were taken away.

Swift was right. The guards started confiscating everything whenever Swift entered Delta, and Hamdan took his anger out on his lawyer. Swift tried to explain that it wasn't his fault and showed Hamdan the folder of letters he had written to Guantánamo's staff judge advocate, detailing why each confiscated comfort item—from cornflakes to flip-flops to the special neoprene wraps that Hamdan liked to wear around his ankles during their visits to prevent the chains from cutting into his legs—was critical to his client. Schmitz even created a spreadsheet for Hamdan listing all the things they had brought down for him and where they now stood—confiscated, pending review, rejected by censors—to prove that they were at least trying. But Hamdan wasn't appeased.

Swift could still bring food to Hamdan, but when their meetings ended, the guards would tell Swift to take anything uneaten with him.

If he refused, the guards would take it away themselves. When Hamdan tried not to relinquish a half-eaten snack, Swift found himself caught in the middle: he didn't want to side with the guards, but he knew that Hamdan was only going to make matters worse for himself by antagonizing them.

IN THE MIDST of Katyal's preparations for the March 8, 2005, oral argument at the court of appeals, his father's condition took a dramatic turn for the worse. The cancer was spreading again, and his mental deterioration was accelerating. After Judge Robertson's decision in November, Katyal's father had seemed able to understand that his son was happy, though he couldn't grasp exactly why. Now he was no longer always able to recognize his own family. In February he underwent an aggressive course of chemotherapy that he did not tolerate well. On the morning of March 1, Katyal's mother called to tell him that his father didn't have long to live.

Katyal knew he needed to get back to Chicago immediately, but the oral argument was only a week away and a group of high-powered lawyers was coming to Georgetown that morning to prep him for it. Katyal decided to go ahead with the moot and then leave for the airport immediately after.

He arrived at Georgetown's moot courtroom to find Swift there in his Navy dress uniform with a camera crew from *60 Minutes*, whom he had invited to film the proceedings. Not only was this the last thing Katyal wanted to deal with, but he was worried about parts of the moot being broadcast on national television, which could give the government an early peek at their strategy. And what if the moot didn't go well? Would they really want it on air?

Katyal took Swift aside and lit into him.

"I thought it would help the case," Swift said.

"The D.C. circuit doesn't care what *60 Minutes* thinks," Katyal spat back.

Swift said he'd talk to the producers to make sure they cleared everything before using it. Katyal still wasn't satisfied. He told Swift that he could do whatever he wanted but that he wasn't going to permit the crew to film him, so they filmed just Swift instead.

On his way to the airport, Katyal called the clerk at the court of appeals about postponing the argument. The clerk told Katyal he would need the consent of the other party. The administration, eager to see Robertson's ruling overturned, had no incentive to agree to a delay, so Katyal figured his only shot was to make a personal appeal to Keisler, the Justice Department lawyer arguing the case for the government. They had never met, but Keisler had been a college roommate of Akhil Amar, one of Katyal's mentors. Amar called Keisler on Katyal's behalf, and Keisler successfully lobbied the administration to agree to reschedule the argument.

By the time Katyal landed in Chicago, his father was in intensive care and only semiconscious. His immune system had been severely compromised by all the chemotherapy medication, so Katyal had to wear a surgical gown and mask in order to see him. After three days his father was moved to a hospice, and Joanna, now seven months pregnant with their third child, flew out with Rem and Calder to be with Katyal and his family. Over the course of the next five days, as his father gradually lost consciousness, Katyal left his side only once, to buy some toys for the boys and a clean pair of pants for himself.

Hoping to keep the *Hamdan* case fresh in his mind, Katyal had brought all of his legal briefs with him, but he found himself unable to drag his thoughts away from the ever more diminished figure in the bed next to him.

Like most children, Katyal had fully come to appreciate his father only once he had become an adult. It wasn't until then that he learned about his father's boyhood in India and his early days in America—how he had arrived in the United States in 1960 with the equivalent of eight dollars in his pocket, the maximum that Indian citizens were allowed to take out of the country; had slept in the back of a dilapidated car until he saved up enough money to pay for an apartment; and had put himself through graduate school at the Illinois Institute of Technology while working the night shift as a chemist. Katyal's father wasn't prone to talking about himself to begin with, but he had deliberately omitted these details whenever discussing his life for the same reason that he had given Katyal and his sister assertively American names, not taught them to speak Hindi (his first language, as well as his wife's), and insisted on celebrating Christmas. He had not wanted anything to stand in the way of their assimilation.

But as Katyal and his sister both became successful adults—and American citizens—his father seemed happy to relax the embargo he had maintained over so much of his history. When Katyal was twenty-two, his parents bought a small piece of property outside Chicago so that Katyal's father could design and build their dream house. The result was like nothing else on the block or perhaps even Illinois. Perfectly round, the house was meticulously organized around a huge circular living room designed for Diwali parties, the Hindu New Year's celebration. Set, as it was, on a tidy suburban street lined with conservative-looking homes, it was about as assimilated as a spaceship.

Katyal came to rely on his father even more once he had children. His parents were at the hospital within five hours of Rem's birth and stayed with Joanna and him for a month afterward to help with the baby. Katyal's father baby-proofed the apartment, as he did every place Katyal ever lived.

As a grandfather, he made a point of seeing his grandchildren at least once a month. Rem called him Papa Cago (his grandfather from Chicago), and only a few months before he became sick, Katyal's father had insisted on driving Katyal's childhood bed, a red race car, to Washington so that Rem could have it. Katyal dreaded the moment he would have to explain to his three-and-a-half-year-old son what was happening.

His mother was an even bigger concern. His parents' marriage had been arranged, but there had never been any doubts about their devotion to and dependence on each other. On a purely practical level, Katyal's mother didn't even know how to fill up her own car with gas.

When his father was about to die, Katyal scrambled to find a friend or relative who had Gunga, holy water from the Ganges River that Hindu custom requires be placed in one's mouth upon death. Surinder Kumar Katyal died just after dawn on March 7, 2005, five days before his son's thirty-fifth birthday. A Hindu priest administered the equivalent of last rites.

After Katyal's father had been cremated, there was a wake at his parents' round house. About a hundred people, mostly relatives and a few of Katyal's childhood friends, crowded into the living room. Katyal delivered a short eulogy. He spoke about his father's compassion, recalling that he had often forgiven the rents of struggling tenants with children to feed. Through tears, Katyal said that he aspired to be like his father, nourishing and protecting the lives of others.

ON THE FLIGHT back to Washington with his family, Katyal wondered what might be left of his friendships, as the *Hamdan* case had consumed almost every waking hour of the last year and a half of his life. A year earlier a friend from law school had lost his father, and Katyal remembered thinking at the time: Who will be there for me when my father dies? He was pleased to return home to dozens of condolence cards from friends, colleagues, even some of his former bosses. Among them was a handwritten note from Judge Roberts.

Katyal wanted to thank him for his thoughts, but was worried about the ethical implications of communicating privately with a judge before whom he had a case pending. After giving it some thought, he came up with a solution: he carbon-copied the solicitor general's office on his note back to the judge.

Katyal had been in Chicago for only a couple of weeks, but his father's death had set him back significantly. It was now mid-March, and he and Swift were due to make their argument to the court of appeals in three weeks. Katyal reread all of the briefs and organized three more moots at Georgetown. He also found himself defending his decision to share the argument with Swift, who skipped two of the moots and came across as problematically bombastic in the third. A number of the panelists again warned Katyal that he was making a mistake. Swift was a showboater, they said, and not familiar enough with the underlying cases. Katyal assured them he was much better on game day.

The argument was rescheduled for 10:00 a.m. on April 7. Swift arrived at the courthouse early and waited for Katyal, who was uncharacteristically behind schedule. The cab Katyal had ordered never showed up, and traffic on Constitution Avenue was snarled because of an accident. He eventually bailed out of his taxi and ran to the courthouse, carrying his briefcase.

By the time he arrived, people were already filing into the ceremonial courtroom on the sixth floor, the equivalent of center court at Wimbledon. The room's bench is unusually high, its gallery unusually large, and its walls are lined with the portraits of many of the judges who have sat on the court. The government had specifically requested the room, no doubt to intimidate Swift and Katyal.

Keisler, who was in his mid-forties, with wire-rimmed glasses and a full head of sandy brown hair, went first. He brought no notes with him and spoke without interruption for five minutes, briefly summarizing Robertson's opinion and then cheerfully eviscerating it, beginning with the judge's decision to wade into the case at all. "We believe the proper course was for the District Court to dismiss this case on the basis of abstention," he said. "We think it was highly premature for the District Court to decide these issues at this very early stage of the proceedings."

Judge Roberts asked why the government was so eager for the court to abstain: wouldn't it rather have the legality of the commissions established before it went forward with them? Keisler conceded that for all practical purposes it would welcome a ruling that the commissions were lawful, but noted that there was a broader principle at stake: the government believed it was important for the court to make it clear that Judge Robertson had overstepped his authority.

Keisler proceeded to hammer away at Robertson's various holdings. "The one that we think cries out most for correction is the holding that members of al Qaeda captured in Afghanistan are entitled to the protections of Geneva," he said. "Al Qaeda is not a signatory to the Geneva Conventions and this isn't simply a question of someone's name on a signature block. They openly defy all the principles of Geneva and under those circumstances, they can't be legally entitled to its protections, because the essence of the treaty is reciprocity."

Keisler's next thrust was the government's *Tel-Oren* argument:

184

Even if Hamdan was entitled to Geneva Conventions protections, the treaty did not confer rights enforceable in the U.S. courts. In order to become part of the law of the land, its various provisions would have to be written into legislation and passed by Congress.

Turning to Robertson's ruling that Hamdan could not be excluded from his own trial, Keisler stressed that the argument was purely speculative, since the government had not yet decided whether to present classified evidence at Hamdan's trial. And even if it did, he assured the court, the government would do everything in its power to accommodate Hamdan by introducing unclassified summaries of the evidence.

NOW IT WAS KATYAL'S TURN.

It had been easy to decide where to start. During his preparations for the argument, Katyal had been almost single-mindedly focused on abstention. He knew the panel was likely to overturn Robertson's ruling. He just wanted to keep *Hamdan* alive and get a second shot at the Supreme Court. If the court of appeals chose not even to wrestle with the substance of their lawsuit, the justices of the Supreme Court were almost certain to do the same. He needed the three-judge panel to engage on the issues, which required rejecting the government's argument for abstention.

"Abstention, Your Honors, is justified when the tribunal to which abstention is sought has demonstrated its fairness, its expertise, and its independence," he said. "None of those can be said about this military commission."

Right away the panel's skepticism was clear. "How many cases has this military commission adjudicated?" Judge Randolph asked.

"The commission itself has not adjudicated any," Katyal answered.

"So, your claim that they haven't demonstrated their competence and fairness is not very fair, is it?"

"Well, Your Honor," Katyal responded, "the test is not . . . 'Might they hypothetically demonstrate fairness?' It's 'Do they have a proven track record, or do they at least have a system of structural safeguards in place that make abstention appropriate?'"

Judge Roberts wanted to know how it would hurt Katyal's client if the court was to abstain for now. "You may prevail before the commission and if you do, fine," the judge said, "and if you don't, you can raise the same arguments you're raising today after the commission's ruling."

To begin with, Katyal answered, if the case was dismissed, the government might very well return Hamdan to solitary confinement. But an even bigger problem with the court's abstaining until Hamdan's military commission had concluded, Katyal continued, was that if his lawsuit was ultimately successful and his commission declared unlawful, the government could simply retry him in federal court, having already gotten a complete preview of Swift's defense at his commission. This would put Hamdan at a severe disadvantage. The prosecution would have had years to research the facts and witnesses presented at his commission.

When his time was up, Katyal turned the lectern over to Swift to defend Robertson's decision that the government could not exclude Hamdan from his own trial.

Swift opened by recounting the story of Hamdan's being kicked out of his own voir dire, noting that the government had been anything but accommodating at the time. The court seemed unmoved: "It's just voir dire you're complaining about . . . We're not talking about excluding the accused from the trial proceedings at all."

Swift explained that voir dire was absolutely critical to any trial attorney. "It is the right of the accused not only to see the witnesses against him but to see those who are judging him and to understand any biases or prejudice they might have."

Wasn't it enough that *he* had been there to question the potential jurors on Hamdan's behalf? Judge Williams asked Swift.

"It's not my jury or my members," Swift replied. "I'm not on trial. He is." Swift then noted that the Nazi saboteurs had been present for the duration of their commission, even though the proceedings were closed to the public for national security reasons: "That was because the fundamental right that had been set down from the Civil War was that the presence of the accused was essential to have a trial."

Keisler had five minutes for a final rebuttal. He began with a tribute to Swift: "Commander Swift filed a next friend habeas petition against his commander in chief and he's argued here that lots of things the president has done are unlawful. In doing that, he's acted consistently with the highest traditions of the legal profession and his military service. He's done his duty. The members of Mr. Hamdan's tribunal have their duty, too, and that's the duty to give a full and fair trial and to decide these issues under the facts and law as they see it . . . That's their job, that's their duty."

The case was submitted.

THIRTEEN

Who We Are

BACK TO THE EXCRUCIATING TASK of waiting, Swift used the spare time to work on his relationships. Moving back in with Debbie after so many years apart had been a bigger adjustment than either of them had anticipated. Debbie had quickly become annoyed at Swift's familiar quirks—his self-absorption, forgetfulness, tardiness, and the general state of frenetic chaos in which he lived. Much of the tension revolved around the house. Debbie had furnished it almost entirely herself, deciding on color schemes and furniture and decorating the walls with her undersea photography and a picture of the two of them on their sailboat in Puerto Rico. For months she had been itching to get the backyard in shape—something for which she needed help— but Swift was always too busy. Tensions grew when they were together and then festered when they were apart, which was often. They discussed couples therapy, but their schedules were too erratic. Instead, they spent a week at a mountain resort in Colorado that specialized in intensive relationship counseling. They returned home rejuvenated and committed to working on some of their problems.

Swift also turned to a professional to help him with Hamdan. After two years, his client still often treated him like the enemy. Swift's resentment was building, which he knew was a dangerous development. So in the spring he asked Emily Keram, a forensic psychiatrist whom he had been planning to use as an expert witness at Hamdan's commission, to sit in on a few of their meetings and analyze their increasingly contentious dynamic.

It didn't take Keram long to get a read on what was happening. She reminded Swift of the uncertainty of existence on Guantánamo, from the arbitrariness of the rules inside Delta to the prospect of indefinite detention. That uncertainty inevitably created rage. "As his lawyer, you're the only outlet for that rage," Keram said. "If you go in there and don't let him vent, if you react defensively, you're basically saying his rage is unjustified. If you do that, you will lose him."

Keram told Swift that he had to stop taking Hamdan's fury personally. It was hardly revelatory advice, but Swift found it reassuring. He had been coming down to Guantánamo for so long that he had started to lose his perspective on the place.

IF SWIFT WAS BECOMING desensitized to Guantánamo, its critics were growing ever more outraged. In April 2005, *Newsweek* published an inflammatory report that a Guantánamo interrogator had flushed a Koran down a toilet. The story was subsequently retracted, but the ensuing investigation uncovered even more egregious examples of Koran abuse; one interrogator had apparently urinated on the Islamic holy book. Emboldened by such disclosures, human rights organizations ramped up their rhetoric: Amnesty International called Guantánamo "the gulag of our times." The administration's defenders answered with hyperbole of their own. "The inmates in Guantánamo have never eaten better, they've never been treated better, and they've never been more comfortable in their lives than in this situation," said the Republican congressman Duncan Hunter.

Pressure was again building on Congress to insert itself into the debate over the executive branch's detention policies. On June 15 the Senate Judiciary Committee held hearings about Guantánamo. Swift was asked to testify. He had gotten the call two weeks earlier, the Monday morning after the *60 Minutes* piece—"Justice at Guantánamo?"—had finally aired. (While it was billed as the story of the military commission defense team, the segment was almost exclusively about Swift.)

Standing before the committee in his Navy whites, Swift focused his brief remarks on the circumstances under which he had been assigned to Hamdan, which he told the panel said everything about the lopsidedness of the commissions: "I was detailed pursuant to an order or a request by the chief prosecutor. That request said that the purpose in detailing me was to negotiate a guilty plea. It also said that my access to Mr. Hamdan was contingent upon the fact that he engage in those negotiations toward a guilty plea, and if he didn't, then we wouldn't have access anymore. In my military career as an attorney I'd never been detailed to represent somebody under those circumstances."

There was one more speaker after Swift, and then the panelists took questions from the senators. It had been a long morning. As he was wrapping things up at the end of the hearing, the committee's chairman, Senator Arlen Specter, noticed Swift shifting about anxiously in his chair.

"Commander Swift, do you have a comment?" he asked. "I note you straining to be recognized, so you are."

"Thank you, sir," Swift answered.

The first part of Swift's final remarks were basically unintelligible, and he very nearly lost his audience. But what followed was a moment reminiscent of that day almost exactly two years earlier in Katyal's office, when Swift had first persuaded him of the importance of the Geneva Conventions. It was as though Swift had ascended to higher ground and, in so doing, gained a fresh vantage point on the morning's debate. He returned once again to the commissions. "When we go to hold accountability, sirs, it says as much about the society that holds the trial, as it does about the individual before it," Swift told the row of senators facing him. "Our trials in the United States reflect who we are," he added, inspiring a subsequent editorial in *The New York Times* headlined WHO WE ARE.

Swift felt on top of the world. "For me personally, that was the peak," he later recalled. "I would never have a day like that again."

THE THREE-JUDGE PANEL was certainly taking its time. Judge Robertson had issued his decision just two weeks after the oral argument. Two *months* had passed since the court of appeals argument, and still nothing.

Katyal's third son, Harlan, named after his favorite Supreme Court justice, was born at 9:52 a.m. on June 22, 2005. It was the first morning in weeks that Katyal hadn't been sitting at his computer, checking the website of the D.C. circuit court of appeals, which posts its latest decisions at 10:00 sharp. Two days later Katyal was back at his computer. "I am shocked it is taking this long," Katyal wrote the team when a decision again failed to materialize.

The court of appeals typically goes on hiatus for the summer at the end of June, so when Katyal arrived at his office a little after ten o'clock on July 15, 2005, he was no longer expecting a decision before Labor Day. Katyal casually scrolled through his e-mails and then checked his voice mail. There was a message from the clerk at the court of appeals, letting him know that a decision had been reached in *Hamdan v. Rumsfeld*.

Katyal called up the court's website. The ruling was already there. It was a 3–0 decision, a clean sweep for the government. The court's opinion was surprisingly short, barely twenty pages—more than enough space, apparently, to dismantle every single one of their arguments. The brevity of the opinion underscored its dismissiveness, as though the lawsuit's many claims didn't even require serious adjudication.

In response to Katyal's separation-of-powers claim, the argument that the president had overstepped his constitutional powers by unilaterally convening Hamdan's war crimes trial, the court agreed with the government: Congress had implicitly authorized the president's military commissions when it gave him permission to respond to the 9/11 attacks with military force.

As for the Geneva Conventions, the court ruled that Hamdan was a stateless terrorist and therefore not entitled to their protections. Even if he did have certain rights under the conventions, the opinion continued, he could not invoke them in an American court because international treaties do not create individual rights. "If a treaty is violated, this 'becomes the subject of international negotiations and reclamation,' not a lawsuit," the opinion stated baldly.

Turning to the procedures of Hamdan's war crimes trial—the procedures that Judge Robertson had said were unlawful because they permitted the court to exclude a defendant from portions of his own trial and, in so doing, violated the Uniform Code of Military Justice—the court found that military commissions weren't obligated to comply with the UCMJ.

The opinion was soon all over the Internet, where it was championed by conservative bloggers and denounced by liberals. The Pentagon described the ruling as nothing less than a vindication of the Bush administration's approach to prosecuting suspected terrorists. In response to numerous inquiries, Katyal tapped out a quick statement for the press: "Today's ruling places absolute trust in the president, unchecked by the Constitution, statutes of Congress, and long-standing treaties ratified by the Senate of the United States. It gives the president the raw authority to expand military tribunals without limit, threatening the system of international law and armed conflict worldwide."

By this point Katyal's in-box was already filled with expressions of sympathy. "Very sorry to see the hatchet job that the D.C. Circuit did to Hamdan," wrote one of his Georgetown colleagues. "My condolences."

Katyal agreed that the decision was a hatchet job, not just wrong but much less thoughtful than he'd been expecting, particularly from Roberts. But he was nevertheless delighted. Never mind that they had lost every one of their claims, every which way. All that mattered was that the panel hadn't abstained and thus given the Supreme Court an easy excuse not to hear *Hamdan* on appeal. Within minutes of reading the opinion, he excitedly wrote Swift and the Perkins Coie team with the news: "hamdan decision released! unan loss, BUT ON MERITS it looks like."

In a few days they would start drafting a new petition to the Supreme Court, but there was a more pressing priority first: preventing the government from restarting Hamdan's trial.

The Pentagon had already said that if Judge Robertson's ruling was overturned, his commission would resume within six weeks. This would be a disaster. Even if they did manage to persuade the Supreme Court to take *Hamdan* on appeal, the case would not be heard for months—until long after Hamdan had already been tried, and almost certainly convicted, on Guantánamo Bay, which would take the wind out of their sails, to say the least. The government's opening statement to the justices would write itself: "This case is about a convicted war criminal." What could they possibly say to that?

The court of appeals decision would automatically go into effect in ten days. Katyal asked one of the members of his Yale team, Lisa Marshall, to research how to stop it. Their only option, she learned, was a request for a so-called stay of mandate, a motion to the court of appeals asking it to hold off temporarily on implementing its decision.

With the help of Marshall and a few other students, Katyal quickly drafted the motion. It argued that the Supreme Court might decide to hear the case, and in the event that it did, "irreparable harm" would be done to their client if his war crimes trial was allowed to proceed on Guantánamo in the interim. The filing of the motion automatically froze the status quo; it was now up to the three-judge panel to deny the motion if it wanted its decision to take effect.

For the time being, Robertson's ruling was intact. Hamdan's military commission couldn't go forward.

AFTER A LONG PERIOD of tranquillity and stability, the past several months had been tumultuous ones at the United States Supreme Court. The eighty-year-old chief justice, William Rehnquist, had taken an extended leave of absence during the winter to undergo surgery for thyroid cancer. He came back to the bench in March 2005 in a visibly weakened state that left little doubt that he would soon need a replacement. No sooner had Rehnquist returned than Justice Sandra Day O'Connor announced her retirement.

President Bush announced her proposed successor in the East Room of the White House on the evening of July 19, four days after the court of appeals handed down its decision in *Hamdan*. Katyal watched the news conference at home with Joanna while they made dinner for their children. After a brief introduction—"One of the most consequential decisions a president makes is his appointment of a justice to the Supreme Court"—Bush turned the microphone over to his nominee, John G. Roberts.

"Before I became a judge my law practice consisted largely of arguing cases before the Supreme Court," Roberts said. "That experience left me with a profound appreciation for the role of the Court in our constitutional democracy and a deep regard for the Court as an institution. I always got a lump in my throat whenever I walked up those marble steps to argue a case before the Court, and I don't think it was just for the nerves." Watching Roberts accept the president's nomination, Katyal's disappointment about the *Hamdan* decision evaporated; he was overtaken by a sense of pride in his old boss.

Only two weeks earlier, while they were still awaiting the court of appeals ruling, Katyal had been invited to dinner at the home of Arlen Specter, the chairman of the Senate Judiciary Committee, which would be vetting the president's Supreme Court nominees. Katyal had never met Specter, but the senator had been briefed on some of Katyal's law review articles and wanted his views on the Supreme Court. For three hours the senator peppered Katyal with questions about constitutional law. When the conversation eventually turned to names, Specter told Katyal he was having breakfast with President Bush in the morning. Whom should he recommend? Katyal answered without hesitation: "John Roberts."

After Roberts's White House news conference, however, Katyal started thinking more closely about the timing of the nomination. *Hamdan* had been decided just days ago, meaning that he must have been interviewing with the president while they were still deciding the case, a case in which the president himself was a defendant. Wasn't this a conflict of interest?

Katyal recalled reading a case many years earlier that presented a similar ethical question. He couldn't quite remember the details, but after Joanna and the kids went to bed he found the case on Westlaw. It concerned a federal judge who was thinking of leaving the bench and was interviewing for other jobs. A headhunter inadvertently arranged for the judge to meet with a law firm that had a case pending before him. A federal court of appeals in Chicago, in an opinion written by the influential judge Richard Posner, concluded that the judge had violated the canon of judicial ethics.

Should Roberts have recused himself from *Hamdan*, and because he hadn't, should the decision now be invalidated? That *Hamdan v.*

194

Rumsfeld had been reached in the middle of the summer, when the court was usually out of session, certainly didn't help appearances. It left the impression that the panel had rushed out the decision in advance of the nomination, to avoid any suggestion that Roberts had acted improperly.

The Justice Department was clearly concerned. Shortly after the announcement, Katyal got a peculiar call from Jonathan Marcus in the Solicitor General's Office. "Who would you say is the defendant in *Hamdan?*" Marcus had asked. Katyal started listing them all: Rumsfeld, Wolfowitz, Altenburg, Bush.

Marcus cut him off. "Didn't we agree to make it just Secretary Rumsfeld when Judge Robertson suggested changing the name of the petitioner from Swift to Hamdan?"

The conversation continued like this for several minutes, with neither Katyal nor Marcus mentioning what was really at issue: if President Bush had no longer been a named defendant in the lawsuit when Roberts ruled on the case, the potential ethics problem might be gone.

Katyal knew the matter wouldn't be so easy for the government to dispense with, but he wasn't sure whether or not to go on the offensive. He had recently started keeping an audio diary as he drove back and forth to his office—he wanted to record the emotional roller coaster of *Hamdan*, but he didn't have time to write in a journal—and for weeks he agonized into his digital voice recorder about what to do. Not only did Katyal still feel loyal to his old boss, but he was worried about the consequences of attacking someone with such a sterling reputation. It could also backfire strategically. For all of the disparate views represented on the Supreme Court, the justices were a tight-knit group. If the Senate did vote to confirm Roberts in the fall, his new colleagues were apt to take a dim view of anyone who had attacked his integrity. And yet Katyal recognized that he had an obligation to defend his client zealously, even if that meant arming congressional Democrats with the information that the new Supreme Court nominee might be guilty of an ethical breach.

Katyal eventually decided to consult a legal ethicist, who asked him if making a big deal out of this issue would invalidate the panel's decision. Katyal gave it some thought and answered that it probably wouldn't. Even if Roberts was retroactively forced to withdraw his vote, there would still be a 2–0 majority. Hearing this, the ethicist told Katyal that it would be okay to let it go. Katyal did just that.

The story hit the papers anyway. Hoping to quiet his critics, Roberts made public the timeline of his interviews with the White House. He had first met with Attorney General Alberto Gonzales on April 1, 2005, six days before the oral argument in *Hamdan*. Later, during the panel's deliberations, he had met with Vice President Cheney, White House Chief of Staff Andrew Card, Jr., and Deputy Chief of Staff Karl Rove. His final interview, with the president, had taken place on July 15, the day the *Hamdan* decision was released.

Katyal received dozens of calls from reporters, but declined to comment. He also fought off an effort by the Center for Constitutional Rights, a left-wing legal group that represented a number of detainees, to force Roberts to withdraw his vote.

Without *Hamdan*'s lawyers challenging Roberts's impartiality, the story quickly lost steam. The ethics issue was now a matter of public record, though, which benefited the *Hamdan* team in an unforeseen way: it discouraged the court of appeals panel from ruling on their request for a stay of mandate. In order for the panel to rule on the stay of mandate motion, Roberts would either have to recuse himself from the decision or not. Either way, he was likely to add fuel to the smoldering ethics controversy. The most prudent thing for the panel to do was simply to sit on the motion, leaving Judge Robertson's ruling in effect and preventing the Pentagon from restarting Hamdan's military commission while the Supreme Court weighed whether or not to hear *Hamdan v. Rumsfeld*.

KATYAL'S VIEW—that the drubbing at the court of appeals had helped the *Hamdan* team's chances for Supreme Court review—was by no means conventional wisdom. A persuasive case could be made, and in fact had been made, that by so summarily dismissing all of *Hamdan*'s claims, the court of appeals had in fact destroyed their chances of a hearing, that the appeals decision was, in the words of one influential legal blogger who had just concluded a clerkship with Justice Kennedy, "cert-proof."

For even the most compelling cases, the odds of gaining a hearing at the Supreme Court are always long. The justices receive about eight thousand petitions every year and agree to hear fewer than one hundred cases. This is partly a matter of resources—even with nine justices and thirty-five law clerks, the Court can do only so much—but it is mostly a matter of design. The Supreme Court knows that its rulings might as well be etched into a stone tablet; once a decision has been rendered, it will stand as the law of the land for generations to come. This is not a responsibility to be taken lightly. "We are not final because we are infallible," Justice Jackson once wrote, "but we are infallible only because we are final."

There are many reasons for the Court not to grant a petition for review. The justices may determine that the issues a particular case raises are not important enough to justify their attention. Or they may agree that the issues are important but conclude that the facts of the case at hand—the vehicle for those issues—are not well suited to speak to them. Sometimes the justices will decide that an issue is simply not yet ready for adjudication, meaning that there has not yet been enough lower-court debate to warrant their intervention.

But above all, the justices are animated by an overarching sense of humility. They know that they are unelected officials, appointed for life and accountable to no one. While they possess the power to resolve controversies by ruling on the lawfulness of actions taken by the other branches of government, they are generally reluctant to insert themselves into the political process. "The most important thing we do is not doing," as Justice Louis D. Brandeis memorably put it.

Never is the Supreme Court more reluctant to act than when faced with a challenge to the president's constitutional war powers in the midst of an ongoing conflict. These are no-win situations for the Court. Should it decide to enter the fray, it has two equally unappealing options: interfere with the president's efforts to keep America safe, or endorse presidential actions that may wind up looking draconian in retrospect. And because of the relative permanence of the Court's decisions, they can endure in infamy, long after the White House has changed hands, as monuments to the Court's poor judgment and dangerous precedents for those inclined to exploit them.

Justice Jackson warned of this very phenomenon in his dissent in *Korematsu v. United States*, the infamous Supreme Court decision that upheld the detention of Japanese-Americans in internment camps during World War II:

> A military order, however unconstitutional, is not apt to last longer than the military emergency. But once a judicial opinion rationalizes such an order to show that it conforms to the Constitution, or rather rationalizes the Constitution to show that the Constitution sanctions such an order, the Court for all time has validated the principle of racial discrimination in criminal procedure and of transplanting American citizens. The principle then lies about like a loaded weapon, ready for the hand of any authority that can bring forward a plausible claim of an urgent need. Every repetition imbeds that principle more deeply in our law and thinking and expands it to new purposes.

The lesson of *Korematsu* and the specter of that "loaded weapon" haunted the Court for years afterward, making the justices even warier of taking cases that dealt with the president's war powers, including his authority to try suspected war criminals before military commissions. In the wake of World War II, some one hundred habeas corpus petitions were filed in U.S. courts on behalf of both foreigners and American citizens who were being prosecuted before military commissions. The Supreme Court didn't hear a single one of them.

THESE WERE the broad historical currents that Katyal was swimming against as he began drafting their petition for Supreme Court review. But there were more specific forces working against him as well.

The Court's decision in *Rasul* made it clear that the government needed to start providing some legal process to the detainees. As far as the administration was concerned, it was doing just that by moving forward with the military commissions. What's more, the Court was now in flux. Roberts had not yet been confirmed, and no one knew if Rehnquist would be returning for the fall 2005 term. This state of uncertainty could deter the justices from taking on a case as significant and contentious as *Hamdan*.

Katyal would also be writing their petition without the benefit of the most common justification for Supreme Court review. Contrary to popular perception, the Court doesn't usually pick cases on the basis of their importance. It's much more common for the justices to choose to hear a case because different appeals courts have handed down conflicting rulings on one or more of the key issues undergirding it. In such instances, the justices often feel a responsibility to step in to lay down the definitive law of the land. But *Hamdan* represented the first challenge to the military commissions, so there couldn't be a conflict among the appellate courts.

Nor did Katyal have the benefit of time. The Supreme Court gives parties ninety days to file their petitions, but with the stroke of a pen the court of appeals could implement its decision at any moment, clearing the way for Hamdan's military commission to resume immediately. Katyal felt it was critical to file for a hearing right away, so the justices could consider whether to hear *Hamdan* at the first conference of their upcoming term. He told the team that the drop-dead date for the petition, their second and final shot at the Supreme Court, was August 8, which gave them just a couple of weeks.

AS A SUPREME COURT CLERK, Katyal had read hundreds of petitions for review and drafted hundreds of so-called cert-pool memos advising the justices on whether or not to take a particular case. He had learned a simple lesson from the process, one that had been powerfully reinforced by his reading of *Supreme Court Practice*, a 1,290-page textbook on Supreme Court litigation. Bad lawyers crammed every issue they could into their 30-page petitions, hoping that at least one of them would stick.

This was the exact opposite of what the justices were looking for. The Court likes to avoid sweeping rulings and thus prefers cases with narrowly defined issues. As Justice O'Connor once said, the Court's duty—symbolized by the bronze turtles that hold up the lampposts in its courtyard—is to move slowly, but steadily, under the light shed by the Constitution: "We guard the ground rules, so that the people, through their elected representatives, can run the country."

Smart advocates understood this. No matter how complex their case was, no matter how many different issues it raised, they selected at most two arguments for inclusion in their petitions for review.

And yet Katyal opted for the kitchen sink approach. Once again he had his student team take a first pass at the various sections, which he then set aside before blocking out his own draft. Unlike their previous petition to the Supreme Court, which they had filed months earlier in an effort to bypass the court of appeals, this one not only enumerated all of their complaints about the commissions but methodically rebutted the various holdings by their three-judge appellate panel. It was quite simply the densest document Katyal had ever written. He circulated the draft to the *Hamdan* team and several other trusted friends on July 21, 2005, six frenzied days after the court of appeals decision, and asked them all to get their comments to him as quickly as possible.

The reaction was almost uniformly negative. David Remes, a partner at the D.C. firm of Covington & Burling and a trusted legal confidant, thought it was too argumentative and unfocused. One of Katyal's Georgetown colleagues, a former lawyer in the Clinton Justice Department named Martin Lederman, told him he was going to overwhelm—and scare off—the Court with so many disparate arguments. Perkins Coie essentially urged him to tear up the petition and start over. Katyal's friend Tom Goldstein, the specialist in Supreme Court litigation, was the only one who didn't consider the petition a train wreck, and even he wasn't exactly enthusiastic about it.

Katyal recognized that the draft needed work, but he had no intention of changing his overall strategy. He was convinced that *Hamdan* was an unusual case that warranted an unusual approach. They weren't staking out a position on a couple of narrow legal issues; they were challenging an entire legal regime—its rules and procedures, not to mention the authorization for its creation. As a veteran of the cert pool himself, Katyal was confident that the clerk who drew the petition would take the time it required to digest and simplify all of the issues for the justices.

Katyal sent around a new draft of the petition on July 30 and got on a plane for Florida with Joanna and their three kids. Months earlier they had planned a vacation at the beach with Katyal's closest friend and his family, who were coming all the way from North Korea. Katyal still might have canceled, but it was the same friend whom he had been scheduled to go skiing with when his father first got sick in early 2004.

The morning after they arrived, McMillan called Katyal to express his concerns about the petition. It was still much too dense, he said, and presumed far too much knowledge on the part of the justices. Instead of wading into so many complicated issues, McMillan thought they should focus squarely on defending Judge Robertson's opinion.

Later that day McMillan sent Katyal a reworked version of the petition. He had jettisoned many of Katyal's arguments and regrouped others beneath new subject headings to make the petition easier to read. "I realize it will be difficult for you to abandon some of the very good material that I felt had to be cut out, but we must prioritize, as you know," McMillan wrote in the accompanying e-mail. He also suggested to Katyal that they forget about his self-imposed deadline and simply concentrate on writing the best petition possible.

Katyal remained adamant that they file the petition on August 8. He thanked McMillan for his edits and promised to circulate a new version soon. For the next several days he holed up in an empty bedroom on the second floor of the beach house—there was no desk in the room, so he sat on the bed with his laptop—and set down another draft. His children were passing around a nasty stomach bug, making it virtually impossible to get anything done during the day. To make up for the lost time, Katyal worked when everyone was in bed, sleeping no more than two or three hours a night.

On August 5, Katyal circulated a new draft. McMillan read it with exasperation. Katyal had incorporated only a handful of his suggestions and ignored his subject headings altogether. (Katyal thought they were an insult to the justices' intelligence.) McMillan called Katyal, and they had a long, testy conversation about the petition.

The house they had rented was right on the ocean, but Katyal didn't get to the beach until their last day. He buried his feet in the warm sand, depressed about the fact that he had just squandered a week with his family and his closest friend. His children were still sick and vomiting on the plane home. Their connecting flight in Atlanta was canceled, and they didn't get back home until after eleven o'clock.

Katyal stayed up until five-thirty in the morning finalizing the petition, which they filed with the Court that afternoon. Katyal thought it could have been better with a little more time, but he was nevertheless happy with it. The thrust of their argument was that if the Supreme Court failed to intervene in *Hamdan*, the court of appeals decision would stand as the law of the land for years to come, denying justice to the detainees and sullying America's reputation abroad, while exposing its troops to additional risks. Summing up their case for a hearing, Katyal wrote that the Court had not spoken on the matter of military commissions since the ratification of the Geneva Conventions and the enactment of the Uniform Code of Military Justice; some "modern guidance" was needed. Otherwise, "the sweeping authority given to the president may be his for several years before the Court has another opportunity to clarify even the most basic ground rules for commissions."

The petition concluded:

> If commissions are worth conducting, they are worth conducting lawfully and being perceived as so conducted . . . Before embarking on a dangerous experiment to break not only from common law and international law, but also from our own traditions of military justice, Americans and the rest of the world should rest assured that these principles will not be abandoned without at least review by the highest Court in the land.

The government aggressively opposed *Hamdan*'s petition, arguing in its own filing with the Supreme Court that the case had gone much too far already: Judge Robertson had taken an "extraordinary and unprecedented" step in halting Hamdan's military commission, and the court of appeals had simply set things straight by allowing the trial to resume. Until Hamdan's trial had run its course, the government wrote, any challenge to its fairness was, by definition, hypothetical and premature.

The government's brief also referenced the Defense Department's latest changes to the rules of the commissions, which it had announced only days after Katyal filed their petition, no doubt in an attempt to undercut the case for Supreme Court review. The Pentagon said the changes would bring the trials "closer to the traditional judge-and-jury system in the American courts." For instance, in a nod to the possibility that a defendant could be convicted on evidence that he was not allowed to personally rebut, the presiding officer would now be required to exclude evidence if he believed its admission would preclude a "full and fair trial."

Katyal too cited the recent changes in his response to the government's brief, their last filing with the justices: "With constantly shifting terms and conditions, the commissions resemble an automobile dealership instead of a legal tribunal dispensing American justice and protecting human dignity. The Government's attempt to evade certiorari through herky-jerky late changes merely demonstrates the system's inherent instability and the constitutional need for immediate judicial review."

By this point, classes were starting back up at Georgetown. For Katyal, it had been another summer consumed by *Hamdan*. Normally a prolific scholar, he hadn't written a substantive law review article since taking on the case. Aside from a few court appearances, almost all of his work had been behind the scenes. This was deliberate. Katyal wanted Swift to be the public face of *Hamdan*. Whenever reporters and TV producers called, he always gave them Swift's cell phone number and suggested they talk to him instead. But it still irked Katyal that he wasn't getting any credit. Over the summer the American Civil Liberties Union had awarded Swift and his JAG colleagues its prestigious Roger N. Baldwin Medal of Liberty, which included a twenty-five-thousand-dollar stipend, for their original amicus brief in the *Rasul* case, which Katyal of course had written.

In a matter of weeks the justices would be making a decision about whether to hear *Hamdan*. This was the moment Katyal had been working toward since his first meeting with Swift and Sundel. He had told them then that the lawfulness of the president's military commissions was too important an issue not to wind up at the Supreme Court. He still believed that now, though it occurred to him that if he was wrong, the enduring legacy of his two and a half years of work would be a unanimous and resounding defeat at the court of appeals.

FOURTEEN

The Supreme Court Responds

SWIFT AND THE REST of the JAGs had spent the summer of 2005 gearing back up for their trials. The appeals court ruling had galvanized the administration. In its wake, Secretary Rumsfeld had announced that eight additional detainees would soon be charged and that President Bush was about to designate more suspected terrorists for the commissions. Rarely a day went by when the Pentagon didn't reiterate its intention to resume Hamdan's war crimes trial as soon as possible.

In June, Swift had finally started the one-year graduate program in trial advocacy at Temple University that he had been slated to begin when he first joined the commissions two years earlier. The workload was light, Philadelphia was a short train ride from D.C., and he was required to be on campus only one day a week, so he could keep working on the *Hamdan* case on TAD—temporary active duty.

Now in its third year of existence, the office of the military commissions defense team was in transition. Sundel had recently left the Navy and taken a job with the International Committee of the Red Cross. Colonel Gunn too announced his intention to retire in July 2005, just as he would have been coming up for promotion to brigadier general, a promotion that had once seemed like a sure thing. Gunn described the decision to leave the Air Force as a personal choice, but it nevertheless confirmed the widespread belief inside the JAG Corps that the commissions were a career killer.

Gunn's replacement, the only applicant for the position, was Col. Dwight Sullivan, a short, blunt, outspoken Marine reservist who was something of a legend in the JAG Corps for successfully overturning the death sentence of a Marine sergeant who had killed his platoon commander. Gunn had felt an obligation to suspend his career concerns when he accepted the assignment as chief defense counsel. Sullivan truly had nothing to lose career-wise; in the Marine JAG Corps, reservists top out at colonel.

Gunn gave the JAGs a parting gift on his way out, a series of e-mails written in March 2004 by two senior military commission prosecutors to their boss, the chief prosecutor, Col. Frederick Borch. The prosecutors, Capt. John Carr and Maj. Robert Preston, both Air Force JAGs, had complained, in pointed terms, about the commissions, which they thought had been deliberately designed to ensure convictions. "I lie awake worrying about this every night," Preston wrote; "writing a motion saying that the process will be full and fair when you don't really believe it will be is kind of hard—particularly when you want to call yourself a lawyer and an officer."

Among other things, the prosecutors' allegations confirmed Swift's suspicions that the government had no intention of providing the defense with exculpatory evidence. Carr had accused Scott Lang of personally suppressing allegations of torture that Sundel's former client, the al Qaeda propagandist Ali Hamza Ahmad Sulayman al-Bahlul, had made to interrogators. "It is difficult to believe that the White House has approved this situation, and I fully expect that one day, soon, someone will be called to answer for what our office has been doing for the last 14 months," Carr wrote.

The defense team knew that Gunn had handed them a bombshell. They had attacked the commissions ad nauseam, but that was their job. For a pair of prosecutors to call the trials unfair gave the criticisms a whole new resonance, all the more so because both Carr and Preston had subsequently quit in protest. The JAGs simultaneously leaked the e-mails to *The New York Times* and *The Wall Street Journal* in late July. Both papers played the story on page one.

Hamdan, meanwhile, was happier than Swift had ever seen him. In July he had been moved to Camp 4, which was reserved for the most compliant prisoners, or Level One detainees, as they were known.

"Your boy's been moved to Camp 4," the deputy staff judge advocate told Swift, informing him of the news. "You'd better be satisfied now."

Unlike the rest of the detention facilities on Guantánamo, Camp 4 resembled a conventional prisoner of war camp. Detainees lived in communal barracks, ate and prayed together, and spent much of the day outside playing soccer and volleyball or just sitting in the shade talking. Hamdan called it Paradise Camp.

Swift's relationship with Hamdan was instantly transformed into that of a normal attorney and client. He would bring Hamdan something to eat, update him on the case, and that was that. "He doesn't need us anymore," Schmitz told Swift.

For Swift, it was a relief not to have to listen to Hamdan complain about his failure to deliver Hamdan's requested comfort items or to have to endure the tantrums that invariably accompanied his departure. But he couldn't help worrying. Swift recognized that he and Hamdan had something in common: they both were hard to miss. The guards all knew Hamdan—not as bin Laden's driver, but as Detainee 149, the prisoner who turned every order into a negotiation. Swift told Hamdan something that someone had told him as a plebe at the Naval Academy: Try to finish every race in the middle of the pack; that way no one will notice you. The message had never sunk in for Swift, but he hoped that it might for Hamdan.

It didn't.

Hamdan lasted all of five weeks in Camp 4. There were conflicting accounts of his ejection from paradise, Hamdan's and the government's. According to Hamdan, a guard had told him and a group of detainees to come back inside, even though their exercise period wasn't yet over. Hamdan had tried to explain that they were still entitled to more time outside, but the guard refused to listen. As it turned out, though, at least according to Hamdan, the guard inadvertently locked the door behind him, leaving Hamdan and the other detainees no choice but to stay outside. Eventually, Hamdan said, the door was unlocked to allow another group of detainees to come out, but at that point the guard was gone, so they saw no reason to go inside. According to the government, Hamdan had argued with the guard about their exercise time, encouraged the other detainees to defy his order, and then become verbally abusive to a senior officer on his cellblock. He had thus lost his Level One, or most compliant, status.

The timing of Hamdan's eviction from Camp 4 was terrible. The detainees had recently launched a prisonwide hunger strike to demand better treatment. The government had been sufficiently worried about the prospect of someone's starving himself to death to begin negotiating with a council of detainees who called for a suspension of the strike, but the talks had quickly broken down, leaving the prisoners more bitter than ever. There were riots in several cellblocks, and in the middle of August 2005 the detainees resumed their strike with fresh resolve. Making matters worse, a prisoner and influential religious leader inside the camp issued a ruling that it was okay for detainees to violate the Islamic prohibition against suicide if it was done for the common good.

Seething over his ejection from Camp 4, Hamdan joined the protesters. In September, he refused to meet with Swift for the first time. A few days after Swift returned to Virginia, he got a call from a civilian defense lawyer on Guantánamo informing him that Hamdan had been rushed to the medical clinic at Camp Delta and put on an IV drip after refusing all food and water for forty-eight hours. Swift flew back down the following day. This time he was able to see Hamdan and even persuade him to eat a few bites of jerk chicken—Swift told him it would give him more strength for the hunger strike—but Hamdan's intransigence and despondency continued.

Swift wasn't just battling Hamdan's anger over his expulsion from Camp 4; he was dealing with the emotional fallout from Katyal's last trip to Guantánamo. Katyal had come down in late August to discuss the status of their lawsuit with Hamdan—he had drawn a new diagram of the court system, this time with an arrow indicating that Roberts had been promoted to the Supreme Court—and to tell him about their petition to the justices. Katyal had told Hamdan that their case was as good a candidate as any for review, but stressed that the odds of getting a hearing at the Supreme Court were always long.

Swift knew all about the defense lawyer's tactic of underpromising and overdelivering, but Hamdan was no ordinary client. They had a more pressing concern than inflated expectations: losing Hamdan altogether. They needed to give him a reason to stay alive and keep fighting.

Swift did everything he could to sound optimistic. Even if the Supreme Court did deny their petition, he told Hamdan, they could still win an acquittal at his military commission. The pressure on the Bush administration to close Guantánamo was increasing. It was a long battle, Swift said, and things were slowly turning in their favor. They had to maintain their resolve.

Hamdan was unmoved by such platitudes. He wanted concrete results. Specifically, he wanted Swift to get him transferred back to Camp 4. Swift said he was trying to and showed Hamdan the letter he had written to the staff judge advocate explaining the "misunderstanding" that had led to his client's having been kicked out. But as he told Hamdan, this wasn't like forcing his transfer into the general population after Robertson's ruling. He didn't have a judge's order to wave in front of the prison's administrators. It was a discretionary call, and Hamdan hadn't done himself any favors by joining the hunger strike.

Hamdan was back to complaining about his comfort items too. Schmitz often took his side, urging Swift at least to allow Hamdan to hang on to his uneaten snacks after their meetings. The worst thing that could happen, Schmitz said, was that they would be confiscated from his cell.

Swift was hardly a stickler for protocol, and he felt enormous pressure to appease Hamdan. Yet with their request for review now pending before the Supreme Court, he knew that all eyes were upon them. They needed to be especially vigilant about following the rules.

Hamdan sank to new depths. "It was worse than the darkest days at Camp Echo," Swift would recall. "Fury followed by tears, followed by withdrawal and depression."

HINDU CUSTOM DICTATES that the bodies of the dead be cremated and their ashes released along the banks of the Ganges River, so in late September 2005, Katyal, along with his mother and sister, headed off to New Delhi. Katyal wasn't exactly thrilled about the timing of the trip. The Supreme Court justices were officially on recess until the first week in October but were scheduled to meet on the last Friday in September to dispense with as many of the summer's petitions as possible. The list of petitions that it had granted would be made public the following Monday; Katyal would still be in New Delhi.

As a child, Katyal had gone to India every year, usually for a few weeks during the summer. His mother was born in what is now Pakistan, but her family, which was Hindu, had been forced to flee during the partition of 1947. She was ten years old when they resettled—with nothing—in the Punjab province of northern India.

The youngest of twelve children, Katyal's mother had grown up in a very poor, close-knit household in which getting through each day was often a group effort. For Katyal, the result of this was a sprawling, intergenerational thicket of cousins, uncles, aunts, and grandparents, all of whom would drop whatever they were doing to play or talk with him when he visited. For a child of immigrants used to grappling with the push and pull of assimilation in a big American city, the trips were enormously comforting.

But by the time Katyal was a freshman in college his family had stopped making regular visits to India. His maternal grandmother had died, relieving his mother's feeling of urgency to go every year, and it was harder to extricate Katyal and his sister from their commitments at home. Katyal spent two months in India after graduating from college but had not been back since then. That had been fourteen years ago.

During the twenty-three-hour flight Katyal thought little about *Hamdan*. He was looking forward to seeing all of his relatives but wished the circumstances were different.

Upon their arrival, Katyal and his family would be staying with one of his more prosperous cousins, Sanjeev Malhotra, an engineer who lived with his family in a relatively spacious apartment in New Delhi. Although their plane landed at two in the morning, Malhotra picked them up at the airport and drove them to his home, where the ritual of deciding who would sleep where began.

As a boy, Katyal had grown accustomed to sleeping on concrete floors when he visited India. It was a concession he had complained bitterly about when he was younger, but as soon as he became an adult, his relatives refused to allow him to sleep on the floor, no matter how much Katyal insisted. (Even more unthinkable, of course, was the thought that Katyal or anyone in his family would ever stay in a hotel.) Katyal almost always ended up in a bed, with one of his cousins or aunts and uncles assuring him that they were quite comfortable on the drafty concrete. This visit was no different, though because of his father's death, people were even more solicitous than usual. Katyal protested for a while but eventually agreed to share Malhotra's bed with his mother and Sonia.

On the third day of their stay, Malhotra took Katyal and his family to the place where they would deliver his father's ashes. It was an intensely emotional day, made all the more so by the otherworldliness of the ritual that it entailed. After a four-hour drive from New Delhi, they stopped just outside a town called Hurduwar, along the Ganges. Once they had crossed into town via a footbridge, Katyal gave his father's name—Surinder Katyal, son of Ramey Katyal—to a random villager, who proceeded to lead them through a series of alleys and into a trinket shop. Katyal was not reassured. Was this a scam? But in the back of the shop was a Hindu priest, one of hundreds in Hurduwar responsible for maintaining the records of tens of thousands of families. In what seemed like a miracle, the priest found the name of Katyal's father quite easily in a huge scroll of names. He then took Katyal and his family out to the crowded banks of the Ganges, where he mixed his father's ashes with some water, said a few prayers, and placed the ashes in the river.

Katyal and his family spent the next several days being hugged, fed, and attended to by friends and relatives. It wasn't until the day of the Supreme Court announcement, about a week into their stay, that Katyal's thoughts returned to *Hamdan*.

The Court's decision on whether or not it would hear the case was expected at 10:00 a.m. in Washington—7:00 p.m. in New Delhi. Katyal's family had been invited to dinner at a cousin's apartment that night. Katyal was hoping to beg off, as he wanted to be at a computer, monitoring the legal blogs for news, but his mother was adamant. The cousins had spent two days preparing all the dishes they remembered

Katyal's liking best from his last visit, and the twenty or so people who were going to be there had been clamoring to see them since their arrival.

The apartment, one of hundreds in an anonymous concrete tower in an industrial part of town, was tiny, crammed with relatives, and suffused with the smell of green banana curry. Relieved to discover that he had cell coverage, Katyal made small talk and waited for his BlackBerry to ring. At a few minutes after seven, it did.

It was Swift, who got straight to the point: "We didn't get it."

Swift was uncharacteristically subdued. He had been deeply disappointed himself when he read the Court's new list of orders only minutes earlier, but he was sure that Katyal, whose sights had been set on the Supreme Court from the beginning, would have an even harder time with the news. Swift also knew there was no way to spin it. Katyal had told him before he left that this was going to be it—their final shot at a hearing.

Swift was right. Katyal was devastated. His mind immediately started tallying up the damage: three years of his life essentially wasted, and—he had to face facts—it might well have been entirely his fault. How many petitions had he read as a clerk? And how well did he know the rule about keeping them simple? Everyone had told him to streamline his argument, but he thought he knew better. He had gambled and lost.

Katyal's mother tried to console him, reminding him of how he'd felt after the 2000 election dispute. Katyal had considered the Supreme Court's decision to halt the recount of ballots in Florida profoundly undemocratic. Having always put so much faith in the wisdom of the justices—their ability to stand above politics—he had been deeply disillusioned by the experience. His bitterness toward the Court had lingered. Katyal had not returned to the Supreme Court building for almost three years afterward.

"Don't you remember what they did to you in the *Gore* case?" his mother said. "Did you really think they were going to go against the president?"

Later that night, after they had returned to Malhotra's apartment, Katyal walked twenty minutes to the nearest Internet café to check his e-mail. He had asked Swift to get Tom Goldstein's read on the situation. It certainly wasn't good news that the justices hadn't granted their petition, but maybe there was some room for hope. Could they still agree to hear *Hamdan* at one of their forthcoming conferences?

"I would say that the tea leaves are poor, but not definitive," Goldstein wrote in an e-mail that Swift had forwarded on to Katyal. "It is possible they talked about it yesterday and wanted to think it over some more. I would say, however, that indications are negative, unfortunately."

Two days later, as he and his family were preparing to return home, Katyal glimpsed some hope when the Court released its first list of rejected petitions, and *Hamdan* wasn't on it. Instead, the case had been relisted for discussion at the next conference. Perhaps, Katyal thought, the justices simply hadn't yet made it through all of the petitions from the summer.

On October 10, when the next list of granted cases was released, again *Hamdan* wasn't included. Neither was it on the list of rejected petitions a few days later. Katyal now felt somewhat more optimistic. Maybe one of the justices was still on the fence.

There was nothing left to do legally, but as a clerk Katyal had observed that the Court's reputation for insularity notwithstanding, the justices were far from ignorant about the outside world. He figured that if he could encourage enough influential people to weigh in on the importance of the issues raised by the case, it might be enough to sway the critical vote.

Over the course of the next several days, Katyal reached out to every law professor, human rights lawyer, and legal journalist he could think of to ask them to write a *Hamdan*-related piece. Articles were soon pouring forth in a wide range of print and Internet publications, all variations on the same theme: "Hear Me, Hear Me: The Case of the Year That the Supreme Court May Duck," as the title of a story in *Slate* magazine put it. In Katyal's mind the outlet didn't matter, as long as there was a link to it on one of the blogs that he knew were avidly read by Supreme Court clerks, who would presumably pass it along to the justices.

On October 14 the justices again took no action on *Hamdan*. Katyal responded by asking one of his researchers, Josh Friedman, to gather signatures from law professors for a petition urging the justices to hear the case.

The justices skipped their next Friday conference but met again on October 28, 2005. Katyal had jury duty on the following Monday, so he couldn't plant himself in front of a computer, but during voir dire Katyal discreetly checked his BlackBerry; the justices still hadn't made a decision on whether or not to hear *Hamdan*.

Katyal was still trying to put a positive spin on things, to somehow will the Court to take the case, but his optimism was starting to fade. Over the past several weeks more than a dozen *Hamdan*-related articles had been published and 450 law professors from across the country had signed the petition to the Supreme Court, and still nothing. If the justices really intended to grant *Hamdan*'s petition, wouldn't they have already done so?

Goldstein thought the most likely scenario was that the justices had already voted to deny their petition but that they were waiting to announce their decision because one of the members of the more liberal wing was writing a dissent. Another theory was that it was the liberal justices who were opposing the petition. They might have thought the Court's conservative wing would carry the day if *Hamdan*'s petition was granted and thus preferred not to make the court of appeals ruling a matter of nationally settled law.

Katyal's colleague Martin Lederman told him over dinner that all of the ink he was generating for the case was a waste of time. Katyal didn't necessarily disagree, but he felt compelled to keep at it. He was already haunted by doubts about his unconventional petition for review. He didn't want to have any more regrets about not doing everything in his power to persuade the justices to hear *Hamdan*.

Swift didn't see the point of Katyal's endless gyrations either. Nevertheless, he mentioned to Katyal in early November that his uncle, the retired admiral who had come to his rescue when he had run into trouble at Annapolis, was friendly with a former big shot in the CIA who knew a ton about Afghanistan. Swift couldn't quite remember his name, but maybe he could write something?

"Was it Milt Bearden?" Katyal asked.

"Yeah, that's him," Swift said.

Bearden was something of a legend in national security circles. During the 1980s he had been in charge of the CIA's covert support to the Afghan resistance against the Soviet occupation. He had subsequently been awarded the CIA's highest honor, the Distinguished Intelligence Medal.

Swift and Katyal tracked Bearden down on the set of the spy film *The Good Shepherd*—he was serving as a consultant—and asked him to write an op-ed. "What would it say?" Bearden asked. Katyal told him about the case, and he agreed to draft something.

Bearden's op-ed ran in *The New York Times* on the morning of Friday, November 4, the day of the Supreme Court's next conference. He focused on the Geneva Conventions, pointing out that when he served in Afghanistan under President Reagan in the 1980s, America's policy had been to urge both the occupying Soviet forces and the Afghan resistance to honor the conventions and treat all prisoners according to established rules. "A unilateral change in those rules dictated by America—the latest in the line of foreign powers to find themselves in Afghanistan—is not only unseemly, but would also put our troops there and elsewhere in the struggle against terrorism in harm's way," Bearden wrote. "The questions of applicability and enforcement of the Geneva Conventions posed by the *Hamdan* case should not go unanswered by the Supreme Court. We are a better nation than that."

MONDAY, NOVEMBER 7, got off to a bad start for Katyal. He had a hard time getting his children fed and out of the house, and his middle son, Calder, then two and a half, was clinging to his leg and refusing to let go when he dropped him off at preschool.

On the drive to his office, Katyal got into an argument with Swift. Neither one of them can remember what it was about, but they had been talking almost every day during this long period of limbo and were on each other's nerves. Katyal was annoyed by the way Swift spoke about the Supreme Court, his habit of referring to the justices by their first names as he unspooled his theories about why they had not yet responded to the *Hamdan* petition ("I'm going to be really disappointed in Nino if he doesn't step up on this"). For his part, Swift, who was accustomed to waiting out juries, was tired of Katyal's stubborn unwillingness to accept that there was nothing more they could do to help their cause.

Katyal finally got to his office at a little before ten, ready to start obsessively refreshing the legal blogs, but his computer froze. He called Swift on his speakerphone to continue their argument while he was waiting for it to reboot. At two minutes after ten o'clock, the announcement came. COURT TO RULE ON MILITARY TRIBUNALS, the headline on SCOTUSblog read.

"We got it!" Katyal screamed. He could hear Swift and the other JAGs, all of whom had been monitoring SCOTUSblog as well, shouting too.

Katyal immediately started firing off e-mails. "WE HAVE CERT!!!!" he wrote to the Yale team. The next one was to the Perkins lawyers, then Goldstein, and then his Georgetown colleagues: "We just got cert in *Hamdan* . . ."

The e-mails were soon pouring in as well, and his colleagues were stopping by every couple of minutes to congratulate him in person.

Katyal called Joanna at the hospital, who was thrilled but then quickly realized what it meant: four more months of briefs and moots, and this time for the Supreme Court. "So, I guess I won't be seeing you for a while," she said. Katyal assured her that it wouldn't be that bad, that he was already up to speed on all of the relevant issues.

It wasn't until he called his sister, though, that the full emotional weight of the news hit him. "I just wish Dad were here," Sonia said, and at those six words Katyal broke down. His father's death eight months earlier had of course been painful, but he hadn't fully absorbed the loss until now. Katyal remembered something a cousin who had recently lost his own father had told him at the memorial service in Chicago: that he would miss his father most when he had done something he knew would make him proud. Alone in his office, Katyal finished the phone call with his sister and wept.

That night, after his children had gone to bed, Katyal opened a Belgian beer, Leffe Brune, that he liked to drink on special occasions, and recorded a message in his audio diary: "I don't know what the future holds. I don't know why they granted the case. I don't even know who will be on the Court. And I am exhausted for now. I know my life is going to change and that there will be enormous pressures put on me. I'm nervous about all of that, and I'm nervous about making sure Charlie understands that this is my case and that I will be arguing it. But for now I'm going to celebrate."

Two days later Swift flew down to Guantánamo to give Hamdan the good news. On his way into Camp Echo, he ran into a civilian defense lawyer, Tom Wilner. "Congratulations on getting cert," Wilner said. "You really surprised a lot of us. But what you need to do now is focus on this bill that Senator Graham just introduced in Congress. If it goes through, you've won for nothing."

FIFTEEN

Getting to Five

KATYAL HAD FIRST HEARD about Graham's bill on Thursday, November 10, three days after their petition had been granted, from a Listserv of lawyers involved in detainee cases. Headlined "URGENT," the e-mail message said that Lindsey Graham, a Republican senator from South Carolina, was about to introduce a bill that would suspend the right of habeas corpus on Guantánamo Bay.

The ostensible reason for the legislation was to unclog the federal courts of the 150-plus pending detainee lawsuits that Graham said were undermining the war against terror. But the timing of its introduction left little doubt about the true purpose of the bill: to kick *Hamdan* off the Supreme Court's docket.

Katyal didn't give it a second thought at the time. He was already busy strategizing for the Supreme Court—their first brief was due in forty-five days—and he figured the human rights lawyer who had sent the e-mail was just being histrionic. Such a sweeping piece of legislation curtailing the power of the courts would surely be debated before the Senate Armed Services and Judiciary committees before coming up for a vote on the floor of the Senate.

Driving home that evening, Katyal heard on the radio that Graham had indeed introduced the measure and that the Senate had passed it, 49–42. Katyal still wasn't too concerned. He assumed that the legislation couldn't possibly apply to pending cases.

But that night, at home, he read the language of the bill in disbelief: "No court, justice or judge shall have jurisdiction to hear or consider an application for a writ of habeas corpus filed by or on behalf of an alien outside the United States who is being detained by the Department of Defense at Guantánamo Bay, Cuba." Katyal could find nothing to suggest that ongoing cases, either *Hamdan* or the dozens of other habeas suits that had been filed in federal court in the past year and a half, would be exempted. On the contrary, the bill stated explicitly that it was to be applied retroactively.

The news coverage the next day, including a front-page story in *The New York Times*, confirmed what Katyal already knew: the legislation was all but certain to render *Hamdan* moot. The instant Graham's bill became law, the government would file a motion to dismiss with the Supreme Court, and *Hamdan* would be finished.

In a panic-fueled rage, Katyal began feverishly contacting everyone he knew with any plausible connection to Capitol Hill, starting with Ron Weich, Senator Harry Reid's legal counsel, whom Katyal had worked with on the Supreme Court project for the Kerry campaign. "My heart goes out to you," Reich told him, "but we're the minority party, and there's already been a vote, so there's not much we can do."

Over the course of the weekend Katyal sent three thousand e-mails, enough to warrant a call from Georgetown's systems coordinator, who thought his computer had been hacked.

He also rang the doorbell of one of his neighbors whom he had never met, a Democratic representative from Michigan named Sander Levin. Levin's wife answered the door and said the representative was out of town. Katyal apologized for disturbing her and then told her all about Senator Graham's bill. She gave Katyal her e-mail address and asked him to write something up that she could forward to her husband.

Representative Levin got in touch with Katyal later that night and told him to expect a call from his brother, Senator Carl Levin, who had voted against Graham's amendment and, as the lead Democrat on the Armed Services Committee, would be the key to any possible change to it.

By the following morning, Katyal's fury had turned into dejection. Not only was *Hamdan* in serious jeopardy, but the Graham bill had rocked one of the central pillars of his judicial philosophy, the idea that the American people should trust their elected representatives over the courts.

Senator Levin called that night with some badly needed good news. He told Katyal that he had approached Graham immediately after the Senate vote and that Graham had agreed to work with him on amending the bill. Katyal stressed to Levin the importance of explicitly exempting *Hamdan* in the new version of the legislation. The senator said he'd be happy to help him and told Katyal to talk to his point person on the legislation, Peter Levine.

Someone had already put Katyal in touch with Levine, and he had gotten nowhere with him. Katyal had tried to explain to Levine that Graham's bill was unconstitutional and that Congress was setting a dangerous precedent by stripping the courts of jurisdiction in an ongoing case. Levine had told Katyal that if he thought the legislation was unconstitutional, he should challenge it in court.

"Senator, with respect," Katyal said, "I did talk to Peter Levine, and he wasn't very helpful."

Levin told Katyal to try him again first thing in the morning, which Katyal did.

"I just talked to you," Levine said, obviously annoyed.

"Well, yeah, but I talked to the senator last night and—"

"You did what?"

"I talked to the senator, and he said—"

"I'm going to get back to you."

Levine called back a few minutes later and explained the situation to Katyal. Senators Levin and Graham were planning to reintroduce the new legislation as a bipartisan measure in a couple of days. All the details had already been worked out. The new bill would give detainees restricted access to the federal courts. Katyal asked about military commission defendants. Those who had been convicted, Levine said, would be permitted to challenge their verdicts at the D.C. circuit court of appeals.

To Katyal, this was hardly a solution. The bill was essentially going to write into law what the government had been arguing all along, that the federal courts should not hear any military commission cases until the trials on Guantánamo were over.

Katyal angrily told Levine that as far as *Hamdan* was concerned, this change was meaningless. Their case had already passed through the D.C. circuit court of appeals. What's more, they weren't appealing a verdict; they were challenging the entire military commission system. They wanted to make their challenge *before* Hamdan's trial, not after, and they wanted to do it at the Supreme Court. Nothing less than a clear exemption would do.

Levine wasn't interested in discussing the matter any further. The deal had been struck between the senators; their staffs were already drafting the new version of the bill.

Katyal needed another strategy. If Congress wouldn't expressly exempt *Hamdan* from the legislation, his only hope was to suggest subtle tweaks to the proposed legislation, tweaks that looked innocuous enough—if they were noticed at all—but that would help him build the argument that the law wasn't intended to kick *Hamdan* out of the Supreme Court.

It was a very particular kind of lawyering, the gentle massaging of a document to open it up to alternative interpretations. Katyal had to suggest as few changes as possible, so as not to provoke the antagonism of Republicans who didn't want Levin watering down the bill. But the changes had to be significant enough to allow them to make a credible argument to the Supreme Court that Congress had intended to grandfather *Hamdan* when it passed the legislation. For instance, by adding the words "effective immediately" to provisions of the bill that did not deal with habeas corpus but leaving it off those that did, they could make a plausible case that the provisions that governed habeas petitions like *Hamdan*'s were not intended to apply retroactively.*

Katyal brought his political skills to bear as well. The wording of laws is often murky, the result of endless rounds of compromise among lawmakers. Thus, when judges are called upon to divine a statute's meaning, they must sometimes look beyond the specific lan-

* Katyal's strategic approach was inspired by the 1997 Supreme Court case *Lindh v. Murphy*, which addressed the question of whether a statute that cut off federal court review applied to pending cases. In that case, the justices had ruled that because Congress had expressly written into the bill that certain provisions *did* apply retroactively, a "negative inference" arose that the rest of the provisions *did not*.

guage to the official statements made by Congress before its passage. Katyal wanted to make sure that he'd be well armed with such statements—legislative history, as they're collectively known—when the time came to beat back the government's inevitable motion to dismiss. Toward that end he lobbied a handful of influential Democrat senators to state for the record that the new bill didn't apply to pending cases. He was essentially urging them to build a paper trail to support his interpretation of the legislation. Even if the legislation was—at best—unclear on this score, its signers could be unequivocal about what they thought it meant.

Levine refused to show Katyal the bill before it was reintroduced in the Senate on November 14, but Katyal managed to get a copy that night from an aide to another senator. Katyal printed it out and read it anxiously at his kitchen table. All of his tweaks to the effective date were there, but so too was the line stating that all challenges to the military commissions were to be made after a verdict had been rendered and could be brought only in the D.C. circuit court of appeals. *Hamdan* was going to be kicked out of the Supreme Court.

Katyal had been dealing with the legislation on his own—the legal work was extremely technical, and neither Swift nor the Perkins lawyers had any contacts on Capitol Hill—but he'd been keeping everyone apprised of all of the twists and turns. Now he e-mailed them with the bad news: "I think we are doomed."

Katyal continued to study the eight-page amendment, looking for a way out. After about thirty minutes he found one. The drafters of the bill had made a subtle but important error: read a certain way, the section of the amendment that limited the challenges to military commissions only to posttrial litigation didn't seem to apply to *Hamdan*. It was a technical mistake, no doubt the inadvertent result of sloppy drafting, yet to Katyal it made all the difference in the world. It would give him a foothold when he had to argue to the justices that the legislation wasn't intended to affect *Hamdan*.*

Katyal e-mailed his interpretation to the team. The Perkins

---

*The amendment's language stated: "The jurisdiction of the United States Court of Appeals for the District of Columbia under this paragraph shall be limited to an appeal brought by or on behalf of an alien . . . for whom a final decision has been rendered." Katyal lawyers remained pessimistic. Goldstein acknowledged that it was their best shot at keeping *Hamdan* on the Court's docket, but he didn't think they were likely to succeed, nor did his colleague, Kevin Russell. Katyal disagreed, and his spirits rose.

The new amendment met with overwhelming approval in the Senate. Senator Levin explained during his brief remarks on the floor that it addressed one of the problems with the first Graham amendment, that it would have stripped the courts of jurisdiction in all pending cases. The new amendment, Levin continued, would do no such thing. "For instance," he added, "the Supreme Court jurisdiction in *Hamdan* is not affected."

Katyal's biggest concern now was that the text of the bill would change for the worse. It still had to get through the more conservative House of Representatives, as well as a closed door conference of the House and Senate Armed Services committees, before returning to both the Senate and the House for a final vote.

The next month was excruciating. The deletion of a single phrase, the words "under this paragraph," would cause Katyal's entire reading of the amendment to collapse. He spent hours on Capitol Hill, impressing upon various House and Senate staffers the importance of preserving the language *exactly* as it was. His greatest worry was that another lawyer might notice his loophole and publicly mention it. He was especially concerned about his Georgetown colleague Marty Lederman, a shrewd lawyer and a prodigious blogger on a legal affairs website called Balkinization. Katyal asked him not to post anything about the issue, and Lederman said he wasn't planning to.

The bill emerged from the conference in the middle of December. After a little prodding, a lobbyist for the detainees told Katyal she had a copy. She wouldn't e-mail it to him, but she agreed to let him come over to her house and look at it. Katyal's heart raced as he read the bill. The loophole had not been closed. He could only hope now that it would be enough to keep *Hamdan* on the Supreme Court's docket.

As Katyal had expected, the government chose to interpret the bill

seized on the words "under this paragraph," concluding that the amendment would require the federal courts to abstain when detainees sued "under this paragraph." However, if they sued using other laws, such as habeas corpus, abstention wouldn't necessarily be required.

differently than Senator Levin. When President Bush signed into law the Graham-Levin bill, now known as the Detainee Treatment Act, he issued a signing statement, an official document in which the president lays out his interpretation of a new statute, declaring that it applied to all cases, including *Hamdan v. Rumsfeld*. It would be only a matter of time before the Justice Department moved to have the case dismissed.

ALL THE WRANGLING over the Graham-Levin bill had prevented Katyal from making much headway on their Supreme Court brief. The deadline was only five weeks away, and he didn't have much more than some notes he'd jotted onto a legal pad and a handful of pages he'd written before disappearing into the fight over the legislation.

The first person Katyal turned to for advice in reframing their argument for its final test was Tom Goldstein. A slight, cheerful-looking man with tightly cropped, prematurely gray hair, Goldstein had, at the tender age of thirty-five, already appeared before the justices sixteen times. This staggering number of arguments notwithstanding, Goldstein was something of an anomaly in the rarefied world of Supreme Court litigation. His résumé was conspicuously devoid of Ivy League pedigree—he had attended American University Law School at night—and he worked not for one of the elite white-shoe firms that handle most of the cases at the Court, but for himself. His firm, himself and two other lawyers, was called Goldstein & Howe, the Howe being his wife, Amy. He had launched the practice several years earlier from the laundry room in his house, cold-calling lawyers and pitching them on his ability to ride one of their cases to the highest court in the land. Driven by the hunger of an outsider, Goldstein had improbably fashioned himself into a prominent Supreme Court advocate. Many of his colleagues at the genteel Supreme Court bar still considered him something of a glorified ambulance chaser, but Katyal had great faith in his understanding of the Court's singular style of reasoning.

Goldstein urged Katyal to approach the argument with modest aims. This was a general rule of thumb when litigating at the Supreme Court, but with respect to *Hamdan*, it seemed particularly advisable. The last time the justices had spoken on the war on terror, they had not said much. As significant as it was, the Court's ruling in *Rasul* was in fact quite narrow: the justices had opened the courthouse doors to the detainees, but had said nothing about what sorts of claims might succeed once they passed through them. Also, *Rasul* had concerned a person who was being indefinitely detained without charges, access to a lawyer, or any sort of judicial process. Hamdan had been assigned a defense attorney, who visited him every month, and had been given the opportunity to argue his innocence in a military commission that was already under way.

But there was an even more compelling reason to tread cautiously: Justice O'Connor, who had delayed her retirement after Chief Justice Rehnquist's death in September, was stepping down at the end of the year, before the Court would be considering *Hamdan*.

Katyal had been convinced from the moment Swift first pitched him on Hamdan that he would make an ideal petitioner for O'Connor. The Supreme Court sits not simply to resolve disputes but to settle matters of law. As a result, most justices care less about the particulars of a case than the larger legal principles undergirding it. But O'Connor was the exception. She was a pragmatist. Unlike the other justices, who tend to ask hypothetical questions, she liked to press advocates on the specific facts of their case. Katyal was certain she would see that Hamdan was a bit player in al Qaeda, not the sort of defendant who warranted flouting international law and rocking America's constitutional order. He had grown only more confident in O'Connor's vote since signing on to represent Hamdan, most notably in the aftermath of Abu Ghraib, when she delivered a speech at West Point implicitly criticizing the Bush administration's decision to set aside the Geneva Conventions in the war on terror. "This country believes in protecting the basic humanity of all people," she said, "and that includes even our adversaries."

O'Connor was a swing justice, more conservative than the Court's liberals, but more liberal than its conservatives. With her on the bench, they had a good shot at a clear majority. But she would be gone, and her successor, Samuel Alito, was a defender of broad presidential power. They had traded a probable vote for to a probable vote against.

Because Chief Justice Roberts had ruled on *Hamdan* at the court of appeals, he would be recusing himself. Considering how he had voted, this looked like good news. The problem was that it left an even number of votes—four liberals and four conservatives. Many Supreme Court watchers, Laurence Tribe among them, were predicting a 4–4 tie, which was tantamount to defeat because it would leave the court of appeals decision intact.

With O'Connor gone, the critical vote clearly belonged to Anthony M. Kennedy. Of the four Republican appointees who would be considering *Hamdan*—Scalia, Thomas, Kennedy, and Alito—he was the one closest to the center and the one whom they had the most realistic shot at persuading. The question was how to get him.

Katyal started with Kennedy's opinion in *Loving v. United States*, a 1996 case concerning the court-martial trial of an Army private who had been convicted of murder. The verdict wasn't necessarily heartening—Kennedy had upheld the death penalty conviction—but the opinion included some promising language about the justice's understanding of the framers' view of military trials. "What they distrusted was not courts-martial *per se*," Kennedy wrote, "but military justice dispensed by a commander unchecked by the civil power in proceedings so summary as to be lawless."

Katyal soon discovered that the notion of the need for one branch of the government to check another was a recurring theme in Kennedy's jurisprudence. He was a full-throated champion of the framers' vision of divided government, and not just as a formula for power sharing among officials but as a means to protect liberty. He wrote in the 1998 case *Clinton v. New York*:

> Separation of powers was designed to implement a fundamental insight: concentration of power in a single branch is a threat to liberty. The idea and the promise [among the framers] were that when the people delegate some degree of control to a remote central authority, one branch of government ought not possess the power to shape their destiny without a sufficient check from the other two. In this vision, liberty demands limits on the ability of any one branch to influence basic political decisions.

The separation-of-powers argument had also been the central theme of Katyal's first forays into the military commission debate, his testimony before Congress and the subsequent law review article in which he and Tribe had claimed that the trials were illegal because Congress had not authorized them. The argument had since fallen by the wayside, though. The Perkins team considered it a sure loser in the lower courts, which would be bound by the holding in the *Quirin* case that the president possessed the authority to convene military commissions. Katyal didn't necessarily disagree. But they were at the Supreme Court now, where different rules apply. The Court's predisposition toward caution notwithstanding, it is less constrained by its own historical precedents than are the lower courts. The justices are chiefly concerned with finding the right answer to the questions before them, even if that means reinterpreting prior rulings to give themselves greater flexibility or overturning them altogether.

THIS WOULD BE the overarching narrative of their argument, but Katyal still needed to figure out which specific issues to emphasize in their brief and at the oral argument. Litigating at the Supreme Court is counterintuitive. In the lower courts, lawyers are generally inclined to present their strongest arguments in the starkest terms. At the Supreme Court, however, successful petitioners don't opt for their strongest arguments; they opt for the ones that are most likely to garner five votes. And they tend to frame those arguments as narrowly as possible, both in deference to the Court's preference to move incrementally and to create less room for disagreement among the justices. The underlying logic is simple: it's a lot easier to persuade five people to agree on something small than on something large.

"How do we get to five?" Katyal asked Goldstein and his partner, Kevin Russell.

After studying the *Hamdan* case record for a week, Goldstein and Russell came back to Katyal with a one-word answer: Conspiracy.

It was an argument that Katyal had treated only glancingly in his previous briefs. The gist of it was that conspiracy, the charge brought against Hamdan, did not constitute an offense against the laws of war.

Goldstein and Russell told Katyal that this was exactly the sort of claim that the justices would feel comfortable accepting in *Hamdan*. It was narrow, discrete, and it didn't require them to invalidate the whole military commission system.

At first blush, Katyal was an unlikely critic of the conspiracy charge. As an academic, he had written extensively in defense of America's conspiracy laws, which he considered a vital weapon in the fight against terrorism. Most criminal offenses don't occur until a crime has been committed, but conspiracy occurs the moment two parties *agree* to commit a crime. Thus, Katyal had argued, America's conspiracy laws allowed the government to stop terrorist plots before they actually took place. And because the conspiracy charge could be brought against any member of a criminal organization, regardless of the extent of his individual responsibility, it gave prosecutors leverage to lean on foot soldiers to testify against the leadership of terrorist groups like al Qaeda.

But Katyal had been advocating the use of conspiracy in *civilian* courts. To his mind, introducing it into the commissions was an entirely different story. Because conspiracy is such a broad, catchall charge, it's an easy one for prosecutors to fall back on when their proof of guilt is thin. The U.S. criminal court system has numerous protections against this: jury trials; judges who are insulated from politics; access to an independent court of appeals, nearly all of which were absent from the commissions.

Katyal liked the conspiracy argument. He was certainly steeped in the subject, and he had already found a powerful historical precedent to support the claim: at Nuremberg, American officials had rejected a Defense Department proposal to file conspiracy charges against German foot soldiers out of fear that it might, in the world's eyes, create a moral equivalence between low-level players and higher-ups and, in so doing, weaken the impact of the charges against the Nazi leaders.

And yet Katyal was worried that winning the conspiracy argument wouldn't amount to much of a victory. Even if the justices agreed that conspiracy wasn't a legitimate war crime, the government could simply re-charge Hamdan for aiding and abetting, and his military commission trial would resume.

Katyal wanted to ask the Court for more. Again, he believed *Hamdan* was unique. Unlike most cases before the Court, it involved numerous matters of unsettled law—from the charge, to the rules of the commissions, to the government's obligation to honor the Geneva Conventions, to the very question of whether or not the war on terror was, in fact, a war, and thus justified the use of war crimes trials.

And so instead of zeroing in on one or two of their arguments, as Goldstein had advised, Katyal decided to leave nothing out of their brief to the Supreme Court. His first draft was over one hundred pages long, more than twice the fifty-page limit. He spent two days cutting it back and then circulated an eighty-page draft to the team on December 12, 2005, three weeks before it was due at the Court.

By this point McMillan and Sipos were working on their own draft. They circulated it a week later, and on December 21 flew east to discuss the brief with Katyal, Swift, Goldstein, and Russell in a seminar room at Georgetown.

Katyal was dreading the meeting. He had already rejected the Perkins draft—he considered it "too facile"—and was not looking forward to rehashing the same debate that he and McMillan had been having for years now about the need to simplify his arguments. Katyal was hoping that Goldstein and Russell would deflect some of McMillan's criticisms, but he knew that they too thought his draft was unrealistically ambitious. (McMillan was actually counting on Goldstein and Russell to help him and Sipos talk some sense into Katyal.)

Katyal opened the meeting by thanking everyone for their hard work and urging them all to be brutally honest. "No one should have any hard feelings," he said. "Our job is to be as frank as possible about our best arguments."

McMillan spoke first. He didn't think the justices would buy Katyal's sweeping separation-of-powers claim, the argument that the commissions were unlawful because they had not been approved by Congress. He was certain the Court would find that Congress had authorized the commissions when it gave the president permission to respond to the attacks of September 11 in any way that he deemed necessary and appropriate. More recently, McMillan said, Congress had implicitly acknowledged the legitimacy of the military commissions when it passed Senators Graham and Levin's Detainee Treatment Act, which made numerous references to the commissions. "We have to move beyond the argument that the president does not have the power to set up this military commission—he does," McMillan said. "Instead, we should deal with the ways in which that power is defined and limited by international law."

McMillan also thought that Katyal was making too many arguments. He wanted to jettison the conspiracy claim altogether. Because its legitimacy as a war crime had not yet been debated in the lower courts, he didn't believe the justices would be ready to rule on it. Instead, he made the case for rebuilding the entire brief around one of their Geneva Conventions claims.

Goldstein and Russell agreed that Katyal's separation-of-powers claim was too extreme and that his draft was generally bulging at the seams, but they wanted him to ditch the Geneva Conventions altogether. They argued that a majority of the justices would agree with the court of appeals ruling that the conventions didn't confer any rights that could be enforced in U.S. courts. They again urged Katyal to focus all his energy on conspiracy.

Katyal had no intention of abandoning the Geneva claims. Ever since Swift had won him over with his first monologue, he had come to see the Geneva Conventions as central to their fight against the commissions. "What I want to do is force the solicitor general of the United States to tell the justices that the United States government does not have to give 'the rights indispensable to all civilized peoples' to those facing war crimes trials at Guantánamo," Katyal told the group, quoting a line from Common Article 3 of the conventions. "It is a claim with no credibility behind it whatsoever. We are going to have trials to decide whom to put to death and we won't even acknowledge that we will give the defendants the most rudimentary set of battlefield rights?"

The meeting lasted ten hours. It was contentious, but far more productive than Katyal had expected. He emerged from it with a new legal strategy. He wasn't going to cut out any arguments or scale back the ambitions of his separation-of-powers claim, but for every issue in the case, he would pair a broad argument with a narrow one. He would argue that Congress had not authorized Hamdan's commission when it authorized the president to answer the attacks of 9/11, but that even if it had, the trial was nevertheless unlawful because, among other reasons, the charge brought against Hamdan did not constitute a legitimate war crime, and the procedures themselves failed to meet the standards required by the Geneva Conventions and the Uniform Code of Military Justice. This way they would leave open the possibility of a dramatic ruling, while also giving the justices a narrower path to a favorable, if modest, decision.

Katyal was still in the midst of overhauling the brief when he and his family flew out to Chicago for Christmas a few days later. There were no desks in any of the bedrooms in his parents' house, so he worked on the dining room table. To drown out the sound of his children, he listened to his iPod; he'd asked a few of his Yale students to send him mixes of whatever they were listening to.

He finished a new draft shortly after midnight on December 27, 2005, and turned his attention to their amicus briefs, which were also due the first week in January. David Remes of Covington & Burling was overseeing the amicus effort, but Katyal had insisted on micromanaging the process. It's customary for parties at the Supreme Court to give blanket consent to anyone who wants to write on their behalf, but Katyal had opted not to, compelling groups to come to him individually for permission instead. He considered the amicus briefs an integral part of his litigation strategy—he hoped that demonstrating the support of a wide array of respected individuals would help offset the Court's natural tendency to defer to the president—and he wanted to control the message.

Katyal assembled thirty-seven amicus briefs in total, their authors ranging from prominent legal scholars to British parliamentarians to ex-American diplomats like Secretary of State Madeleine Albright. He also spent countless hours persuading groups and individuals *not* to file briefs on their behalf. *Hamdan* was already being billed as a landmark case. Virtually every human rights and civil liberties group in America wanted to insinuate itself into the litigation, both to advance its own agenda and to enable it to tout its involvement in this high-profile case to potential donors. Katyal didn't want to overwhelm the justices with amicus briefs and, in so doing, blunt the impact of the strongest ones. What's more, he was worried that some of them—filed ostensibly in support of his client—would wind up hurting their cause by staking out positions that were too radical.

He managed to turn away dozens of unwanted amicus briefs, but he couldn't stop them all. The savvier interest groups knew that even if he withheld permission, they could seek clearance directly from the Court, which virtually always granted it, so Goldstein suggested to Katyal that he ask the authors of the sanctioned amicus briefs to title them as a way of subtly distinguishing them to the Court.

By the time Katyal returned to Washington on Friday, December 30, Goldstein and Russell, the Perkins lawyers, and the student team all had done extensive rewrites on his latest draft of the Supreme Court brief. He borrowed a laptop from Georgetown, set it next to two others on the desk in the office in his attic, and called up the different versions on the various screens. Using a special software program that allowed him to operate all three laptops from a single master computer, he started cutting and pasting what would become the final version.

Katyal was about to spend his third straight New Year's Eve drafting a brief on the military commissions. He took some solace from an e-mail from Col. Larry Wilkerson, Secretary of State Colin Powell's former chief of staff. Katyal had asked Wilkerson to join an amicus brief being filed by a group of retired admirals and generals arguing that the safety of American soldiers captured abroad depended upon applying the Geneva Conventions to all individuals in the custody of the United States. Out of a lingering sense of loyalty to the Bush administration, Wilkerson had declined, but he sent Katyal an unusually heartening rejection letter. "I believe you have the law, both domestic and international, on your side in this brief," Wilkerson wrote. "In a larger sense, I believe you have on your side the Constitution, the intent of its framers (the wiser ones anyway), and the political and cultural values of America. As a citizen and a soldier, I pray for your victory."

Katyal circulated a near-final draft of the Supreme Court brief a few days later. Goldstein and Russell still thought he was overreaching, and McMillan was still pushing for a radical restructuring, but time was running out. Katyal told everyone he was going with this version.

He continued trimming and polishing before finishing the brief at 1:45 a.m. on Friday, January 6, 2006, the day it was due. He slept for four hours, then drove over to Goldstein's home office. Goldstein was out of town, but his wife, Amy, and partner, Kevin Russell, both were there, and Katyal wanted them to proofread the brief before he sent it off. When they printed it, though, something looked wrong to Katyal. He counted the lines, and discovered three extra per page. It was due at the printer in forty-five minutes. Katyal called to say it was going to be a little late, and then hastily cut another page and a half before rushing it to the printer and then filing it with the Court.

The brief was divided into two sections—PETITIONER'S COMMISSION IS NOT AUTHORIZED and PETITIONER'S COMMISSION VIOLATES THE THIRD GENEVA CONVENTION—and began with a short preamble weaving all their claims into a single, coherent story. This "Summary of Argument," as it was called, made no effort to understate the scope of their challenge to the president, but it positioned the administration—not the petitioner—as the revolutionary party.

> The President has claimed the unilateral authority to try suspected terrorists wholly outside the traditional civilian and military judicial systems, for crimes defined by the President alone, under procedures lacking basic protections, before "judges" who are his chosen subordinates. He has further asserted the power to disregard treaty obligations that Congress ratified and the federal courts repeatedly have enforced, obligations that protect not only Hamdan but also American servicemembers. Such assertions reach far beyond any war power ever conferred upon the Executive . . . Our fundamental principles of separation of powers have survived many dire threats to this nation's security—from capture of the nation's capital by enemy forces, to Civil War, to the threat of nuclear annihilation during the Cold War—and those principles must not be abandoned now.

Once the brief had been filed, McMillan and Sipos went out for a celebratory drink near their office in downtown Seattle. McMillan thought it could have been more gracefully written and that it was still too cluttered with unnecessary footnotes and extraneous details, but he nevertheless felt it had turned out okay. Back upstairs, he sent Katyal a congratulatory e-mail. "You did a great job on the brief," McMillan wrote. "Win or lose, I think it's something we can all feel proud to be a part of, as we are discharging a duty we owe our countrymen and our children. Of course, we've still got plenty of work to do, but we should at least take the weekend to catch our breath at this milestone that we have reached, and steel ourselves for the next round."

SIXTEEN

Where's the Food?

JANUARY 12, 2006, marked the fourth anniversary of the opening of the detention facility on Guantánamo Bay. For all of the protests, the prison was still standing. Over the past year the United States had returned some 250 primarily non-Arab detainees to their home countries. This had taken some of the diplomatic pressure off Washington, but it also had the unintended effect of making the 500 or so predominantly Arab detainees who remained all the more cohesive, determined, and radicalized. The ongoing hunger strike had become so serious that the military had flown in five restraint chairs to strap down and force-feed recalcitrant prisoners.

Swayed by the rising tide of militancy and frustrated by the pace of a legal process they didn't understand, detainees had also been firing their American lawyers in droves. This had long been a concern for Swift, and it had become especially acute in the fall of 2005, following Hamdan's ejection from Camp 4.

In November 2005, when Swift told Hamdan that the Supreme Court had taken their case, Swift felt as if he had finally earned some breathing room. "Thanks be to God!" Hamdan had screamed upon learning the news, shouting loudly enough for every detainee within earshot to hear.

Swift was wrong. Less than a week later Hamdan was in trouble again, this time for allegedly shredding a T-shirt and a pillowcase. (Hamdan insisted that they were already torn.) As punishment, he was temporarily placed in solitary confinement in Delta's disciplinary wing. When he emerged in late November, Hamdan was moved into a small cellblock known as Tango, where he had only three cellmates, one of whom was Sundel's former client, Ali Hamza Ahmad Sulayman al-Bahlul, an al Qaeda propagandist with a reputation for persuading detainees to fire their lawyers.

Swift first heard about these developments secondhand. In late December 2005 he had asked Schmitz to go to Guantánamo without him. (Schmitz was not in fact allowed to see Hamdan on his own, but Swift arranged for the paperwork, and no one stopped him.) His first night on the base, Schmitz called Swift to tell him that Hamdan was dejected—they had finally arrived at the Supreme Court, yet his life had gotten worse—and furious; he'd apparently been demanding to see Swift for weeks.

Swift always tried to visit Hamdan at least once a month, but now that their petition had been granted he figured it would be okay to send Schmitz down in his place so that he could stick around and pitch in on the Supreme Court brief. The decision turned out to be a catastrophic mistake. Not only had Swift's efforts to contribute to the brief gone nowhere—he tried to draft some paragraphs on the laws of war and the Uniform Code of Military Justice, subjects he knew cold, but only tied himself in knots and eventually gave up in frustration—but he had just done what he had promised never to do: abandon his client.

Swift knew he had to move quickly and aggressively to mollify Hamdan. As soon as he got off the phone with Schmitz, he drafted an emergency motion to Judge Robertson asking him to compel his client's return to the general population of Camp Delta. He even went so far as to accuse the government of deliberately trying to undermine his relationship with Hamdan in order to jeopardize their pending case at the Supreme Court. And for good measure, the moment he filed the motion, Swift alerted *The New York Times* to its existence.

The Justice Department answered Swift's accusation in its own filing with Judge Robertson, describing Hamdan's transfer to cellblock Tango as a response to "a series of disciplinary problems" that had nothing to do with his relationship with his lawyer. A separate seven-page affidavit in support of the government from Col. Michael I.

Bumgarner, the commander of Guantánamo's detention operations, detailed Hamdan's misbehavior. Bumgarner characterized Hamdan as a rabble-rouser who had tried to incite other detainees to refuse meals during his brief stay in Delta's disciplinary wing. Hamdan had subsequently been transferred to Tango, the colonel wrote, because the other three detainees there "have personalities that are not likely to be influenced by Petitioner's disruptive behavior." At the same time, the government preempted Swift's request, moving Hamdan back into the general population "to avoid even the appearance of an attempt to interfere with Petitioner's relationship to his attorney."

With this, things appeared to have been resolved, but a week before Swift was scheduled to fly to Guantánamo in early January 2006, his first trip down in more than two months, he received a call from Guantánamo's staff judge advocate. Hamdan had been hospitalized after refusing nineteen straight meals and was in a restraining chair, being force-fed water and liquid nutrients.

Hamdan had refused meals before, but never for more than a few days. Swift had always considered his hunger strikes as much a show of solidarity with his fellow prisoners as a genuine form of protest. This one, though, was obviously different.

Two days later Swift was informed that there was some mail for him from Guantánamo at a secure facility in Crystal City. He walked over and picked up two letters from Hamdan, which he converted into PDF files and e-mailed to Schmitz to translate. Both had been written over the course of the past month. In the first, Hamdan said it was urgent that Swift come down to Guantánamo immediately. In the second, written a couple of weeks later, Hamdan told Swift he was fired.

If he didn't know that Hamdan was now being kept alive by feeding tubes, Swift might have been inclined to dismiss the letters as an attention-getting ploy; he had received "get down here now" letters from Hamdan before. Taken together, though, the collective meaning of the two letters and the hunger strike was hard to miss. "It was like a suicide note," Swift later recalled. "The guy was giving up. He was telling me, 'Enough already, I'm going to die.'"

Swift figured that if he flew down to Guantánamo now, Hamdan wouldn't meet with him. And even if he did agree to see him, Swift had nothing to offer Hamdan to appease him—no new pictures, letters, or snacks from home or the promise of a return to Camp 4, which, in light of his recent disciplinary problems, seemed more improbable than ever. Yet Swift knew that if he waited much longer, the situation would be irreparable. He decided to postpone his trip a few days and write Hamdan a letter.

Swift had written to Hamdan in the fall when he was on Guantánamo and Hamdan had refused to see him. But the tone of that letter had been formal and restrained: "Peace and blessings be upon you. I hope that this letter finds you in good health and that we may perhaps meet soon." This one was going to have to appeal to Hamdan's most basic human instincts.

As he thought about what to say, Swift recalled a lecture he'd heard at the Naval Academy given by an officer who had served in Vietnam. The officer said that his platoon had once been pinned down in a rice paddy. They were knee-deep in water with no way out when the sergeant of the platoon charged out of the shielding grasses, firing at the enemy's nest as he went. He was blown to bits, but had managed to give many of his men the cover they needed to escape. The officer telling the story said it had taken him years to figure out why the sergeant had done what he did. He hadn't done it for Lyndon Johnson, democracy, or even the flag. He had done it for the people who were most important to him: his platoon.

In his letter to Hamdan, Swift pressed him to keep fighting for the people who were most important to him, his family. He showed a draft to Emily Keram, the forensic psychiatrist who had been helping him deal with Hamdan. Keram was worried that Hamdan would consider it presumptuous of Swift to speak about his responsibility to his family and would react badly. She thought the letter should be more sympathetic and solicitous.

Schmitz suggested that they get a second opinion from a Yemeni psychiatrist, who gave Swift the opposite advice, counseling him to punch up the letter even more: "Don't let him drown in self-pity. Make him think of others. Remind him of his duties. Tell him to be a man.

Don't worry about being too judgmental. You're not a Muslim, so you can't invoke God, but other than that nothing is off-limits."

Swift took the Yemeni psychiatrist's advice and added a reference to Hamdan's orphaned childhood, urging him not to leave his daughters without a father as well. He knew that he was taking a big risk, essentially gambling that he had earned the right to be this forward with Hamdan, but he didn't feel as if he had much of a choice. Schmitz translated the letter and e-mailed it to Colonel Sullivan, the chief defense counsel for the military commissions, who happened to be on Guantánamo at the time and made sure it was delivered to Hamdan.

Swift flew down a few days later. Hamdan agreed to see him, but the meeting would have to take place in an interrogation trailer at Camp Delta because Hamdan was too weak to handle the little bit of walking required to get to one of the cinder block huts at Camp Echo, the usual site of their visits.

Swift didn't bring Hamdan anything to eat; he was worried that Hamdan was still striking, and he didn't want to seem disrespectful. As Hamdan entered the trailer, Swift was instantly struck by his physical appearance. His weight had fluctuated dramatically during his time on Guantánamo—the hot meals, if eaten, were plenty caloric—but he had never looked this gaunt. Hamdan sat down gingerly, scanned the table separating him from his visitors, and asked, "Where's the food?"

SIX DAYS AFTER they filed their brief with the Supreme Court, Katyal was returning from lunch when he received the call he'd been dreading from the Solicitor General's Office: the government was moving to dismiss *Hamdan v. Rumsfeld.*

Katyal raced back to his office to read the motion, which had already been posted online. The government's argument was straightforward: the Graham-Levin bill—also known as the Detainee Treatment Act, or DTA—had stripped the justices of their jurisdiction to hear the case.

The government's key precedent was *Ex parte McCardle,* a Civil War–era case concerning a Mississippi newspaper editor who had been charged by a military commission with fomenting insurrection. The Supreme Court had agreed to hear McCardle's challenge to the commission, but then promptly dismissed his suit when Congress enacted a law depriving the Court of its jurisdiction in the case. The government quoted the Court's opinion in its motion to dismiss *Hamdan*: "Jurisdiction is power to declare the law, and when it ceases to exist, the only function remaining to the court is that of announcing the fact and dismissing the case."

The government clearly had a compelling case. Not only did the language of the DTA say nothing about exempting pending cases, but the administration's reading of the statute had an undeniable logic: allowing *Hamdan* and the dozens of other detainee cases to continue would defeat the whole purpose of the bill, which was to unclog the courts of lawsuits from America's enemies during a time of war.

Katyal called the Court's clerk to find out when their reply was due. "As soon as possible," he was told.

Kevin Russell, Goldstein's partner, volunteered to help draft part of it. He was going to be at Harvard Law School for three weeks, running a clinic on Supreme Court litigation, and could assign a few of his students to focus on it.

Katyal was thrilled. Russell had been a year ahead of him at Yale Law School and in Justice Breyer's chambers. He was low-key, even laconic, but extremely bright and knowledgeable about the Court. Katyal knew their reply to the government's motion was going to be a massive undertaking. Jurisdiction was a complicated issue—the framers themselves had been deeply divided over how much power to give the courts vis-à-vis the president and Congress—and Katyal was still emotionally and physically spent from the Supreme Court brief. What's more, he was giving a talk at a conference in Aspen in a few weeks and had been planning to stay a little longer to ski and clear his head. He had been looking forward to the trip for months and didn't want to have to cancel it now.

Russell and his Harvard students brainstormed for a few days, and then started blocking out half of the brief. Katyal, meanwhile, was working on the other half, while Goldstein drafted an introduction.

On January 20, Katyal gave Russell and his students some feedback, and they revamped their half and sent it back to him just as he was leaving for Aspen.

Katyal filled a large black Samsonite suitcase with all the law-books, Supreme Court cases, and law review articles he would need during his week in Colorado. He was told at the airline check-in counter that the suitcase was much too heavy to take on board. He pleaded with the ticket agent, and she eventually agreed to let him exceed the fifty-pound weight limit by twenty pounds per bag. Katyal mixed some of the books in with his ski clothes, paid a seventy-five-dollar surcharge for overweight luggage, and boarded the plane.

During his two flights and the long layover between them, Katyal started weaving the three separate pieces—his, Goldstein's, and Russell's—into a single brief. By the time he arrived in Aspen late that night, he was in a bit of daze and slipped on the icy tarmac, landing hard on his knee. He worked a few more hours in his hotel room while his knee swelled up. At about two in the morning he called Joanna, who was asleep back in Washington. She said if he was having trouble walking on it in the morning, he should go to the hospital for X-rays. Katyal's knee was still swollen and throbbing when he woke up, but he could walk. He bought a bottle of aspirin and skied every day, confining himself to the mountains where his BlackBerry worked on the chairlift. When the lifts closed, he went back to his hotel, ordered room service, and worked on the brief until three or four in the morning.

The brief exploited the *Hamdan* team's one big advantage over the government. For the Supreme Court to accept the government's argument that the Detainee Treatment Act had been intended to strip Hamdan of his right to challenge the lawfulness of his trial, it would have to grapple with an enormous constitutional question—namely, the extent of Congress's power to suspend the writ of habeas corpus.* This was something the justices would not want to do. Avoiding knotty constitutional issues was a fundamental tenet of judicial re-

---

* Congress has suspended habeas only four times in the nation's history, most famously during the Civil War.

straint, a natural outgrowth of the Court's tendency to move cautiously, like those bronze turtles.

The *Hamdan* brief offered the Court another option. Congress had intended for the DTA to grandfather pending cases. This was not the most logical reading of the bill, but all of Katyal's subtle tweaks to the text of the legislation had at least made it a plausible interpretation. All they could do now was lay it out for the justices and hope that a majority would be inclined to give them the benefit of the doubt.

Because the language of the law was so murky, the brief relied heavily on the bill's backstory, its legislative history, quoting Senator Levin saying explicitly on the floor of the Senate during the run-up to the bill's passage that it would not prevent the Supreme Court from hearing *Hamdan*.

The government trotted out some legislative history of its own. Senator Levin's coauthors on the Detainee Treatment Act, Senators Graham and Jon Kyl, an Arizona Republican, filed an amicus brief supporting the administration's motion to dismiss *Hamdan* in which they quoted themselves discussing the bill on the floor of the Senate on December 21, 2005, the day of the Senate vote on the Detainee Treatment Act, asserting that it *did* apply to pending cases.

Katyal was stunned. He had been expecting the administration to encourage its allies in the Senate to make these sorts of statements prior to the vote on the DTA and had asked one of his researchers, Josh Friedman, to monitor C-SPAN during the Senate's debates on the bill. Friedman had never mentioned this discussion between Graham and Kyl. Katyal asked if he could have somehow missed it. Friedman was certain he hadn't.

Katyal ordered the DVD of the December 21 Senate proceedings from C-SPAN for five hundred dollars and watched it himself. The exchange had never taken place. This left only one other explanation: it had been added to the *Congressional Record* after the fact and falsely represented as part of the live debate. In other words, Graham and Kyl's colleagues had never heard their interpretation of the DTA before voting on it.

Katyal used this discovery in their response to the government's motion to dismiss to bolster the case that the Senate had not intended to kick *Hamdan* off the Supreme Court's docket when it passed the DTA:

> In response to Senator Levin's explicit and public state-
> ments . . . the government points to contrary statements made
> by Senator Kyl. That legislative history is entirely post hoc,
> consisting of a single scripted colloquy that never actually
> took place, but was instead inserted into the record after the
> legislation passed . . . It is indeed telling that neither Senator
> Kyl nor Senator Graham contradicted Senator Levin's remarks
> during this entire time—over the nearly forty days from start to
> finish while the legislation was being considered.

ANOTHER STRING of sleepless nights preceded the filing of their response to the government's motion, which Katyal finished at four-
thirty in the morning on January 31, 2006. He slept for two hours,
dropped his kids off at school, and went back to bed for another hour
before driving over to Goldstein's house to proofread and submit it.

Several people suggested to Katyal that he file a separate motion
with the Court asking for additional time to discuss the Detainee
Treatment Act at the oral argument. Katyal never even considered the
idea. He was already anxious enough at the prospect of standing before the justices for thirty minutes, the usual allotment for each side
in a Supreme Court argument. The last thing he wanted was to be at
the lectern even longer, debating the extraordinarily complex issues
raised by the DTA. What's more, Katyal knew that if they were lucky
enough to remain on the Court's docket for the argument, he would
be going up against the solicitor general of the United States, Paul
Clement, probably the finest Supreme Court advocate of his generation. More time for him meant more time for Clement.

In early February 2006, Katyal resumed his familiar ritual of obsessively checking SCOTUSblog, only this time he was checking to
see if *Hamdan* had been dismissed. Considering how much was at
stake, he felt relatively calm. He had done everything he could to keep
the case alive. He was hardly convinced that it would be enough,

though. It worried him that the Court had not yet set a date for the oral argument. Even more disconcerting was something he had heard a judge on the D.C. circuit court of appeals, David Sentelle, say at a recent legal society dinner. Sentelle had predicted that the justices were going to cancel the oral argument and send the case back down to his court, which had already made its opinion of *Hamdan* abundantly clear, to figure out what to do.

The justices made their decision a little more than two weeks later. Katyal had told Swift that a ruling might be imminent, and Swift called Katyal from Guantánamo at 10:00 a.m., not even bothering to say hello.

"Is it out?"

"Nothing yet," Katyal answered.

They talked for a little while Katyal refreshed the Web page.

At ten-thirty, the Court's new orders list, the results from the justices' most recent conference, finally appeared. *Hamdan* was still on the docket.

"It looks like we're okay," Katyal told Swift. "We're okay."

For Katyal, relief quickly gave way to anxiety. Without any prompting, the Court had given each side an extra fifteen minutes to dabate the DTA at the oral argument. And the justices had scheduled the argument for March 28, 2006, just five weeks away.

SEVENTEEN

The Countdown

IN THE TWO YEARS since the *Hamdan* team had filed their lawsuit against the government, they had survived *Rasul*, a stinging defeat at the court of appeals, and now an attempt in Congress to kick their case off the Supreme Court's docket. Their chance to persuade the highest court in the land that the president's military commissions were illegal was finally within their sights, yet there were still unresolved questions about how they were going to make their case—and who was going to make it.

Oral argument is often an important part of the Supreme Court's decision-making process. This is partly a matter of timing: the justices meet to vote on cases days after they are argued, so the words of the advocates are invariably fresh in their minds. ("Often my whole notion of what a case is about crystallizes at oral argument," Justice William J. Brennan, Jr., once said.)

But the oral argument was going to be especially influential in *Hamdan*. The team's brief had raised far too many claims to cover in an hour; that meant a lot was going to be riding on how the advocate went about prioritizing them. What's more, the Court's desire to move slowly notwithstanding, *Hamdan v. Rumsfeld* presented stark questions whose answers were impossible to hedge. Wherever the majority ended up, the justices were not going to be able to avoid making a powerful statement about the authority of the president and the rights of our enemies. With so much at stake, the strength and credibility of the advocate were going to be essential.

Katyal, the principal architect of the suit, was the most logical choice to deliver the argument, but Swift was angling to deliver a portion of it himself, and Perkins Coie, which had poured more than forty-five hundred pro bono hours into *Hamdan*—at a value in excess of $1.2 million—thought it might be best to ask an experienced Supreme Court advocate to speak on their behalf.

For his part, Katyal, having long assumed that he would be the one to argue the case if it ever got to the Supreme Court, had started having second thoughts within days of the justices' granting their petition. It's every lawyer's dream to argue at the Supreme Court. When the opportunity presents itself, few are willing to relinquish it to more seasoned hands, even though doing so is almost always in the best interests of their clients. Katyal knew this better than anyone. As a clerk he had seen so many oral arguments botched by inexperienced advocates that he and a couple of his colleagues had joked about starting a malpractice firm that would sue lawyers who had elected not to relinquish their cases to specialists in Supreme Court litigation.

Katyal's doubts were magnified by a conversation with a young law professor, like Katyal a rising star in the legal academy who had recently led a major case to the Supreme Court. The professor, who had opted to do the oral argument, had lost the case and was still plagued by the feeling that a more experienced advocate might have won. "You're not going to want to hear this," the professor told Katyal, "but you should give the argument up."

The conversation haunted Katyal for weeks, all the more so because he knew it wouldn't be hard to find a first-rate lawyer to take his place in such a high-profile case. Goldstein was a good fit; he was already intimately familiar with the issues. The other name that immediately sprang to mind was Seth Waxman, President Clinton's solicitor general and the country's preeminent Supreme Court advocate. Katyal mentioned them both to Richard Lazarus, a law professor and the director of Georgetown's Supreme Court advocacy program, who urged him to hold on to the argument instead: "You bring something to this case that no one else does. You fundamentally and deep down believe in it, and you can make clear what's at stake on so many different levels than an advocate for hire."

Katyal remained unconvinced. In late November 2005, another idea had occurred to him: he could ask a more experienced advocate to split the argument with him. This was not common practice—the Supreme Court's rules state bluntly that "divided argument is not favored"—but Katyal thought it might help protect them; if he bombed, there would be someone else to pick up the slack. He also saw a strategic opportunity to add political diversity to the team. Their claims might find more traction with the conservative justices if pressed by an established Republican, rather than an ex–Clinton staffer like himself.

His first call was to Ken Starr. Katyal had gotten to know Starr a bit when he was in the Justice Department and Starr was the independent counsel investigating Clinton. They had always gotten along well, and Katyal knew they shared the same basic philosophy about executive authority. Both believed that the framers had envisioned a powerful president but that the strength of the office depended on its occupants' vigilantly observing the boundaries defined by Congress, the Constitution, and the courts.

Katyal briefed Starr on their arguments. Starr thought they sounded good, but he wanted Katyal to send him the links to all of their briefs and their petition for certiorari. "Nothing is more threatening to the concept of a strong presidency than claims that go too far and repose the powers of all three branches in one actor," Katyal wrote, doing his best to appeal to Starr's belief in presidential power. "When that happens, the structure collapses or invites a backlash."

Swift, meanwhile, was lobbying on his own behalf, pointing out to Katyal that not only was he an experienced trial lawyer, but he would be wearing the uniform of the United States Navy, which would create a powerful image for the justices.

Katyal had been expecting this. Despite their long-standing agreement that Katyal would be lead counsel for the lawsuit, he knew all along that if the justices granted their petition, Swift wouldn't be happy sitting on the sidelines. Katyal was even worried that Swift might press Hamdan to insist that they share the argument.

Lazarus had seen this coming too, and urged Katyal to resist Swift's entreaties. As Lazarus pointed out, the easiest way to lose votes at oral argument is to exaggerate one's claims. Having watched Swift in a couple of lower-court moots, Lazarus was certain that his trial lawyer's tendency toward hyperbole would be a liability. What's more, arguing at the Supreme Court is as much about listening as it is about speaking. Lazarus was worried that Swift would be too caught up in his own rhetoric to grasp the nature of the questions from the bench and their often hidden subtexts.

Explaining this to Swift was not something Katyal looked forward to, especially because he wasn't convinced that the alternative, Katyal himself, was a much better option. He told Swift that he had been great in the lower courts—"much better than I was"—but that arguing before the justices was different. "All of your years of experience in the military courts have made you master of that domain," Katyal said, "and all of my years studying the Supreme Court have been preparing me for this."

Swift countered by suggesting that if they argued the case together and won, they could someday open their own law practice together. "We got crushed in the court of appeals, three-zip, couldn't get a single judge to buy our position," Katyal replied, "and when we finally won certiorari, it prompted the first action by Congress to strip the courts of habeas jurisdiction since 1867. That's not a very good track record for attracting clients."

Katyal said that if he was going to divide the argument, it would make more sense to bring in a high-profile conservative like Starr to handle part of it. "I think the uniform would be a more powerful weapon," Swift answered. Katyal agreed to give it a little more thought and suggested to Swift that he do the same.

Swift mulled it over that night. Whether he liked it or not, he had made a deal: he had to defer to Katyal's judgment, even if he didn't agree with it. Swift called Katyal in the morning to say that he'd be okay with not being part of the argument.

Starr didn't get back to Katyal, so he instead tried Miguel Estrada, a former clerk for Justice Kennedy, and Maureen Mahoney, a noted conservative Supreme Court advocate whose name had come up as a potential successor to Justice O'Connor. Estrada had just signed an amicus brief in support of the government; Mahoney had an argument before the justices a week before *Hamdan* and another one the week after.

Katyal had just been getting used to the idea of delivering the entire argument himself when in February 2006 the justices extended the time to debate the Detainee Treatment Act, sending him into another spiral of self-doubt. During his moments of insecurity about the argument, Katyal had always reminded himself of Michael Newdow, who had challenged the constitutionality of the words "under God" in the Pledge of Allegiance on behalf of his grade school–aged daughter. It was a monumental case, and Newdow, a nonpracticing lawyer, had insisted on arguing it before the Court. To everyone's surprise, he had done a good job. If Newdow could hold it together for thirty minutes, Katyal had told himself, so can I. Now he was going to have to hold it together for forty-five minutes.

Swift again tried to persuade Katyal to split the argument with him; Katyal again said no. He did take a fresh run at Starr, though. Starr declined, saying he wouldn't be able to give the argument the attention it deserved. Katyal tried several other experienced advocates, even widening the net to include nonconservatives, but no one was able to devote the time necessary to get up to speed on the issues in just a few weeks.

"I really have to steel myself for the possibility that this is going to be a forty-five-minute argument," Katyal confided to his audio diary in early March 2006.

IT HAD BEEN A HARD WINTER for Swift. After Hamdan's hunger strike, he had resumed his monthly visits to Guantánamo, and while Hamdan had emerged from his emotional free fall, the stress of appeasing him, not to mention the cumulative effect of two years' worth of battles with the base's leadership, had taken their toll on Swift. He had once gotten a charge out of his trips to Guantánamo, enjoying the chance to flex his righteousness and win over his client anew. Now it was the ferry ride back across the bay that he looked forward to—"the feeling of everything lifting from your shoulders as you saw things going in the rearview mirror."

Life wasn't much easier for Swift in D.C. His excitement over the Supreme Court's granting their petition had been tempered by the realization that he was not going to be standing before the justices. Even though he was the public face of *Hamdan*, he would be sitting anonymously at the counsel's table during the most public moment of the case, the oral argument.

Swift had never been a central player in the brief-writing process for *Hamdan*, and he had contributed virtually nothing to their various filings with the Supreme Court. He was always more comfortable speaking than writing, and after his failed attempt to participate in their initial brief to the justices, he had been plagued by feelings of self-doubt, which made it even harder for him to put his thoughts on paper, especially since he knew that his audience was Katyal.

After everything that he, Katyal, and the Perkins Coie team had been through, *this* was the moment. Everything was riding on what happened in the next few weeks, and yet Swift was depressingly idle. Katyal had asked everyone on the team not to talk to the media, and with Hamdan's military commission in indefinite recess, there was not much Swift could do on that front either.

The bottom line was that Swift no longer felt like an equal partner in the case. He tried to remind himself that without him, they wouldn't be here. *He* was the one who had made a key argument that had convinced Judge Robertson to halt the commission; *he* was the one who had been keeping their client alive and on board, an increasingly difficult task with each day Hamdan spent on Guantánamo. But that didn't make it any easier for Swift to relinquish the stage.

Over the past few years, even as they bickered and got on each other's nerves, Swift and Katyal had grown close in the way that only two people sharing an experience as intense as the *Hamdan* case can. "We literally finished each other's sentences," Swift later recalled. Once the Supreme Court granted their petition, though, Swift had suddenly felt like a third wheel: "In a sense, I understood. Why would you consult Charlie Swift when you can consult Laurence Tribe? On the other hand, we had come all of this way together, and it really hurt."

Swift withdrew, thinking resentfully that Katyal probably wanted less to do with him anyway. Katyal wasn't aware that Swift felt this way. He knew that some of their routines had changed, but only because he needed to be as efficient as possible with his time; he could no longer, for example, afford to talk to Swift twice a day, once when he was driving to work in the morning and once when he was driving home, whether they had anything important to discuss or not. Katyal now needed that time to dole out research assignments to his student team. In Katyal's mind he tried to reach out to Swift in other ways, if for no other reason than that he knew that when Swift wasn't busy, he tended to spend a lot of time talking to reporters. Yet Swift never returned Katyal's phone calls. "He was just completely AWOL," Katyal remembered.

WHEN KATYAL was debating whether to give up the *Hamdan* argument, he told Richard Lazarus that he was worried about getting flustered in the heat of his first oral argument. "That worry, the worry that you'll find yourself standing before the Court and realizing that you have no clothes on, that you are a fraud and that your arguments are weak—that's what's going to make you good," Lazarus told him. "You will simply work harder than anyone else."

This, at least, was true. Every moment that Katyal wasn't spending on their briefs for the Supreme Court, he devoted to preparing for the oral argument. This was partly a matter of absorbing as much information as possible. Katyal studied *Supreme Court and Appellate Advocacy*, the closest thing to a guidebook on how to argue before the justices, and bought a second copy of *Supreme Court Practice* so that he would have one in his office and one at home. On the weekends he read books about Nuremberg, legal volumes from the international criminal tribunals in the former Yugoslavia, and the Supreme Court's opinions on military commissions, military law, and international treaties. Beside his bed was a copy of the complete case record of *Hamdan*, which numbered about six hundred pages. Katyal methodically made his way through it every night, committing as much as he could to memory so that he wouldn't need to pause before telling an inquiring justice on what page—and in which paragraph—to find a particular fact.

He also went to a handful of arguments at the Court to see the newest justice, Samuel Alito, in action and downloaded many more arguments from Oyez.org, listening to them on his office computer, his car stereo, and his iPod while working out at the gym. Katyal wanted the rhythm of a good oral argument to become second nature. The best Supreme Court advocates treated their arguments as conversations. They rarely, if ever, consulted notes—"Oral argument read from a prepared text is not favored," the Court's rules state—and they responded to questions from the bench promptly yet efficiently, using their answers to pivot back to points of their own. Katyal kept a list of especially deft transitions and quickly discovered that one of the nimblest practitioners of this verbal pirouette was his opponent, Paul Clement.

But the centerpiece of Katyal's preparation was his moots. Some Supreme Court advocates don't do dry runs, preferring instead to test out their ideas on colleagues and practice their arguments in private. (Thurgood Marshall hadn't done any before arguing *Brown v. Board of Education*.) It's more typical to do one, maybe two moots. Like preseason scrimmages, they help expose one's strengths and weaknesses but typically provide diminishing returns. There is also a danger of overmooting. Advocates need to be fresh when they engage the justices. Their answers should feel crisp and spontaneous, not tired and rehearsed. Also, doing too many moots can lull advocates into a false sense of security: questions from moot court panelists—typically supportive colleagues—are rarely as tough as those from the justices themselves.

Beginning in late January, two months before the argument, Katyal did fifteen moots in five different cities, Seattle, Boston, New Haven, New York, and Washington. He wanted to get as comfortable as possible at the podium, and he knew he didn't have to worry about maintaining his intensity; his anxiety about the argument would take care of that. He also wasn't concerned about being lulled into a false sense of security. When he decided to deliver at least a portion of the argument, Katyal had directed everyone on the *Hamdan* team to be unsparing in his criticism and stingy with praise. "I want to be relentlessly attacked," he said. "I don't want to be stroked in any way."

Katyal also took out a legal pad and jotted down the name of every lawyer and legal scholar who intimidated him and then asked each one of them to moot him. Nearly all of them agreed.* The group of more than a dozen lawyers cut across the ideological spectrum and had done a combined total of more than five hundred arguments among them. It included Ivy League law school deans, former Supreme Court clerks, high-profile law firm partners who billed as much as one thousand dollars an hour for their time—though they would be doing this pro bono—and former solicitors general from both Democratic and Republican administrations.

The moots all were structured the same way. Katyal would enter the mock courtroom and start in on his opening statement. Before long, one of the panelists would interrupt him with a question, and the argument would be under way. Someone would let Katyal know when his time was up, but the sessions typically lasted about two hours, after which the panelists would spend another hour or two critiquing his performance.

At night, with the moot still fresh in his head, Katyal would listen to a recording of it. He was principally concerned with tone. He had to be at once assertive and respectful, a difficult balance for first-time advocates to strike. After an early moot at Harvard, Laurence Tribe, one of Katyal's panelists, said he looked "small" at the podium, by which he meant that Katyal was coming off as too deferential. "Most of your answers are fine," Tribe said, "but you aren't being aggressive enough about driving the argument forward."

At the same time, Katyal didn't want to sound defensive or petulant no matter how aggressive the questioning. As Lazarus had put it,

---

*The exception was Charles Fried, a professor at Harvard Law School and former solicitor general under Reagan, who made no excuses for declining. "I am afraid I am so out of sympathy with your side of this dispute that I would not feel right helping you to make your case," he wrote to Katyal. "I could say I am busy, but that would not be the honest reason, and I respect you too much to make lame excuses. Good luck!"

he needed to "revel" in hostile questions. The justice would at least be making it clear what he thought and, in so doing, giving Katyal a chance to persuade him otherwise.

KATYAL FELT progressively better over the course of the first month of moots. He was honing his answers for maximum precision and economy, both to make the most of his time at the podium and to avoid getting snagged by an ill-considered word or phrase. He was learning which theories he wanted to emphasize, and he felt like his argument was gaining force.

But as the moots wore on, the enormity of the case began to weigh on him. In late February Katyal's confidence started to crack. Not only was the team still beating up on him, per his instructions, but everyone was telling him that he was doing too many moots, and that he wasn't going to have anything left in the tank when the argument arrived. Worse still, McMillan and Goldstein were maneuvering to persuade him to relinquish at least a portion of the argument—"Is Tom still available?" McMillan had asked on more than one occasion—only magnifying Katyal's anxiety. "The degree of manipulation is quite intense," Katyal confided in his audio diary on February 28, 2006. "It would be one thing if I felt I were Seth Waxman and awesome at advocacy, but I don't, so I have to agonize over this stuff."

It didn't help matters that Katyal's performance would be judged instantly and by millions. Until recently Supreme Court oral arguments were largely anonymous affairs. Not until the 2000 election dispute did the Court first depart from its long-standing custom of withholding recordings of arguments until after cases had been decided. Since then the Court had agreed to allow almost real-time broadcasts of a handful of arguments in which there was a "heightened public interest." *Hamdan* was going to be part of this elite group. C-SPAN had even called for a photograph of Katyal to accompany its audio broadcast.

Katyal had gone through intense periods of single-mindedness before—at the Justice Department, during *Bush v. Gore*, and repeatedly during *Hamdan*—but this was of a different order. It had never been a problem for him to go weeks on three or four hours of sleep a night, but his anxiety about the argument and the performance aspect of the moots took an additional toll on him. He was tired. And though he managed to maintain his daily routine with the kids, often rushing out of his D.C. moots so that he could make the school pickups, help get dinner ready, and put the older boys to bed, he felt he still needed more time to prepare.

So weekends too became a casualty, putting more pressure on Joanna, whose own life was already so compressed that she was pumping breast milk for Harlan in the car as she drove to and from work. With Katyal often gone from breakfast to dinner, she was left to herd and cajole the children through the weekend days alone. Sometimes her parents came in from New York to lend a hand and give Katyal more time to work, but more often than not it was three on one.

Coursing through all of this was the first anniversary of the death of Katyal's father on March 7. The anticipation had been nagging at him for months, and as March approached, he felt profoundly guilty for not flying to Chicago to spend the day with his mother. But he just couldn't spare the time. As Katyal worked through the moots, thinking about his father invariably upped the ante. He had a chance to make a difference, to do something he knew would have made his father proud. It was a privilege he didn't want to squander.

There were a few moments of escape: Katyal saw a New Pornographers concert, and he and Joanna hosted a joint birthday party—his thirty-sixth and her fortieth—at their house, a rare night during which he was not somehow working on his argument. But Katyal felt on the verge of being overwhelmed, a state he was not at all familiar with.

His anxiety about the argument peaked at a moot at Yale on March 9. One of the panelists was Harold Koh, now the dean of the law school and a former professor of Katyal's, who stopped the moot only a few sentences into his opening statement—"You're going to lose if you walk into the Supreme Court with an opening like that." In the recollection of several students who attended the moot, Koh proceeded to berate Katyal for the next two hours.

Then, as abruptly as Katyal's confidence had been shaken, it was restored by a pair of moots at two high-powered D.C. law firms, Covington & Burling and WilmerHale. The panelists included several of the country's most respected Supreme Court advocates, Seth Waxman among them. Katyal thought his answers were crisper and sharper than ever, and the feedback was almost uniformly positive. "So what do you need me for?" Waxman remarked at the close of the WilmerHale moot.

Katyal felt even better after working with Joshua Karton in mid-March. Although he knew the experience would be uncomfortable verging on unpleasant, given how slowly and deliberately Karton uttered every word, Katyal could see he needed work loosening up at the podium and asked Karton to come to D.C. to help him out. A few weeks later Karton breezed into Katyal's office, and soon enough the men were holding hands, with Karton's eyes fixed meaningfully on Katyal's. Later in the afternoon, at Katyal's house, Karton lined up eight of Katyal's children's stuffed animals along a table so that Katyal could practice making eye contact with the various justices.

Katyal also practiced making eye contact with the justices in person. A week before the argument, he moved Swift for admission into the Supreme Court bar so that Swift could sit with him at counsel's table. Swift's application could have been processed through the mail, but Katyal opted to present him in open court instead. As a clerk he had stood at the Supreme Court podium when the courtroom was empty, but he wanted to see what it felt like to stand before the justices when the Court was in session.*

NOT EVERYONE on the *Hamdan* team was feeling as confident as Katyal.

McMillan had been worried from the start. He attended the very

---

*Katyal also wanted to acquaint himself with the new seating configuration of the Court. For more than ten years Breyer had been the juniormost justice, meaning that he sat on the far right of the courtroom. The justice with the least seniority after him, Justice Ginsburg, sat on the far left of the courtroom. But now that Justice O'Connor had been replaced by Alito, he and Ginsburg were on the right of the courtroom and Breyer was on the far left.

first moot at the Perkins Coie offices in Seattle in late January 2006 and thought that Katyal sounded rambling and unfocused. Since then McMillan had been tracking the evolution of Katyal's arguments—Josh Friedman had been keeping a spreadsheet of all the questions and answers from the various moots—and had grown only more concerned. It looked to him like Katyal was drifting further and further away from the terrain where McMillan believed they needed to be to win. Specifically, he was worried that Katyal was allowing himself to get sidetracked by broad, theoretical questions rather than focusing ruthlessly on the unlawful aspects of Hamdan's military commission. "I was very unhappy," he would remember. "I felt like Neal's northeast tour in front of the academics was not serving him well."

Over the past two years, McMillan had personally devoted two thousand pro bono hours to *Hamdan*. Perkins Coie had been understanding about the demands of the case, but the firm still expected him to at least come close to meeting his billable hour expectations too. That meant squeezing in *Hamdan* whenever he could. Like Katyal, McMillan too had grown accustomed to working on holidays and late at night, in addition to sacrificing numerous weekends with his family. He had gone through endless rounds with Katyal over every single document they had filed, fighting for even the smallest concession—a topic sentence, a transitional phrase, the deletion of a footnote, anything that would make the filing even the slightest bit more readable and persuasive.

Now, with the most important moment in the case approaching, McMillan knew it was his last chance to be heard. So instead of flying in the night before the argument, as he had been planning to do, he decided to go to D.C. a week early to encourage Katyal to rethink his approach.

Shortly before leaving, McMillan called Swift to sketch out his concerns about the direction of the argument and to tell him that he and Sipos were coming to town earlier than expected. At that point Swift had not attended a single one of Katyal's moots. He had volunteered to go to one in early March at New York University, but Katyal, who was worried about Swift's monopolizing the floor in front of a group of high-priced law firm partners, had asked him not to. Katyal

had since invited him to several moots in D.C., but Swift, feeling inse-
cure and irrelevant, had never shown.

Swift had long admired McMillan's stubborn willingness to endure one rebuff after another from Katyal and was amazed he hadn't
quit many briefs ago. Hearing his concerns about the direction of
the argument now, Swift felt that maybe there was a role for him after
all. If McMillan was going to give it another try, Swift thought, so
would he.

Several days later, after McMillan and Sipos had arrived in D.C.,
Swift turned up at Georgetown for a meeting with them and Katyal.
Swift kept mostly quiet, still feeling a bit tentative. McMillan spoke
freely and candidly. "I felt like, okay, this is our last shot," he recalled. "I
need to be very vigorous in asserting my views."

McMillan could tell that Katyal wasn't exactly eager for his input:
"I got the impression that he felt I was coming in trying to overturn
what was already the product of a lot of weeks of work."

He was right. Katyal had no intention of changing directions now.
The positive feedback from Waxman and several others had only reinforced his faith in his overarching strategy. As a trial lawyer McMillan was naturally inclined to emphasize the individual facts of their
case, the specific flaws with Hamdan's military commission. But
Katyal remained convinced that the key to victory was winning Justice
Kennedy, and the key to winning Kennedy was to focus on the big picture and stress that the president's power cannot go unchecked.

ON THE FRIDAY AFTERNOON before the argument, Katyal did his
fourteenth moot. It was held in the mock courtroom at Georgetown.
Of all the rooms in which Katyal had practiced his argument over the
course of the past two months, none more closely resembled the
Supreme Court courtroom, right down to its red, rellow, and blue patterned carpet. About thirty minutes into the moot, Katyal was asked if
he considered 9/11 an act of war. This was a popular question at the
moots; it cut to the heart of the issue of whether the use of military
commissions, which were, at bottom, wartime courts, was appropriate in the context of the war on terror. The problem was that the an-

swer Katyal liked to give, the one he believed to be correct—yes, the war on terror was a war, but it was a very different kind of war—was too nuanced and invariably led to a hostile question to the effect of, Well, is it or isn't it?

In the previous moot, Katyal had started in on his usual answer—"Yes, but . . ."—and Swift had interrupted him: "Why? Because some guy who knows nothing about war says it is? Did the president call up his judge advocates and ask *them* if it was an act of war?" Swift had then gone to the podium to demonstrate to Katyal how to answer the question. "War has dignity," Swift said. "War has honor. These terrorists don't have dignity. They don't have honor. Let's call 9/11 what it was: a criminal act."

It had sounded interesting when Swift said it, so Katyal now gave it a try. Coming from him, though, the same words fell flat. They lacked the moral force that Swift had infused them with. Substantively, they seemed likely to provoke a backlash from the Court, which would almost certainly be unwilling to overturn the president's entire paradigm for fighting terrorism.

"I remember feeling at that point like things were unraveling," McMillan would recall. "The war on terror may be nothing more than a political slogan, but we are not going to be able to win this case by going in and telling the Supreme Court that we are not at war."

Swift too was worried: "I was there, good Lord; should I go in and say, Let me do the argument, because you ain't got this?"

KATYAL SPENT the Sunday before the argument rereading all the amicus briefs, filling three legal pads with notes by the time he was finished. On Monday morning he did a final tune-up at Georgetown. The Friday moot was supposed to be his last. Everyone thought that doing another, and only twenty-four hours before the argument, was a mistake. He should try to unwind and recharge his batteries instead. But the members of his Yale team were now in town, and Katyal wanted them to have a chance to question him.

McMillan thought the final moot went much better than the previous two; some of his advice from the previous week must have sunk in, he figured. Katyal was less satisfied. He thought his students were deliberately lobbing him softballs. He was particularly annoyed when they gave him a standing ovation at the end. The applause felt staged, as if they were trying too hard to boost his confidence.

Katyal had lunch with McMillan, Sipos, and his student team in the Georgetown cafeteria and then went for a run, following New Jersey Avenue over to the Capitol building and down the National Mall, past the various monuments and memorials—Washington, Jefferson, Vietnam, World War II, Lincoln. He showered in the law school gym, had a massage at the Mandarin Hotel, and went to see *V for Vendetta*, the story of a freedom fighter who uses terrorist tactics to bring down a futuristic fascist government. It was the first time in months that he had shut off his BlackBerry.

By the time Katyal emerged from the movie theater, the sun was setting. He turned on his BlackBerry and discovered seventy new e-mail and voice messages, nearly all of them from reporters seeking comment on a letter that had just been filed with the Court seeking Justice Scalia's recusal from *Hamdan*.

A couple of days earlier, the tape of a provocative speech that Scalia had recently delivered in Switzerland had surfaced in Washington. Not only had Scalia said that detainees should not be given access to the federal courts—"It has never been the case that when you captured a combatant you have to give them a jury trial in your civil courts"—but he had suggested that he had a personal stake in how *Hamdan* was decided: "I had a son on that battlefield, and they were shooting at my son."

Knowing that judges are forbidden by law to hear cases in which they cannot be impartial, Katyal had briefly considered filing a recusal letter with the Supreme Court himself but had decided against it. He figured that if Scalia thought he had done something unethical, he would step down on his own volition. A letter from a self-interested party would not affect him either way. What's more, the request could easily backfire by angering not just Scalia but his brethren on his behalf.

Outside the movie theater, Katyal called Swift to find out what was going on. Swift was out to dinner with Debbie and David Remes, the lawyer who had coordinated their amicus briefs. He got up from the table and explained to Katyal that it was in fact Remes who had filed the letter on behalf of a group of generals and admirals who had authored one of the amicus briefs.

Katyal lit into Swift. "You knew my views on this. How could you have let this happen? What the hell were you thinking?"

Swift told Katyal that Remes thought it was a good idea and that he didn't think he could stop him. So Katyal called Remes on his cell phone to yell at him too.

Now Remes stood up from the table and defended the decision, insisting that he had an obligation to his clients, the generals and admirals whom he had brought together to file the amicus brief, to do what he thought was best for the case—namely, trying to force the recusal of a justice who was so obviously partisan.

Katyal was rattled. He had already been worried about getting attacked by Scalia on the substance of his argument. Now the Court's most conservative, confrontational justice would have another reason to go on the offensive.

Still fuming, Katyal went home and ate dinner with his family, including his mother and sister, who had flown in for the argument. Not long after they sat down, Karton called to offer Katyal some final tips. He should try to imagine that Justice Scalia was actually his wife wearing a Scalia suit, Karton said, and sing "Oh, What a Beautiful Mornin'" in the shower in the morning so he'd be accustomed to the sound of his own voice when the argument started.

SWIFT WAS BACK and fully engaged now. He had attended two of the last three moots and had ducked out of the last one just as it was getting started because he had agreed to debate a conservative legal scholar at the Cato Institute in a kind of preview of the Supreme Court argument. It was a packed house, and Swift was very much on his game. He left feeling exhilarated, and his spirits rose even higher when McMillan called him later in the afternoon to tell him that Katyal's final moot had been superb.

Swift was too excited to fall asleep that night. He finally managed to doze off for an hour or so when his alarm woke him at three in the morning. It was time to drive Debbie to the courthouse. She hadn't been planning to attend the argument but had managed to change her flight schedule at the last minute. It was too late for Swift to secure a ticket for her, so the only option was to get to the Supreme Court early and wait in line for one of the courtroom's 180 unreserved seats.* By the time they arrived at the courthouse, a crowd of 200 people had already gathered outside. Fortunately, one of Katyal's students had held a place in line for Debbie.

Emily Keram, the forensic psychiatrist, was among those waiting. She spotted Swift in his Navy sweatshirt and blue jeans and called him over to meet a group of high school students from Wisconsin who had been studying *Hamdan* in class. Swift commended them for coming and told them that they were about to witness history. "Only in America can a military officer challenge his commander in chief," he said. "Everywhere else they call that a coup."

The sun was just beginning to rise when Swift drove home to Falls Church, showered, made a pot of coffee, changed into his dress uniform, and took the Metro back into the city for the argument.

---

*An additional 60 are reserved for tourists who are cycled in and out at three-minute intervals to get a quick glimpse of the Court in session.

262

EIGHTEEN

The Argument

MARCH 28, 2006, dawned clear and brisk in Washington. Katyal awoke early, having slept better than he expected. He felt less anxious than he'd felt in a while: in six hours, win or lose, it would all be over. He put on a dark gray suit and Gucci tie that his mother had given him for the occasion and stashed his father's wristwatch in his pocket for good luck.

Katyal had received some threatening voice mail messages over the past few weeks and had hired two bodyguards for the day. They picked him up a little after eight and drove him to the Supreme Court in his minivan while he listened to music on his iPod. Katyal had made a special mix for the occasion: U2's "The Hands That Built America" and "The Ground Beneath Her Feet"; The New Pornographers' "Sing Me Spanish Techno"; Blur's "Song 2"; and Blink 182's "What's My Age Again?" The songs amplified the jumble of contradictory emotions he was experiencing, the mixture of nervousness, exhilaration, fear, pride, and awe at the task before him.

The Supreme Court's tradition of humility and restraint appears to have been the last thing on the mind of the courthouse's architects. An early occupant, Justice Harlan Fiske Stone, once described the Supreme Court building as "almost bombastically pretentious." One of Stone's colleagues suggested that the only way he and his brethren could live up to the pomp of their surroundings would be to enter the courthouse on elephants.

As one of the day's advocates, Katyal had been asked to enter through a side door, but he wanted to use the main entrance instead. Somewhat counterintuitively, he felt that absorbing the full grandiosity of the setting—the long marble staircase, the sixteen Corinthian columns, the words "Equal Justice Under Law" etched into the stone below the pediment—would have a calming effect, putting things in perspective for him. Whatever the stakes of *Hamdan*, he was still just one lawyer arguing one case in the long history of this great institution.

By the time Katyal arrived, the plaza facing the courthouse was flooded with people. Electronic devices are not permitted inside the Supreme Court, so he left his iPod and BlackBerry inside the marshal's office. It was 8:45 a.m., roughly two hours before *Hamdan*, the second argument of the day, would be heard.

The interior of the Supreme Court building, with its soaring ceilings, ornate friezes, bronze busts, and still more marble columns, is no less imposing than the building's exterior, but Katyal felt at home there. He still knew some of the security guards, and behind the counter in the cafeteria was a woman who had often made him breakfast during his clerkship. She gave him a hug and wished him luck.

Arguing advocates may request a card that entitles them to roam certain parts of the Supreme Court building not open to the public. Goldstein had suggested to Katyal that he procure one and hole up in the law library to relax and gather his thoughts before the argument. Katyal had planned to do this but was overtaken by an irrational fear that he might get stuck in the library, which was upstairs, and miss his argument. So when he finished eating his bagel and cream cheese, he instead did the one thing that Goldstein had urged him not to do: he went into the courtroom and listened to the argument preceding *Hamdan*.

The lawyer at the podium, who looked to be even younger than Katyal, parried complicated questions from the bench with ease and grace, thrusting Katyal into a fresh spiral of self-doubt: Why didn't I give the argument away? I can't answer any of these questions! Then it dawned on him that he wouldn't have to. This wasn't *Hamdan*. It was a health insurance case that turned on an especially obscure subsection of the Employee Retirement Income Security Act of 1974.

Katyal left the courtroom at 10:35, twenty-five minutes before his argument was to begin. He had not sung in the shower in the morning because he hadn't wanted to wake up Joanna, who was going to be coming to the courthouse later with his mother and sister, so he went into a stall in the bathroom of the lawyers' lounge and belted out the theme song from *Mister Rogers' Neighborhood.* (He couldn't remember the words to "Oh, What a Beautiful Mornin'.")

Katyal returned to the courtroom. Chief Justice Roberts closed the prior argument—"The case is submitted"—rose from his black leather chair and walked off the bench, leaving the ensuing proceedings in the hands of the Court's seniormost justice, John Paul Stevens. A brief moment of drama followed when Scalia too stood up, as if to recuse himself, but then quickly sat back down.

"We'll hear argument in 05-184, *Hamdan Against Rumsfeld,*" Justice Stevens said at 11:01. "Mr. Katyal, you may proceed."

The lawyer who had preceded Katyal was still clearing his papers as Katyal moved to the podium. He brought with him a white binder with one sheet of paper attached to the front and another attached to the back. One sheet contained his opening statement; the other, a page of typewritten notes. Taped to the side of the page of notes was a blank check, a reminder to use the resonant phrase that Justice O'Connor had penned in an opinion in 2004: "A state of war is not a blank check for the President."

All five hundred of the courtroom's seats were occupied. At counsel's table, just behind and to the left of the podium, were Swift and McMillan. Several rows back, in the section reserved for members of the Supreme Court bar, were Charles Sipos, Harry Schneider, the senior partner at Perkins Coie who had first agreed to sign onto the case, and Katyal's former nemesis, Ben Sharp. Joanna and Katyal's mother and sister were in the seats reserved for the general public, as were Debbie and fourteen members of Katyal's student team, past and present. Most of the JAGs from the military commission defense office were there too, as was Sundel.

Moments before the argument started, Swift overheard a brief exchange directly behind him between an unlikely pair: the Pentagon's adviser for the military commissions, General Hemingway, and a human rights lawyer who was working with some of the Guantánamo detainees. They agreed that Katyal was in for a long morning.

Katyal was now at the podium. Standing before the justices, he was struck by the intimacy of the setting. He took a moment to compose himself, to think about his family and make eye contact with each of the justices—as Karton had taught him—and began: "Justice Stevens, and may it please the Court . . ."

AS HE HAD DONE in their Supreme Court brief, Katyal opened by positioning the government as the revolutionaries and the *Hamdan* team as the defender of American tradition. Some thought this was the wrong way to go. They had urged Katyal to open more boldly, with a more affirmative assertion of America's role as a modern beacon of human rights, a role that had been betrayed by the administration's treatment of the detainees. But Katyal felt strongly about anchoring his argument in the country's wartime history, and in the simple notion that the president must abide by the nation's statutes and treaties.

"We ask this Court to preserve the status quo to require that the president respect time-honored limitations on military commissions," Katyal said. "These limits do not represent any change in the way military commissions have historically operated. Rather, they reflect Congress's authority under the Define and Punish Clause to codify limits on commissions, limits that this Court has historically enforced to avoid presidential blank checks. And because this commission transgresses those limits, it should be struck down."

Scalia rocked forward in his chair, ready to pounce. Katyal subtly, almost unconsciously, raised his hand and stared back at him. The justice gently rocked back, permitting Katyal to continue. He had soon reached the end of his opening statement. In fifteen moots this had never happened. He paused, momentarily flustered, and then launched into his discussion of the Detainee Treatment Act.

As near as the justices were, the length of the bench made it impossible to see them all at once, and their voices were piped into the courtroom via a single bank of overhead speakers. The only way to know who was speaking was to identify each justice by his or her voice. The pugnacious tone of the first questioner was unmistakable. It was Scalia, taking aim at Katyal's claim that the DTA was not intended to apply to pending cases like *Hamdan*.

Moments later Alito chimed in. Katyal had been arguing that Hamdan had the right to challenge his military trial *before* it had actually taken place, that this was a right that "goes all the way back to the founding."

"Criminal litigation review *after* the final decision is the general rule," came Alito's retort. "There generally is not . . . any interlocutory appeal."

Katyal saw an opening and charged through it. "Justice Alito, if this were like a criminal proceeding, we wouldn't be here. The whole point of this is to say we're challenging the lawfulness of the tribunal itself. This isn't a challenge to some decision that a court makes. This is a challenge to the court itself."

Katyal had been told by an experienced Supreme Court advocate that he would be nervous at the beginning, but that once he'd answered a few questions, his self-awareness would disappear; he'd be in the thrall of the argument. That moment had just arrived. Katyal rested his arms on the lectern, leaned forward, and continued with his line of thought, observing that normal criminal trials were governed by rules established by an independent body, Congress. The rules of the commissions, by contrast, were written by the prosecution, the president. "The thing that makes this different than the ordinary criminal context, the thing that, as this Court said, stops military justice from being lawless is the Congress of the United States setting clear limits on the use of military justice. Now, if those limits had been observed . . . we wouldn't be here. Our whole point is that they don't," Katyal said. "This is a military commission that is literally unbounded by the laws, Constitution, and treaties of the United States."

THE MOST IMPORTANT MOMENT in the argument followed, though to the casual listener it probably didn't seem especially significant.

During his many moots Katyal had struggled to avoid getting bogged down in the Detainee Treatment Act. It was an argument they had to win—if they didn't, *Hamdan* would be dismissed—but it was only a threshold issue. In other words, if they won *only* the DTA, they would have won nothing more than the right to walk into court. The justices had added fifteen minutes to discuss the Detainee Treatment Act, but a buzzer wasn't going to sound when the time had elapsed. Katyal needed to hit a few key points in support of the argument that the DTA didn't apply to *Hamdan* and then quickly find a way to pivot away from it and into the substance of the lawsuit. He had learned that the most effective way to do this was to underscore that the two were inextricably linked—that in order to see why Hamdan was entitled to challenge the legitimacy of his military commission *before* it took place, it was necessary to understand the myriad flaws of the commission.

It was, of all people, Scalia who inadvertently opened the door for Katyal to make this point when he chided him for conflating the timing of the challenge and the challenge itself. "You're running in a circle," Scalia said.

"Well, that's precisely, Justice Scalia, our argument, that I don't think one can consider the abstention claim . . . without considering the underlying merits . . . So, if I could turn to the merits."

The utterance of this line produced a silent cheer among the *Hamdan* team. The DTA—specifically, the question of whether the bill had stripped Hamdan of his right to bring a challenge to the military commissions at the Supreme Court—had routinely cannibalized as much as a half hour of Katyal's moots. He was now only thirteen minutes into the argument.

Moving to the substance of their claims, Katyal tackled conspiracy first. As he started in, Stevens wanted to know where in the case record he could find the government's charge against Hamdan. Without hesitation, Katyal directed him to 63(a) of the appendix to their petition for certiorari.

"Conspiracy has been rejected as a violation of the laws of war in every tribunal to consider the issue since World War II," Katyal said.

"It has been rejected in Nuremberg, it's been rejected in the Tokyo tribunals, it's been rejected in the international tribunals for Rwanda and Yugoslavia, and, most importantly, it's been rejected by the Congress of the United States, in 1997."

The argument didn't seem to be finding much traction with Kennedy, who pointed out that the government could simply recharge Hamdan if need be, a concern of Katyal's from the beginning, so he quickly transitioned to their claim that Hamdan's commission violated his right under the Uniform Code of Military Justice to be present at all portions of his own trial.

At this, Scalia became a bit sarcastic.

"You acknowledge the existence of things called commissions," Scalia said. "Or don't you?"

"We do," Katyal replied.

But why even have military commissions, Scalia continued, if they are obligated to follow the same rules as court-martial trials? "I mean, I thought that the whole object was to have a different procedure," the justice snapped.

Katyal answered by drawing a distinction between the 867-page Army manual governing court-martial trials and the much shorter Uniform Code of Military Justice. The president is free to depart from many of the trial rules set out by the Army in the court-martial manual, he explained, just not from the fundamental rules established by Congress in the Uniform Code, including the defendant's right to be present at his own trial.

Now Justice Breyer spoke, echoing Scalia's question: "But if you have to have approximately the same procedures, what's the point of having a military commission?"

Katyal felt a little nervous addressing his old boss, and he stammered for the first time since the beginning of the argument. He recovered his composure and explained that military commissions had not been created to allow the president to try people in whatever way he wished. They were courts of necessity that had historically been used only when no other options were available. "Essentially, the worry is one of forum shopping, that you give the President the ability to pick a forum and define the rules," Katyal said. "And that fundamentally open-ended authority is what I believe this Court rejected . . . when it rejected the blank check."

Katyal wasn't sure how much time he had left. The white light on the lectern that flashes when an advocate has five minutes remaining had not yet been illuminated, but he knew he had to be close by now, and he had not yet touched on the Geneva Conventions.

Katyal quickly zeroed in on what he believed was their most compelling Geneva argument, the fact that Hamdan's commission violated Common Article 3 of the conventions. In the aftermath of September 11, the Bush administration had staked out the position that this provision, like the rest of the conventions, didn't apply to the conflict with al Qaeda. Katyal thought this was dead wrong. He had spent a lot of time studying the history of the drafting of the Geneva Conventions and was convinced that the authors of Common Article 3 had meant for it to guarantee a floor of humane treatment to combatants captured in *any* conflict. As Katyal now pointed out to the justices, this minimum baseline included the right to a trial by a "regularly constituted court" following judicial standards recognized as "indispensable to civilized peoples." Hamdan's commission did not qualify.

Scalia again played the antagonist, peering through his gold-rimmed glasses as he challenged Katyal's definition of a regularly constituted court. His tone verged on patronizing: "In your brief, I gather . . . what you meant is a court that was preexisting. It doesn't necessarily mean that . . . It could mean one that was set up for the occasion, but was set up for the occasion by proper procedures. Wouldn't that be a 'regularly constituted court'?"

KATYAL: Well, I think the way that it has been interpreted, "regularly constituted court," is not an ad hoc court with ad hoc rules.

JUSTICE SCALIA: Well, I mean, not ad hoc in that sense, "I'm creating one court for this defendant, another court for the other defendant," but setting up for the occasion, and for trying numerous defendants, a new court. I

> don't think that, just because it's a new court, you
> can say that it's not a "regularly constituted court."
> KATYAL: So long as it is, (a) independent of the executive . . .
> and, (b) affords the rights known to civilized
> peoples. And here, we think this military
> commission strays from both of those.

Kennedy interjected and brought the conversation around to Hamdan himself for the first time: How should the Court view him? Should it accept the government's claim that there is probable cause to believe that he was an unlawful combatant who had fought out of uniform and conspired with al Qaeda?

No, Katyal, answered, because Hamdan had never had a proper hearing, which was also required under the Geneva Conventions, to determine whether he was a prisoner of war; the president had simply declared him an unlawful combatant. And even if he wasn't found to be a POW, Katyal continued, he was still entitled to the minimum baseline of protections provided by Common Article 3.

The white light was now illuminated, and Katyal wanted to make sure that he had at least a little time left for his rebuttal, if for no other reason than to prevent the government from having the last word. Katyal reserved the balance of his time and sat back down at counsel's table. He was happy with his performance. He had managed to hit all of their claims, which he knew was extraordinarily rare at Supreme Court arguments.

ALL EYES NOW TURNED to Paul Clement, a slender, bespectacled man with a high forehead in a morning coat and striped pants, the traditional outfit worn inside the Supreme Court by the United States solicitor general.

Two months shy of his fortieth birthday, Clement, an ex–Scalia clerk, had already argued thirty-two cases before the Court and had won the vast majority of them. He brought no notes to the lectern with him and addressed the justices with a casual confidence, almost as though he were lecturing a graduate school seminar on the president's long-standing authority to try enemy combatants before military commissions. "That authority was part and parcel of George Washington's authority as Commander in Chief of the Revolutionary forces, as dramatically illustrated by the case of Major André,"* he said. "And that authority was incorporated into the Constitution. Congress has repeatedly recognized and sanctioned that authority."

Stevens was the first to interrupt, asking what sorts of laws these commissions were to enforce. "Well, what I would say, Justice Stevens, is, they basically enforce the laws of war," Clement answered.

Souter seemed a little puzzled: Why, then, weren't the commissions observing the Geneva Conventions, which were an integral part of the laws of war? This seemed like circular logic. The government couldn't claim to be operating under the laws of war and at the same time assert that the Geneva Conventions didn't apply to the commissions, could it? "I don't see how you can have it both ways," Souter said.

"We're not trying to have it both ways, Justice Souter," Clement answered, a trace of irritation in his voice. "The fact that the Geneva Conventions are part of the laws of war doesn't mean that Petitioner is entitled to any protections under those Conventions."

But isn't the Petitioner—Hamdan—at least entitled to make a claim that he is protected by the conventions? Souter asked.

Of course, Clement answered: He is free to make that claim at his military commission.

Now Kennedy entered the fray. He was "having trouble" with the government's argument that a challenge to the legitimacy of the military commissions be brought at the commission itself.

Scalia intervened on Clement's behalf for the first of several times during the argument to say that the discussion under way was irrelevant. A challenge to the validity of a court shouldn't be considered anyway until the trial was over.

Clement, happy for the help from his old boss, agreed. "That's ex-

---

*During the Revolutionary War, American forces captured the British Army's major general John André with the defense plans for West Point and tried him before a military court for spying.

actly right, Justice Scalia. And this Court made clear that it doesn't intervene—"

Kennedy cut him off, somewhat incredulously. "If a group of people decides they're going to try somebody, we wait until that group of people finishes the trial . . . before habeas intervenes to determine the authority of the tribunal to hold and to try?"

The normally unflappable Clement bristled at this. "With respect, Justice Kennedy, this isn't a 'group of people.' This is the president invoking an authority that he's exercised in virtually every war that we've had."

Clement added that Congress too had spoken on this issue in the Detainee Treatment Act and had agreed with the president: "Congress has made it clear that, whatever else is true, these military commission proceedings can proceed, and exclusive review can be done after the fact, after conviction, in the D.C. Circuit."

Now Breyer jumped in, taking issue with Clement's interpretation of the DTA or, rather, pointing out that in order to accept the government's reading of the bill, the justices would be forced to grapple with "the most terribly difficult and important constitutional question" of whether Congress can deprive the Supreme Court of authority to hear an ongoing habeas corpus case.

Stevens put an even finer point on it. By limiting the jurisdiction of the federal courts to hear detainee lawsuits in the DTA, had Congress suspended the great writ of habeas corpus or not?

"I think both," Clement replied.

"It can't be both," Stevens snapped, eliciting laughter from the courtroom.

By now Clement's ease and grace had curdled into defensiveness. He dug in his heels. "I don't see why I can't have alternative arguments here, and anywhere else, Justice Stevens."

Clement elaborated on the government's position: it did not believe that Congress had consciously intended to suspend detainees' rights to habeas corpus when it passed the DTA, but that even if it had inadvertently done so, such an extraordinary move—the Constitution permits the suspension of habeas only in times of "rebellion" and "invasion" or when "public safety" requires it—would have been justified by 9/11. "My view would be that if Congress, sort of, stumbles upon a suspension of the writ, but the preconditions are satisfied, that would still be constitutionally valid."

Souter appeared stunned by the suggestion that Congress might have accidentally "stumbled on" the suspension of habeas corpus. "Isn't there a pretty good argument that a suspension of the writ of habeas is just about the most stupendously significant act that the Congress of the United States can take?" he asked. "And, therefore, we ought to be at least a little slow to accept your argument that it can be done from pure inadvertence?"

Clement tried to draw a distinction between the right to habeas corpus as it applied to enemy combatants and regular aliens.

At this, Souter's face reddened in anger. Normally the least confrontational of the justices, a man with the placid demeanor of a small-town librarian, he rocked forward abruptly and cut Clement off. Numerous Court watchers later remarked that they had never seen him so exercised. "Now, wait a minute," Souter sputtered in disbelief. "The writ is the writ. There are not two writs of habeas corpus, one for some cases and one for others."

Mercifully for Clement, the conversation soon turned away from habeas corpus and toward the legitimacy of the military commissions themselves. But the battering continued.

"If the President can do this, well, then he can set up commissions to go to Toledo, and, in Toledo, pick up an alien, and not have any trial at all, except before that special commission," Breyer said.

Clement replied that America was at war and that war justified the use of military commissions.

But the president, not Congress, had defined the laws, such as the prohibition against conspiracy, that the commission would enforce, Breyer noted. "Isn't there a separation-of-powers problem there?"

"I sure hope not, Justice Breyer," Clement answered, "because that's been the tradition for over two hundred years."

"But I don't think, Mr. Clement, the two hundred years have approved of his adding additional crimes under the laws of war. I don't think we have ever held that the president can make something a crime which was not already a crime under the laws of war."

When the red light flashed and Clement finally sat down, he looked a bit dazed, like a heavyweight champion returning to his corner after an unexpectedly tough fight.

KATYAL HAD MISSED much of the fight. He was by now well acquainted with Swift's tendency to provide a running commentary when the opposing side was at the podium. He had asked Goldstein to sit between the two of them at counsel's table so he could concentrate on Clement's argument, but Goldstein's wife had gotten sick that morning and he had never made it to the courthouse. Katyal had shushed Swift several times, at one point even threatening to get up and move, but Swift had soon resumed editorializing.

Katyal wasn't sure how much time was left when he stood up for his rebuttal. The chief justice usually tells advocates, but Stevens, who was unaccustomed to the presiding role, had forgotten to do so. Knowing that it would cost him precious seconds to ask, Katyal instead dived right in. He took issue with a few of Clement's points and then quickly moved toward his final remarks. He wanted to end as he had begun, by stressing that there was nothing radical about what he was asking the Court to do, that it was the president who had broken with American history and tradition: "If you defer to this system and give the president the ability to launch all of these tribunals for seventy-five individuals with these charges, with these procedures, you will be countenancing a huge expansion of military jurisdiction."

Katyal closed with a quote from Thomas Paine that he had cited in his original law review article on the commissions and that was now printed on the back of the military commission defense team's office T-shirts. He had been debating whether or not to use the line right up until now—it was purely rhetorical, and he was worried that it would prompt an eye roll or even a snicker from Scalia—but the mood in the courtroom seemed right. "It was a great American patriot, Thomas Paine, who warned, 'He that would make his own liberty secure must guard even his enemy from oppression, for if he violates this duty he establishes a precedent that will reach to himself,'" Katyal said. "That's what we're asking you to do here, just enforce the lawful uses of military commissions and the historic role of this Court."

At 12:31 p.m. on March 28, 2006, *Hamdan v. Rumsfeld* was submitted.

Katyal turned to shake Clement's hand, but the solicitor general was already moving to the door, apparently so out of sorts that he had forgotten about this post-argument ritual.

For his part, Swift spun around, hoping to catch Hemingway's eye, but the general was already gone.

As Katyal joined the throngs of people spilling out of the courtroom and into the Great Hall, he felt exhilarated. There had been a few hiccups, but not even his best moot had gone this well. Katyal thought instantly of the young law professor who had advised him to give up the argument. Whatever happened from here, at least he knew that he wasn't going to regret arguing the case.

Katyal, Swift, McMillan, Sipos, and Schneider descended the courthouse steps together. When they reached the bank of microphones at the bottom of the long marble staircase, Katyal introduced the Perkins lawyers and turned the podium over to Swift.

"First of all, I'd like to thank Professor Katyal," Swift said. "Three years ago, after meeting Mr. Hamdan, I came to him and asked him to help me prove that there was law in Guantánamo, that there was law everywhere. And he undertook that with me. Then, shortly thereafter, Perkins Coie joined me. And what you've seen today is the culmination of our efforts."

For years Swift had envisioned a moment like this one, although in his mind it had followed a performance by him. But over the past few weeks, and especially over the last ninety minutes, as he watched Katyal argue almost flawlessly before the justices, his feelings of disappointment had melted away. As he faced the cameras, Swift was just happy to be there. Before taking questions, he concluded with a final jab at the commissions: "If you believe that this is a full and fair trial, then you believe the Bill of Rights is irrelevant."

The JAGs from the military commission defense office had gathered nearby and were rehashing the argument. Sundel stood among them in civilian clothes. "Whoops, I think I just accidentally suspended habeas!" Colonel Sullivan joked.

That night Perkins Coie hosted a dinner for Katyal and Swift and their wives at an upscale restaurant near the White House called the Oval Room. The wine was flowing, and the mood was festive. The whole Perkins team was there, even Sharp, who toasted Katyal's performance.

Before dinner was served, Swift stood up to make a presentation to Katyal, and felt a rush of gratitude. Who but Katyal, for all his bullheadedness, could have brought them all to this moment? Swift produced an American flag enclosed in a clear plastic case and read the text that accompanied it: "This is to certify that the accompanying flag of the United States of America was presented to Neal Katyal by LCDR Charles Swift, detailed defense counsel in the case of *Hamdan v. Rumsfeld*, for his tireless pursuit of liberty and justice for all. The flag was flown over the northeast gate which separates communist Cuba from the United States naval base, Guantánamo Bay, Cuba. Every day, United States Marines watch and wait as they protect the freedom for which so many have fought and died."

Katyal, obviously moved, took the flag. Later that night, when Joanna went out to get the car and Katyal was saying his goodbyes, McMillan came to speak to him privately. His eyes were moist, and his voice cracked as he spoke. "Neal, your performance today . . . your service to the Constitution . . . everything our country and our profession was built on. I've never been so proud. Thank you for letting me be a part of it."

At home, Katyal opened a bottle of Hungarian dessert wine that his father had given him for Christmas in 2003, just a few months before he got sick, and drank it with Joanna and his mother and sister. He woke up the following morning startled by the realization of how little he had to do. For the next several weeks, he taught his classes, went to the gym—he had gained twenty-five pounds since starting the case—and spent his evenings and weekends with his family.

Georgetown posted an audio recording of the *Hamdan* oral argument on the law school's website, and it automatically downloaded onto Katyal's iPod. He listened to it during a run one afternoon and was pleased. A more seasoned advocate might have been smoother, but he didn't want to change any of his answers.*

AS KATYAL'S LIFE was finally returning to normal, Swift's was falling apart.

A few weeks after the argument he graduated, with honors, from the trial advocacy program at Temple. His parents came to Philadelphia for the commencement ceremony and spent the weekend with Debbie and him in Virginia. When Swift returned home from driving them to the airport on Monday morning, Debbie told him she wanted a divorce.

Swift was stunned. He knew their marriage wasn't perfect, but in his mind he had been working on his end of it, trying to be home more, to help around the house, and to shut up and listen. He was also in the final stretch of the *Hamdan* case; life would be returning to normal soon enough.

To Debbie, it was in many ways surprising that they had stayed together for so long. She had been only eighteen years old when Swift proposed, and had he not just gotten orders to go to Guam, they could easily have just continued dating and never married. Even though Debbie had grown up in Annapolis, she hadn't been prepared for the shock of Navy life. "I was one very young, innocent, naive girl being shipped off three thousand miles only to find that her husband takes off for six months at a time," she later recalled. She had encouraged Swift to apply to law school, and even helped him type up his applications, in the hope that their life would stabilize if he became a lawyer, not realizing that she'd still be losing him for long stretches, only to his cases rather than to Navy cruises.

---

* Several weeks after the argument, Katyal also found himself in the unusual position of having to introduce Clement, who was being honored at an event at Georgetown's law school. If that wasn't strange enough, the other speaker was Justice Scalia. Katyal wrote out his remarks in their entirety, just to make sure he didn't say anything that might adversely affect the justice's consideration of *Hamdan*. He told the audience that he was "darn nervous" the night before he went up against Clement: "I'm not sure if you remember the news, but there were reports of unusual cries coming from the zoo that were blamed on the baby panda. Well, it turns out that was me at about 3:00 a.m."

The Argument

There was no question that *Hamdan* was the precipitating event. Debbie had never taken much interest in Swift's cases, and while it had initially been exciting to see him in the newspapers and on TV, she had grown tired of his constantly pacing around the house, chatting up reporters, or bickering with Katyal—the relationship between the two lawyers reminded her of that of Lucy and Ricky in *I Love Lucy*—that is, when he wasn't in his office or on Guantánamo.

But Debbie could see that *Hamdan* had really just turned Swift into a more exaggerated version of who he had always been. He was someone who truly felt like himself only when he was completely consumed by some cause; downtime seemed always to disorient him. Children might have drawn his focus away from his work, but they had not been able to have any. Swift was not going to change, and Debbie had decided that life with him was no longer what she wanted.

Swift did everything he could to talk her out of it, but she nevertheless moved out of the house in May 2006. A few weeks later, though, they were unexpectedly brought back together when Debbie's grandmother, who had essentially raised her, became fatally ill. Swift had never particularly liked her grandmother—he found her to be ungenerous and judgmental—but he wanted to be by Debbie's side during this tough time. Being back in Annapolis, where they had met and fallen in love, made the prospect of their marriage's ending that much more painful for Swift, and he convinced Debbie to at least try couples counseling before giving up on nineteen years of marriage.

LIKE EVERYTHING ELSE at the United States Supreme Court, the deliberative process follows a time-honored ritual. Within days of the oral argument, the justices gather in an oak-paneled conference room lined with bound volumes of all the Court's prior opinions. After the customary shaking of hands, they take their seats around a large rectangular table, beneath a portrait of the most influential figure in the history of American constitutional law, John Marshall. The chief justice summarizes the facts of each case under consideration—with respect to *Hamdan*, that task would have fallen to Stevens—and the justices vote, one by one and in order of seniority.

This is just the beginning of the process, though. Next, the se-niormost justice on the side of the majority designates an author for the Court's main opinion. Once the opinion is written, which can take as long as six weeks, it is circulated, both to give the justices who are joining it the opportunity to comment and to give dissenting justices something to respond to. Then the justice or justices writing for the minority circulate their dissents. This back-and-forth can go on for weeks, with the justices repeatedly reworking their drafts to take those of their colleagues into account.

Once all the opinions are complete, the decision is announced in the courtroom. Rulings are never made available to the public before-hand, nor does the Court ever disclose which cases will be decided on what day. Advocates or interested parties who wish to hear the opin-ions directly from the justices' mouths can only show up on decision days and take their chances.

Katyal went to his first decision day on Monday, May 22, 2006. The justices had stopped sitting at the end of April, making the Court a much quieter, more subdued place than when it was in session. Inside the courtroom Katyal ran into Clement, who had come in hopes of hearing the opinion in one of his other cases. "What are *you* doing here?" Clement asked, surprised. "*Hamdan* won't be coming down un-til the last day of the term."

Katyal knew Clement was probably right: not only was *Hamdan* a complicated case, but it was one that the justices obviously felt pas-sionate about. Their respective opinions would almost certainly be ricocheting among the various chambers for weeks. Still, he didn't want to risk missing it.

So began a weekly or, depending on the week, twice-weekly ritual. Katyal would put on a suit and tie—with the students now on summer vacation, he would otherwise wear jeans or even shorts to the office—drop his kids at school, drive to Georgetown, and walk over to the Supreme Court building, a twenty-minute trip, in time to watch the justices take their seats on the bench and hand down the day's deci-sions at ten o'clock sharp.

It was an excruciating process. Swift met Katyal there most days—they had by now resumed their routine of talking on the phone twice a day, endlessly speculating about when the justices might rule and what they might say—and they would be in suspense right up until the moment Chief Justice Roberts announced which decision was next. Katyal couldn't help searching for clues in the justices' faces as they filed into the courtroom. One morning he was sure Kennedy was looking at him with a dour expression, and he became convinced they had lost. But it was just another day without a decision.

SWIFT AND KATYAL weren't the only ones in agony. Hamdan had been a little agitated when Swift visited him after the argument in early April, but when Swift returned in May without any news, Hamdan was a mess.

Swift knew that this moment, the period between the trial and the decision, was always especially stressful for defendants. He tried to ease Hamdan's mind, assuring him that no news wasn't necessarily bad news, but he was wary of raising his client's hopes too much, not just about winning but about what exactly a victory would mean. The truth was, Swift had no idea himself. Would it be the end of the commissions? An opening to make a deal? Or would the government simply find a way around the decision and proceed with its plan to try his client as a war criminal? "Win, lose, or draw," Swift told Hamdan, "we are going to have to get up the next morning and keep fighting."

On June 10, 2006, the news broke that two unnamed detainees had hanged themselves in Camp Delta. Swift instantly thought of Hamdan. He made several panicked calls to the Defense Department, but by now he had made too many enemies at the Pentagon to get a call back. Katyal made some calls as well, and after an hour and a half of anxiety, he learned through someone at the Justice Department that Hamdan was okay.

The justices gradually worked through their winter and spring caseload, yet week after week passed without a decision on *Hamdan*. With July, the traditional end of the Supreme Court's term, approaching, the pace of the hand-downs accelerated. There was a rumor that *Hamdan* was coming on Wednesday, June 28, the three-month anniversary of the argument, and the courtroom was packed. Three other cases were handed down instead, leaving just *Hamdan* and one other undecided case, *Clark v. Arizona*. Before banging his gavel to adjourn the Court, Chief Justice Roberts said both opinions would be announced the next morning, Thursday, June 29, 2006. Katyal e-mailed the Perkins lawyers with the news and told his students to meet him at four o'clock the following afternoon at a bar in Dupont Circle for either a celebration or a wake.

SWIFT WAS UP at 6:00 a.m. the following morning, walking the dog, when his cell phone rang. He was surprised to hear the voice at the other end, Charles "Cully" Stimson, a former colleague of his in the legal offices at Mayport who was now serving as the deputy assistant secretary of defense for detainee affairs in the Pentagon.* "I just wanted to congratulate you," Stimson said. "Whatever happens today, you've done a tremendous job."

Swift drank a few cups of coffee before putting on the same dark blue dress uniform he'd been wearing to all of the Supreme Court's hand-downs and had been struggling to keep clean. On the Metro into D.C., he took a legal pad out of his backpack and jotted down the seven central issues in *Hamdan* so he could keep track of what they had won and lost while the opinion was being announced.

Katyal, meanwhile, was driving to his office, already exhausted. His three-year-old son, Calder, had somehow contracted hand, foot, and mouth disease, making it impossible for him to eat or drink, so Katyal and Joanna had been up most of the night shooting fluid into his throat with a syringe to keep him hydrated.

Katyal parked his car at Georgetown and then walked over to the Supreme Court building one final time. He had recently figured out a shortcut, reducing his walking time to just eleven minutes. Everyone at the Court knew the *Hamdan* decision was coming; even the guards were looking at Katyal differently. Several lawyers wished him luck as

---

* In January 2007, Stimson became embroiled in controversy after giving a radio interview in which he criticized white-shoe law firms for representing prisoners on Guantánamo.

he moved through the Great Hall and entered the courtroom with Swift by his side.

Because the decision day had been added at the last minute to the Court's calendar, the room wasn't even half full. Katyal and Swift sat in the first row of the section reserved for members of the Supreme Court bar. McMillan and Sipos, who had flown in on the red-eye from Seattle, settled in directly behind them. A handful of Katyal's students were a little farther back, in the section of the courtroom for the general public.

At ten o'clock a high-pitched bell rang, and the justices emerged from behind the red velvet curtains. As Chief Justice Roberts took his seat at the center of the bench, he flashed Katyal a broad grin. Katyal scribbled a note to Swift: "I think we won."

The agony continued, though. *Clark v. Arizona*, a criminal insanity case, was announced first, with Justice Souter reading a detailed summary of his majority opinion.

Five minutes and forty-seven seconds later Justice Stevens cleared his throat and spoke in his flat Chicago monotone. "I have the disposition to announce in number 05-184, *Hamdan Against Rumsfeld*."

Stevens's language threw Katyal. He had used the word "disposition" rather than "decision." Katyal whispered to Swift that the Court might have been fractured, and that no clear majority had emerged.

Stevens laid out the background of the case for one more excruciating minute before finally saying: "We now reverse the court of appeals."

Katyal and Swift both felt a surge of joy. It was not unqualified joy, though. Supreme Court decisions are not necessarily like jury verdicts, with clear winners and losers. The justices could easily have reversed the court of appeals on a narrow, technical point. Their victory could be limited, even insignificant.

Stevens continued. It was a 5–3 decision, with himself and Justices Breyer, Ginsburg, Souter, and Kennedy voting with the majority. Stevens had written the Court's opinion himself, and he now proceeded to summarize it from the bench. His manner was understated, even matter-of-fact, as though he were trying to downplay the historic nature of the Court's ruling, which was nevertheless unmistakable.

The eighty-six-year-old justice moved methodically through the opinion, starting with the Court's determination that the Detainee Treatment Act had not been meant to strip the justices of their authority to hear the case. As Katyal had hoped, the Court had opted not to wrestle with the question of whether or not Congress had the constitutional authority to suspend Hamdan's habeas rights. It had simply concluded that Congress had never intended to do so when it passed the DTA.

Turning to the lawsuit itself, Stevens acknowledged that the president has the power—"in some circumstances"—to convene military commissions. He quickly added, though, that this power is "carefully circumscribed" by the laws of war, including international treaties and statutes like the Uniform Code of Military Justice, which requires that military commissions follow the same rules as court-martial trials unless there are compelling reasons to depart from them. "The danger posed by international terrorists, while certainly severe, does not by itself justify dispensing with usual procedures," Stevens said.

As a result, he continued, "we conclude that the commission lacks power to proceed."

"For similar reasons," Stevens went on, "the commission lacks power to proceed under the Geneva Conventions." Specifically, the Court had determined that Hamdan's commission violated Common Article 3 of the conventions, which mandates that all captured combatants be tried by a "regularly constituted court affording all the judicial guarantees recognized as indispensable by civilized peoples." Hamdan's commission had failed to meet this standard, Stevens said.

The justice moved next to conspiracy: "No treaty or domestic statute makes conspiracy a war crime, and the historical materials from this country as well as international sources confirm that it is not a war crime under the common law of war . . . Because the jurisdiction of a law-of-war military commission stands and falls with the validity of the charge, we conclude that the defect with the charge against petitioner precludes this military commission from proceeding."

Katyal was taken aback. He had been expecting a modest ruling, one consistent with the Court's tradition of deferring to the president during wartime. Instead, the justices had accepted nearly every one of their claims. He turned to Swift and said, "We won everything." Swift, who had been keeping track of their claims on his legal pad, was already thinking the same thing.

STEVENS SPOKE for almost fifteen minutes. When he was done, two of the three justices who made up the Court's minority in *Hamdan*, Scalia and Thomas, exercised their right to summarize their dissenting opinions from the bench as well.

Scalia went first. He too began unemotionally, but as he continued, his disgust with the majority gradually overtook him and he became alternatively biting, dismissive, and incredulous. His opinion focused almost exclusively on the Detainee Treatment Act, which he said had clearly and unambiguously deprived the Court of its jurisdiction to hear *Hamdan*. His colleagues in the majority, he said, had ignored the plain language of the bill as well as a long line of Supreme Court precedents that had established that a statute eliminating jurisdiction applies to pending cases unless it contains an explicit reservation saying that it does not. And they had done so, Scalia said, for "the flimsiest of reasons." He was talking about the legislative history that Katyal had made a concerted effort to generate. His fury rising, Scalia chided his colleagues for relying on "fragments of senatorial speeches that were quite clearly deliberately prepared by the staff of a tiny handful of senators to be cited in the briefs in this very litigation."

Even if the Court did still have jurisdiction over *Hamdan*, Scalia continued, it should have abstained from hearing the case until after Hamdan's military commission had been completed: "Our interference in this case over the executive's objections creates significant and wholly gratuitous inter-branch conflict in an area where we have no expertise." The Court's time-honored practice of erring on the side of caution in cases involving military conflict had just "come crashing down," Scalia said. He closed with a subtle but powerful gesture, replacing the customary words "I respectfully dissent" with "I vigorously dissent."

JUSTICE THOMAS opened by announcing that in his fifteen terms he had never read a dissent from the bench, "but today's decision requires that I do so."* In a deep voice and sober tone, he proceeded to dispute every one of the majority's conclusions, summoning a range of historical and legal precedents to support his claims. The conclusion that conspiracy was not a legitimate war crime was "unsupportable." The Court's holding that the Uniform Code of Military Justice requires that military commissions observe the same procedures as court-martial trials was "similarly unpersuasive." The majority had "fared no better" with respect to its analysis of the Geneva Conventions, which Thomas said could not be enforced in U.S. courts. And even if they could, he continued, the president's determination that Common Article 3 did not apply to the conflict with al Qaeda was entitled to the Court's deference. "This is a straightforward case involving fundamental principles and controlling precedents," he said. "The Court of Appeals, by adhering to these principles and precedents, unanimously rejected petitioner's claims in a mere eighteen pages. This Court should have done likewise."

Katyal hadn't paid much attention to Scalia's comments. He was often bombastic, and Katyal had still been in a fog of euphoria over the majority decision. But he now found himself shushing Swift. Katyal was surprised at how badly he had misread Thomas—he had thought they had a realistic shot at winning his vote†—but was nevertheless moved by the justice's conviction. The past several years had shaken Katyal's faith in both the executive branch and Congress. Little of the debate over Guantánamo Bay and the military commissions had risen above the level of demagoguery. As he listened to Thomas, though, it was clear to Katyal that the justices had engaged in a vigorous debate about the issues raised by *Hamdan*. What's more, his arguments had stood up. Thomas's defense of the administration and denunciation of the Court's majority seemed to enhance their victory, not detract from it.

When Thomas was done, Chief Justice Roberts rapped his gavel

---

*This turned out to be inaccurate. Thomas had in fact read one prior dissent.

†Katyal's optimism about Thomas was rooted in an opinion the justice had written in a 2004 detainee case in which he asserted that prisoners being tried and punished are entitled to greater rights than those simply being detained.

and adjourned the Court for the summer. Katyal gathered the *Hamdan* team together and told them to walk out of the courtroom quietly, with an air of humility. Before confronting the media, they reconvened briefly in the lawyers' lounge to take a closer look at the opinion. A Supreme Court page brought a copy in, and Katyal read it out loud, with Swift, McMillan, Sipos, and a group of his students gathered around him.

PRESIDENT BUSH was in a meeting with the prime minister of Japan, Junichiro Koizumi, when the *Hamdan* decision was released. When asked about the ruling at a press conference later that morning, Bush stuck to generalities, explaining that he hadn't yet had a chance to fully review the findings, but suggested that he wasn't necessarily going to give up on the idea of the commissions.

A few miles away at the Supreme Court building, dozens of reporters and news crews were waiting for Katyal and Swift as they descended the courthouse steps. Katyal felt, as he would later describe it, "thick with emotion about the role of the Court." There was no lingering bitterness about the government's various maneuverings to undermine their case. On the contrary, he felt grateful that they had been able to see their lawsuit through.

Standing before the media, Katyal first thanked Perkins Coie. For all the friction between them, he knew that the constant questioning of the Perkins lawyers—McMillan in particular—had made their case immeasurably stronger.

Katyal would ordinarily have turned the microphone over to Swift next, but he had jotted something down on a legal pad earlier that morning—before he knew whether they had won or lost—that he wanted to say first: "What happened today, a man from Yemen with a fourth-grade education accused of conspiring with one of the most horrendous individuals on the planet, being able to sue the most powerful man in the world, the president of the United States, and have his case heard—that is something that is fundamentally great about America and something we should be celebrating to the rest of the world. In no other country would that be possible."

Swift followed in his Navy blues, his barrel chest thrust forward as if actually swelling with pride. "Our values are what won here today," he said, "our values for the rule of law, for the idea that every individual and that human rights were protected under the rule of law. That's what won."

Katyal had arranged in advance for them to call Hamdan from Georgetown that afternoon. He and Swift would be going down to Guantánamo in a few days to discuss the decision with him in detail, but win or lose, they wanted to be the ones to deliver the news. Katyal knew that Hamdan would be on a satellite phone and was worried that they wouldn't be able to hear him on speakerphone, so he set Swift up in a colleague's office and conferenced him in.

"What's going on?" Hamdan asked, confused. "They won't tell me anything."

"You won your case," Katyal answered.

"Thanks be to God," Hamdan said.

"This doesn't mean you go free," Katyal quickly added. "It just means you have a better chance at a fair trial."

KATYAL STOPPED BY the bar in Dupont Circle for only a few minutes. He had agreed to go on the *NewsHour with Jim Lehrer* and had to pick up Rem, who was now four, at school first. Joanna had left work early to take Calder to a pediatric clinic for an IV. She called Katyal on his way to the *NewsHour*'s studio in suburban Virginia to let him know that Calder was doing much better but was going to have to stay at the clinic for several more hours. Rem waited in the greenroom during the interview, and he and Katyal drove back home for dinner. Once the children were in bed, Katyal drank a Leffe Brune that he had put in the refrigerator that morning, hoping he would have something to celebrate, and went to sleep himself.

Swift didn't stay long at the bar either. He had been giving interviews all day and was exhausted. He could also already feel his excitement over the decision draining out of him. Swift experienced all his wins and losses acutely, but they never stayed with him long. This was partly a matter of training—busy trial lawyers can't afford to wallow or preen—but it was also a product of his restless nature. Swift instinctively sought stimulation. Once a trial was complete and a verdict had been rendered, he was ready to move on.

From Dupont Circle, Swift took the Metro back to his house in Virginia. It was still filled with Debbie's things, even though she was now living temporarily in an apartment near LaGuardia. For the first time in weeks, Swift didn't miss her intensely. He had never shared his posttrial moments with her—or anyone else, for that matter.

Before going to bed, Swift sat on his deck and smoked a cigar, as he always did following a big trial. It was his way of getting closure. If he won, he would congratulate himself on a job well done; if he lost, he would beat himself up over what he could have done differently. Either way, when he woke up, the case would be over. He knew that this case would be different, that Hamdan was not going anywhere anytime soon, but he didn't have a clue what the government's next move was going to be.

He got his first inkling the following morning when the Pentagon's general counsel, William Haynes, turned up at the military commissions defense team's office to speak with him and the other JAGs. "Congratulations to all of you—especially you, Commander Swift," Haynes said. "The decision does not change anything in this office. Keep working on your cases."

NINETEEN

The Heroes of Guantánamo?

FOLLOWING THE DECISION, Swift and Katyal were deluged with interview requests. Katyal, who had in the past steered virtually all media inquiries to Swift, agreed to cooperate with a few stories, and even went on *The Colbert Report*. He prepped carefully for the appearance and brought a couple of props with him, including a poster-size copy of the Constitution that he picked up at the Supreme Court gift shop and heavily redacted with a thick black marker: the Constitution according to President Bush.

Swift, already something of a public figure, was everywhere. To CNN's Bob Franken, he was the man who had "for so long been a voice in the wilderness." To *The Washington Post*'s William Arkin, he was simply "the hero of Guantánamo." *Vanity Fair*'s Marie Brenner started work on a long profile—"Taking on Guantánamo"—and *Esquire* asked Swift to write something himself about the military commissions and the war on terror. "Yes, I am the military officer who sued my commander in chief and the secretary of defense on behalf of a Guantánamo Bay detainee named Salim Hamdan," it began.

The *Hamdan* decision led all of the nightly news broadcasts, and the next day's papers. JUSTICES, 5–3, BROADLY REJECT BUSH PLAN TO TRY DETAINEES, *The New York Times*'s four-column front-page headline read. In the accompanying story, reporter Linda Greenhouse described the decision as "a sweeping and categorical defeat for the administration" and "a defining moment in the ever-shifting balance of power among branches of government."

Students of the Supreme Court picked up on an interesting bit of historical symmetry with respect to the *Hamdan* decision. Its author had once clerked for one of the Supreme Court's lesser-known justices, Wiley B. Rutledge, who had himself written a memorable opinion in a World War II–era military commission case concerning a Japanese general named Tomoyuki Yamashita. The Court heard the case in 1946—one year before the twenty-seven-year-old John Paul Stevens would arrive in Washington for his clerkship—and upheld Yamashita's conviction by a U.S. military commission, despite some glaring procedural deficiencies in his trial, most notably the admission of hearsay evidence and the use of unnamed witnesses. Rutledge had dissented powerfully from the Court's majority:

> More is at stake than General Yamashita's fate. There could be no possible sympathy for him if he is guilty of the atrocities for which his death is sought. But there can be and should be justice administered according to law. In this stage of war's aftermath it is too early for Lincoln's great spirit, best lighted in the second inaugural, to have wide hold for the treatment of foes. It is not too early, it is never too early, for the nation steadfastly to follow its great constitutional traditions, none older or more universally protective against unbridled power than due process of law in the trial and punishment of men, that is, of all men, whether citizens, aliens, alien enemies or enemy belligerents. It can become too late.

It was easy to discern Rutledge's influence in Stevens's seventy-three-page *Hamdan* opinion, which legal pundits and scholars were already comparing to such landmark executive authority rulings as *United States v. Nixon*, the 1974 decision that compelled President Nixon to turn over the secret White House tapes that led to his impeachment.

Court watchers instantly recognized that *Hamdan* was about much more than the president's military commissions; it was about nothing less than the president's obligation to comply with the law. Less than twenty-four hours after the decision, Walter Dellinger, a former solicitor general and law professor at Duke, called *Hamdan* "the most important decision on presidential power ever." As he put it, "The farther back you stand, the more significant it appears. Up close, it's a case about Mr. Hamdan, or maybe about Hamdan and a dozen others . . . But that is not what *Hamdan* is really about. *Hamdan* is about the OLC [Office of Legal Counsel] torture memo, and it's about whether the president can refuse to comply with the McCain Amendment.* It's about all those laws the president says, as he signs them, that he will not commit to obey . . . And, by the way, he won't even commit to tell Congress he is not obeying the law."

Without question, the Court's most significant holding in *Hamdan* was that Common Article 3 of the Geneva Conventions applied to America's conflict with al Qaeda—and that Hamdan's military commission had violated it. With this ruling, the justices had done much more than demolish the president's military commissions. They had struck a major blow to the foundation of the administration's entire system for detaining and interrogating prisoners.

The idea undergirding Common Article 3 is simple: Every captured combatant, no matter how heinous the crimes he stands accused of, is entitled to a floor of humane treatment. That includes a fair trial, but it also includes a good deal more. Among other things, Common Article 3 prohibits "outrages upon personal dignity," "humiliating and degrading treatment," and "cruel treatment and torture."

The legal basis for many of the administration's practices in the war on terror had been built on the now false presumption that it would be unconstrained by the protections guaranteed by Common Article 3. As such, *Hamdan* would force a variety of dramatic policy shifts inside the administration, beginning with a Pentagon memo issued days after the decision stating that all Defense Department personnel would now be required to comply with Common Article 3. A classified CIA program to detain and interrogate "high-value" detainees in secret prisons abroad would be terminated, as would the use of "enhanced interrogation techniques" like waterboarding, an ancient form of torture that simulates the experience of drowning.

---

*The McCain Amendment, which banned the inhumane treatment of prisoners, was passed by Congress and signed into law in 2005.

Hamdan had rendered vulnerable some non-Geneva-related antiterrorism policies as well. For instance, by asserting that the war against terror does not give the president the right to defy the laws of Congress, the justices had effectively declared illegal the National Security Agency's so-called terrorist surveillance program, which authorized warrantless wiretapping in violation of a 1978 statute, the Foreign Intelligence Surveillance Act.

Yet *Hamdan* was less a rebuff to the Bush administration than an affirmation of the majesty of America's constitutional government and the critical role of the courts within it. The framers wanted the people to govern the country through their elected representatives, but they also created a third branch of government, the independent judiciary, to ensure that these politicians remained true to the system set forth in the Constitution. Unelected and unremovable (absent impeachment), justices represent something of an antidemocratic force in America's political system. Yet the fact that they are not accountable to the electorate insulates them from the public's baser instincts. And under the system designed by the framers, when the justices speak, both the president and Congress must listen.

At bottom, *Hamdan* was a reminder of the resilience of the principles upon which this country was built. The system worked: the president broke the rules, and the justices, acting equally as the nation's conscience and the defender of its traditions, stopped him. In so doing, they restored to America a measure of dignity that had been badly eroded by Abu Ghraib, the torture memos, the secret CIA prisons, and numerous other post-9/11 antiterrorism policies. Swift had told the Senate in June 2005 that our treatment of detainees was about us—who *we* are—and the Supreme Court had now answered that question resoundingly and unambiguously. America was strong enough to withstand a challenge to its commander in chief and to treat even its worst enemies according to the law.

SWIFT AND KATYAL flew down to Guantánamo a few days after the decision. Swift was relieved to be finally seeing Hamdan under more positive circumstances. Katyal was still riding the high from their victory. As it happened, the date of their trip was July 4. By the time they cleared security and were checking into the bachelor officers' quarters, the sun had set and fireworks were exploding over the bay. Katyal had never felt so patriotic.

The following morning they went to see Hamdan. They had arranged the visit days earlier, but Hamdan hadn't been moved to Camp Echo for the meeting yet, so Swift and Katyal were left baking in the hot sun for thirty minutes. When they were finally cleared to enter the prison, one of the guards at the gate went through Katyal's papers and pulled out a copy of the Supreme Court opinion that he had brought for Hamdan.

"You can't bring this in," the guard said. "Security reasons."

Katyal pointed at Hamdan's name on the decision in disbelief. "But this is *his* case!"

"We're under orders," the guard replied. "No outside information inside the camp."

Katyal had always played the good cop when they ran into trouble on Guantánamo, but this time he went on the offensive. Full of righteous anger, he demanded to see the guard's superiors. Another thirty minutes passed before the guard eventually relented, returning the opinion and waving them through.

When they broke for lunch a couple of hours later, Katyal and Swift went out to the Naval Exchange and brought back a cheesecake, Hamdan's favorite treat, for a proper celebration. Hamdan couldn't eat without approved utensils, though, and the guards didn't bring them in until the late afternoon, when they came to announce that the visit was over. Hamdan managed one bite of the wilted dessert before Swift and Katyal were instructed to leave, and to take the melted cheesecake with them.

Despite this inauspicious start, it was a good week for Hamdan. Katyal and Swift went through the opinion line by line with him and laid out some of the administration's potential next steps. After such an embarrassing defeat at the nation's highest court, there was some chance they might even offer a short sentence for a guilty plea in an effort to save face.

Hamdan paid close attention and took copious notes. His spirits were higher than they had been since his brief stay in Camp 4 a year earlier. He didn't expect to be going home immediately, but he couldn't help but absorb Swift's and Katyal's enthusiasm about the ruling.

BY THE TIME Swift and Katyal returned to Washington on July 9, 2006, the administration had made its next move: the president had urged Congress to move quickly to pass a bill authorizing his military commissions.

The White House soon floated a proposed version of the legislation that it had in mind. Katyal got his hands on a copy and was astonished. *This* was the president's reaction to being told by the Supreme Court that he had violated his oath to support and defend the Constitution? Not only were the trials envisioned virtually identical to the ones the justices had just declared unlawful, but the bill effectively gave the president statutory authorization to circumvent the Geneva Conventions, including Common Article 3.

During the congressional debate over the military commissions, Katyal testified at a July 19 hearing of the Senate Armed Services Committee. He rehashed yet again the myriad flaws with the president's commissions, urging lawmakers to tread cautiously—"The eyes of the world are indeed upon us, and what Congress does here may establish a legal framework for the war on terror for generations to come"— and stressed the importance of preserving the Court's opinion in *Hamdan*: "Only America is wise enough to let such a decision stand as the law of the land and to celebrate it as a vindication of the Rule of Law."

Katyal's visions of a relaxing summer were quickly shattered. Unable to find a lobbying firm to help them press their case against the proposed legislation on Capitol Hill, he spent most of July and August on the Hill himself, trying to persuade any lawmaker who would meet with him to reject the president's proposal.*

The Democrats were a lost cause: the 2006 midterm elections were

---

*Among those Katyal met with—for two hours—was the Illinois senator Barack Obama, who ultimately voted against the legislation.

looming, and they were wary of being labeled weak on national security. But a handful of Republican senators—most prominently, John Warner, a former secretary of the Navy, and, to a lesser extent, John McCain and Lindsey Graham—came out against particular aspects of the president's proposed legislation. So too did a number of military leaders, who were especially troubled by the idea of setting aside Common Article 3, which had long protected America's armed forces abroad by ensuring universally accepted norms of civilized behavior.

Gen. John Vessey, chairman of the Joint Chiefs of Staff under President Reagan, wrote a letter to McCain urging him not to allow the White House to gut the Geneva Conventions. In it, Vessey quoted Gen. George Marshall's reminder to America's troops of their moral obligation to those in U.S. custody in the aftermath of World War II:

> The United States abides by the laws of war. Its Armed Forces, in dealing with all other peoples, are expected to comply with the laws of war, in the spirit and the letter. In waging war, we do not terrorize helpless non-combatants, if it is within our power to avoid so doing. Wanton killing, torture, cruelty, or the working of unusual hardship on enemy prisoners or populations is not justified under any circumstance. Likewise respect for the reign of law, as that term is understood in the United States, is expected to follow the flag wherever it goes . . .

SWIFT TESTIFIED before the Senate Judiciary Committee and pitched in as much as he could with the lobbying, but he was now consumed with more pressing concerns. He was suddenly grappling not simply with a failing marriage but with a failing career.

The small yet portentous slights from the military had been accumulating for months now. At the end of 2005, all of the JAGs in the defense office had been presented with medals for their work on the commissions. Everyone's but Swift's was a Meritorious Service award; his was the less prestigious Commendation. Not a single member of the Navy brass had called to congratulate Swift on *Hamdan*, and not only had he not been given a hero's welcome on Guantánamo after the decision, but he had been treated with mock reverence in the form of "we are not worthy" bows.

In mid-July 2006, just a couple of weeks after *Hamdan* was decided, Swift learned that he had not been selected for promotion to commander. It was the equivalent of receiving a pink slip; under the military's "up or out" system, officers who aren't promoted are expected to resign.

The military doesn't disclose details from its selection board meetings, so it's impossible to know if the decision was politically motivated. There's no question that Swift's tenure in the JAG Corps had been unconventional. Most upwardly mobile JAGs get out of the courtroom as quickly as possible and focus instead on diversifying their résumés. Swift had done nothing but litigation, and only defense work at that. On the other hand, his fitness reports in the JAG Corps had been excellent, and they'd been especially good since he'd joined the military commissions. Gunn had called him "tremendously creative, hardworking and dedicated." His accomplishments had been recognized outside the military as well: *The National Law Journal* had named him one of the nation's top one hundred lawyers for 2005.

Swift was crushed, if not entirely surprised. From the beginning, he had figured that his public approach to defending Hamdan wasn't going to sit well with his superior officers, and he had already been passed over for promotion once before, a year earlier. You only got two tries, though, so this time it was final. But what bothered Swift most was that no one had even given him a heads-up. He had been forced to learn that his twenty-year naval career was about to end by logging on to the Internet and vainly searching for his name on the 2006 promotions list.

The *Navy Times* reported Swift's non-promotion, and a number of major newspapers picked up on the story, casting Swift as a martyr. *The New York Times* devoted an editorial to the event, headlined THE COST OF DOING YOUR DUTY. "With his defense of Mr. Hamdan and his testimony before Congress starting in July 2003, Commander

Swift did as much as any single individual to expose the awful wrongs of Guantánamo Bay and Mr. Bush's lawless military commissions," the *Times* wrote. "It was a valuable public service and a brave act of conscience, and his treatment is deeply troubling."

The tributes were nice, and Swift took some pleasure in sticking it to the military on his way out the door, but the notion of leaving the Navy terrified him. As much as he chafed against the system, he was comfortable playing the antiestablishment figure—"the nonconformist in a conformist society," as he would later put it. Swift knew that without the structure and discipline the military provided, his life could very easily spin out of control. What's more, his identity was totally bound up in the Navy. He was a romantic, and he connected deeply to the military's history and traditions. A born trial lawyer, he saw his life in storybook terms: he was the JAG Corps maverick who was married to his Naval Academy sweetheart. In the span of just a few months, the whole narrative had unraveled.

ON SEPTEMBER 6, 2006, the president formally unveiled a modified version of his proposed legislation for the military commissions in the East Room of the White House. To raise the drama of the occasion, the administration filled the audience with families of the victims of 9/11 and coupled the announcement with the news that fourteen so-called high-value detainees, including Khalid Sheikh Mohammed, the alleged mastermind of the 9/11 attacks, had just been transferred to Guantánamo Bay to await trial. "As soon as Congress acts to authorize the military commissions I have proposed," Bush said, "the men our intelligence officials believe orchestrated the deaths of nearly three thousand Americans on September 11, 2001, can face justice."

Arlen Specter provided a last gasp of resistance to the president's proposal, introducing an amendment that would also preserve the rights of detainees to file habeas suits in the federal courts. "The right of habeas corpus was established in the Magna Carta in 1215, when, in England, there was action taken against King John to establish a procedure to prevent illegal detention," Specter said during the debate over his amendment. "What the bill seeks to do is set back basic rights by some nine hundred years."

The Senate narrowly rejected Specter's amendment. He had vowed to vote against the president's bill, which he called "patently unconstitutional," but when the legislation reached the floor of the Senate the following day, his resolve crumbled, and he and the rest of the Republican dissidents all cast their votes in favor of the Military Commissions Act, or MCA. It passed overwhelmingly, 65–34.

Katyal was again disillusioned with Congress for its unwillingness to stand up to the president, and he was less than thrilled with the particulars of the legislation. Among other things, he considered it discriminatory: because the Military Commissions Act applied only to foreigners, non-American enemy combatants would be tried in a system that afforded fewer protections than those guaranteed to American enemy combatants in the civil court system. Not even the government's infamous policy of interning Japanese-Americans during World War II, which applied equally to citizens and noncitizens alike, had gone that far.

Still, Katyal wasn't discontent. The trials were *fairer* than those initially envisioned: detainees could no longer be kicked out of the courtroom, they would be able to see all of the evidence against them, and there was now a much stronger prohibition against the use of testimony obtained through torture. Most of all, the White House had backed off its proposal to gut Common Article 3. America's commitment to the Geneva Conventions would remain intact.

Despite Katyal's qualms about Congress's performance, it had at least spoken on the matter of military commissions. Two of the three light switches had been thrown. Now it was up to the third, the courts, to determine whether or not the Military Commissions Act was lawful. At least with respect to the separation of powers envisioned by the framers, America's constitutional order had been restored.

In a sense, Katyal's favorite opinion in *Hamdan* belonged to his old boss, Justice Breyer. It was all of two paragraphs long and wasn't exactly headline worthy, but to Katyal it represented a powerful vindication of the idea that had been animating his opposition to the commissions from the beginning. Breyer wrote, concurring with the Court's majority:

The dissenters say that today's decision would "sorely hamper the President's ability to confront and defeat a new and deadly enemy." They suggest that it undermines our Nation's ability to "preven[t] future attacks" of the grievous sort that we have already suffered . . . That claim leads me to state briefly what I believe the majority sets forth both explicitly and implicitly at greater length. The Court's conclusion ultimately rests upon a single ground: Congress has not issued the Executive a "blank check" . . . Where, as here, no emergency prevents consultation with Congress, judicial insistence upon that consultation does not weaken our Nation's ability to deal with danger. To the contrary, that insistence strengthens the Nation's ability to determine—through democratic means—how best to do so. The Constitution places its faith in those democratic means. Our Court today simply does the same.

So, begrudgingly, Katyal made his peace with the Military Commissions Act, even though it hadn't been the outcome he had hoped for. There was no question that *Hamdan* had sent his professional stock soaring. He was offered high-paying partnerships at a number of top D.C. law firms; law schools and legal societies around the country invited him to come talk about *Hamdan*—in a matter of months, he earned back in speaking fees the forty thousand dollars he had spent on the case; and the *Harvard Law Review* asked him to write a lengthy article about the experience.

Best of all, though, during the cocktail hour of a black-tie dinner on judicial independence in September 2006, a smiling John Roberts approached a cluster of people to whom Katyal was talking to congratulate him on *Hamdan*. "I know I speak for myself and my colleagues when I say that I hope you'll come see us again," the chief justice said, according to several people in the room.

THE ADMINISTRATION wasted no time moving ahead with its plans to try Hamdan. In October 2006, days after the president signed the Military Commissions Act into law, the government filed a motion with Judge Robertson, who had been charged with figuring out how to implement the Supreme Court's decision in *Hamdan v. Rumsfeld*, seeking the dismissal of the case. Robertson granted the government's request in December, concluding that the legislation had stripped Hamdan of his right to habeas corpus.

By this point, Katyal had told the team that he was going to be cutting back on *Hamdan*. Swift was in good hands with McMillan and the rest of the Perkins lawyers, and Katyal was burned out. He wanted to spend more time with his family and refocus his energy on his legal scholarship.

It proved harder to let go than Katyal had anticipated, though. The moment Robertson dismissed the case, he drafted an entirely new thirty-page petition for review at the Supreme Court—the case was now called *Salim Hamdan v. Robert Gates*; Gates was the president's new secretary of defense—mounting a whole new litany of claims against the commissions, including the argument that their inherently biased treatment of noncitizens violated the Constitution's guarantee of equal protection.

On April 30, 2007, the Supreme Court voted 5 to 3 against granting the petition.

HAMDAN'S OPTIMISM quickly faded over the course of the summer of 2006. A couple of weeks after Swift and Katyal visited him in early July, his notes from their conversations as well as his copy of the Supreme Court opinion were confiscated from his cell. Not only were there no offers of a deal from the government, but the administration seemed more determined than ever to try him as a war criminal under the Military Commissions Act. Swift told him that they were going to challenge this new legislation too, but Hamdan didn't much care. He had heard this kind of talk from Swift before, and his situation still hadn't changed.

Once again Hamdan's focus returned to his day-to-day life, which was only getting worse. In October 2006 he was moved into Camp 6, a brand-new maximum-security facility where the conditions were tantamount to solitary confinement.* Hamdan lived in an eight-by-twelve-foot steel cell, and his meals were handed to him through a slot in the door. He had only an hour or so of indirect contact with other detainees during his daily recreation period. (He had to exercise alone, but his chain-link recreation pen adjoined several others.) Hamdan was despondent, though his unhappiness took on a different cast now. He no longer swung dramatically between hope and disappointment. He was now resigned to his miserable fate of staying on Guantánamo indefinitely.

SWIFT TOO was feeling less and less optimistic about his own life. Despite his promises to do whatever it took to keep them together, couples therapy had only steeled Debbie's resolve to split up. In the fall of 2006 she asked Swift for a divorce. He agreed to buy out her share of the house, and she moved into a beachfront condominium in Tampa.

Like many adopted children, Swift was especially vulnerable to the feeling of abandonment. And he wasn't just coping with the loss of Debbie. With Katyal now pulling back on *Hamdan*, they were no longer in constant contact, and soon Swift wouldn't have the Navy to help anchor him either.

It didn't help matters that Swift still hadn't figured out what he was going to do when he left the JAG Corps. For months his head spun with possibilities. He embraced every idea completely, trying each new career on for size. One day he was going to be the pro bono coordinator for Perkins Coie in Seattle, the next day the political strategist for a human rights group in D.C., a lawyer for Major League Baseball, or a candidate for Congress. Nothing seemed to live up to *Hamdan*,

---

*Camp 6 had initially been envisioned as a medium-security prison, but after a rash of uprisings inside Camp Delta—among other incidents, a group of detainees had lured several guards into a cell by faking a suicide attempt and then attacked them with fan blades and broken pieces of fluorescent light fixtures—it had been refashioned as a maximum-security facility.

though, in terms of both the unique sense of purpose it had provided and all the attention the case had brought him. Swift also felt an obligation to see things through with Hamdan, even if that meant representing him as a civilian. And in a funny way, with Debbie gone and Katyal busy with other things, Hamdan was all Swift had left.

At the same time, he desperately wanted the case to be over. He was tired of the monthly trips to Guantánamo—the constant battles on the base and the thankless task of managing his precarious relationship with Hamdan—and he knew that the military commission itself would be little more than a postscript to *Hamdan v. Rumsfeld*. Swift envied Katyal, who had not only returned to his normal life after *Hamdan*, but had benefited enormously from the case. And here he was, still slogging away in the trenches.

In March 2007, Swift sold the house in Falls Church and moved back in with his uncle, with whom he had stayed when Gunn first summoned him to Washington four years earlier. He had been planning to keep the house, but without Debbie's undersea photographs and furniture it had become a depressing place, a constant reminder of their failed relationship. He also couldn't afford both the mortgage and the $19,000 a year he now owed in alimony payments.

Around the same time, Swift was contacted by a film and literary agency about doing a book on the *Hamdan* case. A ghostwriter, the same writer who had worked with him on his *Esquire* story, would put together a proposal, which they would sell first to a book publisher and then to a Hollywood studio.

As the process started moving forward, Swift began having second thoughts, but it seemed too late to put the brakes on the project. The twenty-three-page proposal for *Honor Bound: The True Story of Lieutenant Commander Charles Swift and His Fight to Defend American Justice* went out to publishers and movie studios in June. Katyal got a copy thirdhand; reading it, he grew incensed. It was filled with exaggerations and inaccuracies. Katyal urged Swift to withdraw it immediately, and Swift, painfully aware of his moral collapse, agreed.

A few weeks later, over a three-hour dinner, Swift apologized profusely to Katyal. He confessed to having been seduced by the prospect of stardom and the promise of making millions. He told Katyal that he loved him like a brother, that he would never again do anything to jeopardize their friendship. The experience served as a reality check for Swift. Between the dissolution of his marriage, his effective termination by the Navy, and the knowledge that this once-in-a-lifetime case was ending, he had lost his grip on himself.

Coming back from Guantánamo only a few weeks earlier, Swift had waited in line at the airport with an enlisted sergeant who was leaving the service and felt anxious about her uncertain future. "There are no worries, if you really think about it," Swift had told her. "You're single. You don't have anybody to support. You could get a job at Starbucks and live fine. It's okay not to know exactly where you're going and to say, 'Hey, look, the world is not a secure place.' You've done your duty; now your only responsibility is to yourself."

It occurred to Swift now that the same was true for him. He was just like anybody else leaving the military. He didn't have anything to prove. His moment was over, and it was time to move on.

Swift was gradually starting to see his relationship with Debbie in a new light as well. They were very different people who had come together at a time of mutual need. Swift had been struggling to get through the Naval Academy; Debbie, whose self-confidence had been undermined by her judgmental grandmother, had found a badly needed champion in Swift. For years their marriage had been held together by their common interests—sailing, scuba diving, backpacking. All the while, though, they had been growing further apart. Their problems had been obscured by the peripatetic nature of Navy life: whenever things got difficult, a fresh start on a new base was always just around the corner.

Swift had stayed with Debbie for almost twenty years, never once considering the possibility of separation, much as he had never thought about leaving the Navy even though he knew the military was at best an awkward fit for him. In both cases he had stuck it out because the prospect of the alternative, being on his own, was too crippling to even contemplate. But it dawned on Swift now that he had lived through his worst fear, the fear of being abandoned, and he had come through it okay.

In the late spring of 2007, with the end of his military career just a couple of months away, Swift finally made a decision about his future. When he left the military, he was going to quit the *Hamdan* case and become a death-penalty defense lawyer somewhere out West, ideally Seattle.

By this point, Hamdan had been re-charged with material support for terrorism and conspiracy, which had been codified as a war crime under the Military Commissions Act. More than two and a half years after it had been halted, Hamdan's military commission was finally going to resume.

Swift flew down to Guantánamo with McMillan for the arraignment in June 2007 with the intention of telling Hamdan that he was going to be leaving the case, but the moment Swift saw him, he realized he couldn't do it.

The military commission proceedings didn't get very far. On the very first day, the new presiding officer, Navy captain Keith Allred, ruled that Hamdan's commission lacked the authority to try him because the Military Commissions Act only allowed for the trial of "unlawful enemy combatants." Hamdan had been found to be an "enemy combatant" in his combatant status review tribunal, but never an "*unlawful* enemy combatant," the designation required by the Geneva Conventions in order for a prisoner to be prosecuted before a military commission.

The effect of the ruling was dramatic: Salim Hamdan's war crimes trial was once again halted before it had even gotten under way. This time, though, Hamdan didn't see much reason to celebrate; he had been here before. Sure enough, the government soon expressed its intention to convene a hearing to establish that Hamdan was, in fact, an unlawful enemy combatant. The commission would proceed.

BACK IN VIRGINIA, Swift canceled all his interviews for death-penalty defense jobs. A few days later, another opportunity emerged. Swift was offered a one-year visiting professorship at Emory Law School. Swift wasn't sure that teaching was really what he wanted to do for his next act—he knew that he was going to miss being in the courtroom—but he thought it was worth a try. One of his brothers lived near Atlanta, and his parents, in North Carolina, wouldn't be far away. Perhaps most of all, the job would also allow him to continue representing Hamdan, along with his new military defense counsel and the Perkins team. Swift wouldn't be as intimately involved, in part because he'd now have to pay his own way to Guantánamo, but he would at least be able to honor his commitment to Hamdan.

Swift finished out his service to the Navy and elected not to have a retirement ceremony, instead opting to leave the military in a style antithetical to the manner in which he had existed in it—quietly. On August 1, 2007, Swift's last day of active duty, he went to Anacostia Naval Station in D.C. to fill out the paperwork for his discharge. While he was there, he bumped into an old friend from Mayport, Mike Holyfield, who had just been promoted to commander. Holyfield consoled Swift, mentioning a few other worthy candidates they both knew who had been passed over and a few unworthy ones who'd made the jump to commander.

"This was the weirdest selection board in recent memory," Holyfield said.

"I'm okay with it, Mike, really," Swift replied.

Swift had already driven his car down to Atlanta, so Holyfield offered him a ride to the Metro. Swift wished Holyfield good luck, slung his backpack over his shoulder, and took the Blue Line toward Reagan National Airport.

Epilogue

AS OF THIS WRITING, the fate of both Salim Hamdan and the military commissions remain uncertain.

In the fall of 2007, the chief prosecutor for the commissions, Air Force colonel Morris Davis, resigned in protest, publicly accusing the Pentagon of interfering with his ability to do his job by pressuring him to pursue "sexy" cases in advance of the 2008 presidential election. A couple of months later, Davis elaborated on his criticism of the Pentagon's handling of the commissions in a February 17, 2008, op-ed for *The New York Times*. Davis wrote that he had argued, unsuccessfully, against using evidence obtained through waterboarding at the war crimes trials: "To do otherwise is not only an affront to American justice, it will potentially put prosecutors at risk for using illegally obtained evidence."

Days after the op-ed was published, Davis publicly recounted a conversation with Jim Haynes, the Pentagon's general counsel, which cast further doubt on the fairness of the commissions. "We can't have acquittals; we have to have convictions," Davis recalled Haynes telling him. "If we've been holding these people for so long, how can we explain letting them get off?"

A new challenge to the lawfulness of the Bush administration's detention operations, *Boumediene v. Bush*, reached the Supreme Court in December 2007, with Seth Waxman arguing for the detainees and Solicitor General Paul Clement speaking on behalf of the government. At the center of the dispute was whether or not the Military Commissions Act, which barred the federal courts to the defendants, represented an unconstitutional suspension of the right to habeas corpus.

The Bush administration has shown no sign of backing away from the commissions. In February 2008, the Pentagon announced that it was filing charges against six "high-value detainees" accused of plotting 9/11, including the alleged mastermind of the attacks, Khalid Sheikh Mohammed. If they are convicted, the Pentagon said it intends to seek the death penalty.

Hamdan's commission started again too, following a December 2007 hearing on Guantánamo to determine whether he was a lawful prisoner of war as defined by the Geneva Conventions or an unlawful enemy combatant who could therefore be tried in a military commission. Judge Allred ruled against Hamdan, finding that he was not part of a legitimate army and had been actively engaged in hostilities against the United States. The pretrial hearings resumed in February, with Joe McMillan and Hamdan's new military lawyer, Lt. Brian L. Mizer, arguing for the defense.

In late 2007, Hamdan was transferred from Camp 6 to Camp 5, another maximum-security facility with minimal contact among the prisoners. Hamdan's mental state continued to deteriorate. According to Emily Keram, who had by now spent more than seventy hours with Hamdan, he was suffering from both post-traumatic stress disorder and major depression. In an affidavit dated February 1, 2008, Keram wrote that Hamdan was already unable to materially assist in his own defense and was in danger of developing more serious psychiatric symptoms, including suicidal behavior.

Shortly before Hamdan's final pretrial hearings in late April 2008, McMillan and Mizer asked Judge Allred to halt their client's military commission until he was moved out of solitary confinement. They argued that Hamdan was no longer able to meaningfully assist in his own defense—that he was suicidal, heard voices inside his head, and talked to himself. Even in his more lucid moments, they said, Hamdan refused to talk about his case. Instead, he remained fixated on getting transferred back to Camp 4.

At the hearings themselves, Hamdan announced his intention to boycott his own trial—nor, he added, would he allow his lawyers to speak on his behalf. "There is no such thing as justice here," Hamdan said.

"Mr. Hamdan," Judge Allred replied, "I think you should have great faith in American law. You have already been to the Supreme Court. The Supreme Court of the United States said to the president, 'You can't do that to Mr. Hamdan.' You were the winner. Your name is printed in our lawbooks."

When the hearings resumed the following morning, Hamdan refused to leave his cell.

May 2008

A NOTE ON SOURCES

This is primarily a book of reporting. My principal sources were the book's two main characters, Charles Swift and Neal Katyal, each of whom sat for hundreds of hours' worth of interviews as I followed their stories from early 2004 to early 2008.* Whenever possible, when writing about something I didn't witness, I supplemented their recollections with those of others who were present for the conversation or event. Some of these people are quoted in the book; others are mentioned in the acknowledgments.

My portrait of Salim Hamdan, whom I was not permitted to interview, was drawn primarily from the accounts of Swift, Charles Schmitz, Ali Soufan, and conversations with Hamdan's family, including his brother-in-law and best friend, Nasser al-Bahri, whom I interviewed at length in Yemen in the fall of 2005.

In addition to interviews, legal documents, and court transcripts, I relied on the reporting of a variety of newspapers, wire services, and magazines, most notably *The New York Times*, *The Washington Post*, *The Wall Street Journal*, *The Boston Globe*, *The Miami Herald*, *USA Today*, the Associated Press, *Slate*, *Legal Times*, and *The New Yorker*. Several legal blogs kept me informed about the case and educated me on its constitutional complexities, including SCOTUSblog, Balkinization, and How Appealing.

A selected bibliography of especially helpful books, articles, and documents follows:

Anderson, Kenneth. "Who Owns the Rules of War?" *New York Times Magazine*, April 13, 2003.

*There were certain matters Katyal could not discuss for reasons of attorney-client confidentiality or attorney-client work product privilege, nor could he go into detail about the particulars of his assignments at the Clinton Justice Department. Swift was similarly bound by his attorney-client relationship with Hamdan; he also couldn't talk about any subjects that had been deemed classified by the government.

A Note on Sources

———. "What to Do with Bin Laden and al Qaeda Terrorists? A Qualified Defense of Military Commissions and United States Policy on Detainees at Guantánamo Bay Naval Base." *Harvard Journal of Law & Public Policy*, Spring 2002.

The Army Lawyer: A History of the Judge Advocate General's Corps, 1775–1975. Washington, D.C.: U.S. Army, 1975.

Bass, Gary J. "Atrocity & Legalism." *Daedalus*, January 1, 2003.

Bazelon, Emily. "Invisible Men: Did Lindsey Graham and Jon Kyl Mislead the Supreme Court?" *Slate*, March 27, 2006.

———. "Tight Briefs: The Government's Tricky Lawyering in the Guantánamo Bay Cases." *Slate*, February 24, 2006.

Belknap, Michael. "Frankfurter and the Nazi Saboteurs." *Supreme Court Historical Society Yearbook*, 1982.

Berkowitz, Peter (ed.). *Terrorism, the Laws of War, and the Constitution: Debating the Enemy Combatant Cases*. Stanford: Hoover Press, 2005.

Bishop, Joseph W., Jr. "The Quality of Military Justice." *New York Times Magazine*, February 22, 1970.

Bloch, Susan Low, and Thomas G. Krattenmaker. *Supreme Court Politics: The Institution and Its Procedures*. St. Paul: West Publishing Co., 1994.

Bradley, Curtis A., and Jack L. Goldsmith. "The Constitutionality of Military Commissions." *Green Bag*, Spring 2002.

Brenner, Marie. "Taking on Guantánamo." *Vanity Fair*, March 2007.

Caton, Steven C. *Yemen Chronicle*. New York: Hill & Wang, 2005.

Cooper, Phillip J. "George W. Bush, Edgar Allan Poe, and the Use and Abuse of Presidential Signing Statements." *Presidential Studies Quarterly*, Fall 2005.

Danner, Allison. "Beyond the Geneva Conventions: Lessons from the Tokyo Tribunal in Prosecuting War and Terrorism." *Virginia Journal of International Law* 46, 2005.

Danner, Mark. *Torture and Truth*. New York: New York Review of Books, 2004.

Dobbs, Michael. *Saboteurs: The Nazi Raid on America*. New York: Alfred A. Knopf, 2004.

Draper, Theodore. *A Very Thin Line*. New York: Simon & Schuster, 1991.

Dresch, Paul. *A History of Modern Yemen*. New York: Cambridge University Press, 2000.

Dworkin, Ronald. "What the Court Really Said." *New York Review of Books*, August 12, 2004.

Eastland, Terry. *Energy in the Executive: The Case for a Strong Presidency*. New York: Free Press, 1992.

Fisher, Louis. *Military Tribunals and Presidential Power: American Revolution to the War on Terror*. Lawrence: University Press of Kansas, 2005.

———. "Military Tribunals: The *Quirin* Precedent." *Congressional Research Service*, March 26, 2002.

Fonte, John. "Democracy's Trojan Horse." *National Interest*, Summer 2004.

Glazier, David. "Kangaroo Court or Competent Tribunal?: Judging the 21st Century Military Commission." *Virginia Law Review*, December 2003.

A Note on Sources

Golden, Tim. "Administration Officials Split over Stalled Military Tribunals." *New York Times*, October 25, 2004.

———. "After Terror, a Secret Rewriting of Military Law." *New York Times*, October 24, 2004.

———. "The Battle for Guantánamo." *New York Times Magazine*, September 17, 2006.

Goldsmith, Jack. *The Terror Presidency: Law and Judgment Inside the Bush Administration*. New York: Norton, 2007.

———, and Cass R. Sunstein. "Military Tribunals and Legal Culture: What a Difference Sixty Years Makes." *Constitutional Commentary*, Spring 2002.

Greenberg, Karen J., and Joshua L. Dratel (eds.). *The Torture Papers: The Road to Abu Ghraib*. New York: Cambridge University Press, 2005.

Greenburg, Jan Crawford. *Supreme Conflict: The Inside Struggle for Control of the United States Supreme Court*. New York: Penguin Press, 2007.

Guttman, Roy, and David Rieff (eds.). *Crimes of War: What the Public Should Know*. New York: Norton, 1999.

Haney, Craig, and Mona Lynch. "Regulating Prisons of the Future: A Psychological Analysis of Supermax and Solitary Confinement." *New York University Review of Law and Social Change*, 1997.

Harr, Jonathan. *A Civil Action*. New York: Random House, 1995.

Jinks, Derek, and David Sloss. "Is the President Bound by the Geneva Conventions?" *Cornell Law Review* 97, 2004.

Katyal, Neal Kumar, and Laurence H. Tribe. "Waging War, Deciding Guilt: Trying the Military Tribunals." *Yale Law Journal*, April 2002.

Klaidman, Daniel, Stuart Taylor, Jr., and Evan Thomas. "Palace Revolt." *Newsweek*, February 6, 2006.

Kluger, Richard. *Simple Justice: The History of* Brown v. Board of Education *and Black America's Struggle for Equality*. New York: Random House, 1975.

Krislov, Samuel. "The Amicus Curiae Brief: From Friendship to Advocacy." *Yale Law Journal*, March 1963.

Lewis, Anthony. *Gideon's Trumpet*. New York: Random House, 1964.

Lithwick, Dahlia. "Because I Say So: The Supreme Court Takes the Military Tribunals out for a Spin." *Slate*, March 28, 2006.

Mackintosh-Smith, Tim. *Yemen: The Unknown Arabia*. Woodstock: Overlook Press, 2000.

Margulies, Joseph. *Guantánamo and the Abuse of Presidential Power*. New York: Simon & Schuster, 2006.

Mayer, Jane. "The Hidden Power: The Legal Mind Behind the White House's War on Terror." *New Yorker*, July 3, 2006.

The 9/11 Commission Report: Final Report of the National Commission on Terrorist Attacks upon the United States. New York: Norton, 2004.

O'Brien, David M. *Storm Center: The Supreme Court in American Politics*. New York: Norton, 1986.

O'Donnell, Pierce. *In Time of War: Hitler's Terrorist Attack on America*. New York: New Press, 2005.

A Note on Sources

Packer, George. *The Assassins' Gate: America in Iraq*. New York: Farrar, Straus and Giroux, 2005.

Paust, Jordan J. "Antiterrorism Military Commissions: Courting Illegality." *Michigan Journal of International Law*, 2001.

Persico, Joseph E. *Nuremberg: Infamy on Trial*. New York: Viking Penguin, 1994.

Rehnquist, William H. *All the Laws but One*. New York: Random House, 1998.

Resnik, Judith. "Court Stripping: Unconscionable and Unconstitutional?" *Slate*, February 1, 2006.

Rosen, Jeffrey. "The Power of One: Bush's Leviathan State." *New Republic*, July 24, 2006.

Rules of the Supreme Court of the United States. Available at supremecourtus.gov.

Russell, Sharman Apt. *Hunger: An Unnatural History*. New York: Basic Books, 2005.

Savage, Charlie. "Hail to the Chief: Dick Cheney's Mission to Expand—or 'Restore'—the Powers of the Presidency." *Boston Globe*, November 26, 2006.

Schlesinger, Arthur M., Jr. *The Imperial Presidency*. New York: Houghton Mifflin, 1973.

Spiro, Peter J. "The New Sovereigntists: American Exceptionalism and Its False Prophets." *Foreign Affairs*, November–December 2000.

Starobin, Paul. "Long Live the King!" *National Journal*, February 18, 2006.

Stone, Geoffrey R. *Perilous Times: Free Speech in Wartime*. New York: Norton, 2004.

Sweetman, Jack. *The U.S. Naval Academy: An Illustrated History*. Annapolis: Naval Institute Press, 1979.

Swift, Charles. "The American Way of Justice." *Esquire*, March 1, 2007.

Talbot, Margaret. "Supreme Confidence: The Jurisprudence of Justice Antonin Scalia." *New Yorker*, March 28, 2005.

Thai, Joseph T. "The Law Clerk Who Wrote *Rasul v. Bush*: John Paul Stevens's Influence from World War II to the War on Terror." *Virginia Law Review*, April 19, 2006.

Timberg, Robert. *The Nightingale's Song*. New York: Simon & Schuster, 1995.

Toobin, Jeffrey. "Killing Habeas Corpus: Arlen Specter's About-Face." *New Yorker*, December 4, 2006.

——. *The Nine: Inside the Secret World of the Supreme Court*. New York: Doubleday, 2007.

Wright, Lawrence. *The Looming Tower: Al Qaeda and the Road to 9/11*. New York: Alfred A. Knopf, 2006.

Yoo, John. *War by Other Means: An Insider's Account of the War on Terror*. New York: Atlantic Monthly Press, 2006.

ACKNOWLEDGMENTS

THIS BOOK GREW out of a profile I wrote of Lt. Cmdr. Charles Swift for *The New York Times Magazine* in the spring of 2004. Since then, the magazine and its talented staff of editors have been by my side every step of the way. Ilena Silverman, Vera Titunik, Jamie Ryerson, Scott Malcolmson, and Alex Star all helped shape my reporting on Yemen, Guantánamo Bay, the military commissions, the Supreme Court, and the *Hamdan* case itself. The magazine's unrivaled fact-checking department, overseen by Aaron Retica, saved me from many mistakes. Thanks to Gerry Marzorati for his enthusiasm and ability to always tell me what the story is, even when I'm not sure myself.

I am fortunate to have Farrar, Straus and Giroux as a publisher. Thanks to Jonathan Galassi, Jeff Seroy, Gena Hamshaw, Susan Goldfarb, Sarita Varma, Laurel Cook, and especially to my editor, Eric Chinski, for his patience, insight, and wisdom. I am indebted to Josh Kendall, who left Farrar, Straus when this book was still in its infancy but remains a valued friend. At the Wylie Agency, thanks to Andrew Wylie, Edward Orloff, Kate Prentice, and above all, Sarah Chalfant, for her endless encouragement and impeccable judgment, and Scott Moyers, for his indispensable wisdom.

This book took a good deal longer to complete than I anticipated. I never would have made it to the finish line without the generous financial support of George Soros's Open Society Institute. Through Columbia University's Hertog Research Fellowship program, I was also blessed with a gifted and conscientious researcher, Vrinda Condillac. And thanks to Coburn Architecture, I had an office and plenty of coffee.

I am grateful to a number of people inside the military for their cooperation, including Maj. Gen. Thomas Romig, Col. William Lietzau, and Col. Lawrence Morris. In particular, I want to thank Col. Will Gunn and Lt. Cmdr. Phil Sundel—both now retired—for their assistance and indulgence. A great many civilians helped me along the way too, several of whom deserve special mention: on matters Guantánamo, David Remes and Marc Falcoff; on the Supreme Court, Tom Goldstein and Kevin Russell; inside the government, Pierre Prosper and Brad Berenson. Chuck Schmitz was a vital resource on both Swift and Hamdan. Larry Wright was kind enough to introduce me to Ali Soufan. Marty Lederman gave the (near) final manuscript a close and much appreciated vetting. And thanks to Nasser Arrabyee, a first-rate translator and an extraordinary individual, for taking such good care of me while I was in Yemen.

The Perkins Coie team was invaluable. My heartfelt thanks to Joe McMillan and Harry Schneider for all of the (nonbillable) hours, not to mention the warm welcome in Seattle (the highlight of which was a Mariners game in the firm's box at Safeco Field). Roxann Ditlevson went above and beyond the call of duty, sending me thousands of pages of court filings and transcripts. Also in Seattle, my old friend Mike Dix was a gracious host, and even better company.

I am lucky to have such smart, supportive friends; I exploited their intelligence and generosity to their fullest while writing this book. Mike Sokolove helped me navigate some rocky patches in the early going (and as if that wasn't enough, put me up at his home in D.C.). William Brangham, Roger Burlingame, and Jonathan Rosen provided critical moral support and priceless editorial advice. Seth Mnookin, Tom Watson, Blake Eskin, Tucker Nichols, Sam Sifton, Joel Lovell, Kate Porterfield, Deirdre Dolan, Ginia Bellafante, Seth Lipsky, Kevin Baker, Matt Bai, David Greenberg, Scott Medintz, Daniel Gross, Deak Nabers, Mark Bailey, and Manny Howard were all there when I needed them. So too were Dave Leopold and the Mattoons—Ashley, Lyn, and Skip. Above all, I am deeply indebted to my parents and my

Acknowledgments

sister, Susan, for their bottomless love and encouragement and for filling our home with books. And thanks to Sonia Charles, for making my day-to-day life possible.

There is simply no way for me to adequately thank the two main characters of this book, Neal Katyal and Charles Swift, who not only spent hundreds of hours with me discussing the intricacies of the Hamdan story but also invited me into their lives without any conditions, an act of courage on the order of suing the commander in chief. The talents and commitment of both men consistently humbled me and taught me an enormous amount about patriotism, the Constitution, and sacrifice. I also owe a great debt to Joanna Rosen and Deborah Swift for tolerating my constant intrusions into their homes and for sharing their memories of *Hamdan* with me.

Speaking of sacrifice, my greatest debt is to my wife, Danielle Mattoon, and children, Gus and Nora, who sustained me for the duration of this project. Danielle has been a constant source of love and support, but that's only half the story. She also dove into the manuscript and made it immeasurably better. With apologies to every editor I've ever worked with, no one compares. It is to her that this book is dedicated.

INDEX

Index

Index

Index

Index

Index

Index

Nuremberg war crimes trials, 42, 228, 251, 269

Obama, Barack, 295*n*
O'Connor, Sandra Day, 60, 193, 200, 225, 226, 248, 256*n*, 265
One L (Turow), 50
O'Neill, John, 80

Pace, General Peter, 31–32
Padilla, Jose, 123–24
Paine, Thomas, 275–76
Pakistan, 32, 83, 84, 126, 131, 210; Hamdan's family in, 10, 94, 95
Palestine Liberation Organization, (PLO), 169
Pan Am Flight 103, 25
Paper Chase, The (film), 50
Parker, Robert, 51
Parliament, British, 46
Parsons Clarke, Julia, 102–103
Patriot Act (2001), 56–58, 60
Pentagon, 53, 71, 82, 86, 144, 153, 205, 281, 282, 307, 308; and Abu Ghraib scandal, 115; adviser for military commissions at, 84, 265–66; Brownback named presiding officer for trials by, 125, 132; on changes to commission rules, 203; and defense counsel for military commissions, 39–41, 46, 62, 85, 99; general counsel of, 29, 35, 40, 75; hierarchy of, 43; indictment of Hamdan delivered to, 76; JAG offices in, 34; media and, 45, 78, 96; and *Rasul* amicus brief, 74–75; and Robertson's ruling, 192, 196; target letter on Swift's access to Hamdan issued by, 92; terrorist attack on, *see* September 11, 2001, attacks; and Vieques weapons-testing ground accident, 23; *see also* Defense Department, U.S.

Perkins Coie, 102, 110, 146, 150, 192, 216, 246, 250, 265, 276, 277, 302; and filing of habeas petition, 104–105; and Graham-Levin bill, 222–23; in Hamdan's defense before military commission, 301, 306; Katyal's briefs reviewed by, 143–45, 149, 173–74, 227, 229, 232; oral argument moots at offices of, 257; request for pro bono assistance from, 102–103; and unsealing of Hamdan's affidavit, 112–13; Washington, D.C. offices of, 147
Philbin, Patrick, 29, 33–35, 200
Pledge of Allegiance, 249
Podesta, John, 64
Pope, Brent, 21
Posner, Richard, 194
Powell, Colin, 31, 44, 113–14, 232
Preston, Major Robert, 206
pro bono work, 55, 102, 257, 302
Prosper, Pierre-Richard, 25, 28, 31–32
Puerto Rico, 22–23

Qala, Muhammad al-, 122, 127–29
Quirin, Richard, 37–39; see also *Ex parte Quirin*
Quran, *see* Koran

Ramadan, 6–7, 162, 163
Randolph, Arthur R., 171, 185
Rasul, et al. v. George Bush (2004), 66, 69, 98, 104, 106*n*, 108, 146, 153, 245; JAG amicus brief on, 70–71, 74–75, 203; lower court decisions on, 66–67; Supreme Court decision on, 109, 111, 122–23, 125, 141, 147, 177, 198, 225
Rathburne (frigate), 15
Reagan, Ronald, 27, 28, 171, 215, 253*n*, 296
Reagan Doctrine, 27, 28

Index